A TASTE OF OREGON

JUNIOR
LEAGUE
OF
EUGENE

The purpose of the Junior League of Eugene, Oregon is exclusively educational and charitable, and is to promote voluntarism, to develop the potential of its members for voluntary participation in community affairs, and to demonstrate the effectiveness of trained volunteers. Profits received from the sale of *A Taste of Oregon* will be used to fund the Junior League's projects within the community, through the Community Trust Fund.

Junior League of Eugene, Inc.
2839 Willamette Street
Eugene, Oregon 97405

First Printing	October 1980	10,000
Second Printing	September 1981	10,000
Third Printing	February 1982	20,000

ISBN 0-9607976-0-2

KANSAS CITY PRESS, INC.
1012 Locust
Kansas City, Missouri 64106

Oregon

To many of the early western settlers who had completed the long, treacherous journey from the East, Oregon was the pot of gold at rainbow's end. It was a chance for a new life in a land with promise of bounty more precious than wealth.

Eugene Skinner, the founder of Eugene, wrote a letter March 18, 1860, to his sister in Canada trying to explain the new life in the Oregon country:

My Dear Sister;

We are strangers to this far-off land and those who inhabit it, and the beautiful scenes which surround us in Oregon, but could you but see our land of enchantment! Though the country is new, we have no aristocracy and no high style of living. Still, we enjoy life as well as those who roll in luxury. . . 'tis not wealth but contentment of conscience clear of offense that makes the sum total of this life.

Oregon was a panorama of varied western landscape. From the rugged coast, to the fertile Willamette Valley, to the high snow covered peaks of the central Cascades, to the sage desert and the rolling hills of Eastern Oregon, the pioneer was treated to constantly changing scenes. Fishermen, loggers, sheep and dairy farmers, wheat growers, and fruit producers settled in Oregon from their native lands.

It is not surprising that many settlements of Old World cultures still thrive within Oregon, Mr. Skinner's "land of enchantment," and the foods enjoyed by Oregonians reflect the heritage of these settlers. The influence of the Native American as well as the pioneers, and the richness of the land, is evident in the recipes used by their descendants.

The members of the Junior League of Eugene would like to share with others some of the flavor of Oregon. Throughout this cookbook are notes on the history of Oregon, its culture, and recollections of the lifestyle experienced by the early settlers. It is through the recipes, old and new, and the use of many of the foods produced within the state, that we hope our readers can experience a true *Taste of Oregon.*

Acknowledgements

The Junior League of Eugene would like to thank those who contributed to this book: the historical associations for the information used in many of the historical notes; the artists who generously allowed the inclusion of their artwork; the restaurants for the use of their recipes; Mr. Roger Rutan for his wine expertise; members and friends who donated and tested recipes.

HISTORIC ASSOCIATIONS

Josephine County Historical Society; Josephine County, Oregon
Klamath County Museum; Klamath County, Oregon
Oregon Historical Society; Portland, Oregon
Tillamook County Pioneer Museum; Tillamook, Oregon
St. Peter's Landmark, The Dalles, Oregon

ARTISTS

Elizabeth Fisher Gough has spent much of her life studying and teaching art, painting, and drawing. She has served as chairman of the Art Department at Park School, University of Buffalo. She currently runs the Country Studio Gallery and Gift Shop in Eugene, Oregon. Her drawings include many historic buildings and Pacific Northwest scenes.

Darlene Kosoff has worked with pen and ink illustrations as well as with pastels and oil media. She has published a series of three coastal calendars of pen and ink drawings. Her pastels and oil paintings have been on display at a one-man show at the Kodiak, Alaska Airport.

Terry Maddox began drawing in 1975, plunging into his newly found avocation with great enthusiasm. His pencil drawings, though diverse, have a recurring outdoor theme. He has done numerous drawings of historic Oregon scenes. His works are on display in many Northwest galleries and his shows are a frequent occurence.

Gwyneth O'Connell has taught at Tongue Point Job Corps and Treasure Valley Community College. She is currently teaching at the University of Oregon, Lane Community College, and Maude Kerns Art Center. Her works include printmaking, calligraphy, photography, and illustration.

Kenneth O'Connell is an artist, film maker, and designer. He was chairman of the Art Department at Treasure Valley Community College. Presently, he is an assistant professor in the Masters of Fine Arts Program at the University of Oregon. Drawings of old Oregon buildings are included among his works of art.

Bonnie Bausor Phipps teaches design and drawing at Maude Kerns Art Center in Eugene, Oregon. She works primarily in oils and gives her paintings a fantasy quality in both color and style. Her paintings are on display at many Northwest Galleries and have been shown throughout the country.

Betty Rogers Stockman has always enjoyed drawing, painting, and crafts. In 1951 she helped in the formation of the Maude Kerns Arts Center in Eugene, Oregon. Her drawings of people, local scenes, and historic buildings are well represented by her note cards.

Joan Zenick has taught illustration, watercolor, and color harmony in painting. Her drawings of animal life and historic scenes have decorated greeting cards since 1958. Her realistic yet veiled style projects the feeling of looking into the past.

Dan and Louis Oyster Bar Portland, Orego

The Oyster Bar is a favorite in the Portland area for those who love oysters. The restaurant looks like it was once a fish house and the dining room i designed to resemble the hold of a ship. Fresh oysters from Oregon's Yaquin Bay are the mainstay of the menu. Other delicious offerings include fres seafood appetizers, salads, delicious chowders, and a specialty of the chef, cra and shrimp Louis.

The Gables Corvallis, Orego

The Gables Restaurant was named for the building in which it is housed, a lo structure with gabled roof and beautiful stained glass window. The restauran has been at the same location for 22 years and has doubled in size. Prime ri and fresh Oregon seafood are the specialties of the chef. The wine cellar boast a selection of over fifty varieties.

Henry Thiele's Portland, Orego

Established in 1908, Henry Thiele's has long been a favorite restaurant in th Portland area. It has a large, varied menu and historic atmosphere that com- plements leisurely dining. Specialties of the restaurant include pastries, desserts, German pancakes, and fresh Oregon seafood.

Jacksonville Inn Dinner House Jacksonville, Orego

Housed in Gold Rush Jacksonville's early permanent structures, the Jacksonvil Inn Dinner House has been restored to reflect that bygone era. The sandston walls in the dining room were quarried locally and flecks of gold ore are sca tered throughout the mortar. The building has served many purposes since i construction in 1863 and now is a fine eating establishment and also offe rooms furnished with western antiques. The restaurant's gourment specialties i clude prime rib, veal parmesan, veal scallopini, Oregon salmon and raz clams.

L'Auberge de Vieux Moulin Eugene, Orego

Although only a few years old, L'Auberge is fast becoming a popular restauran for very special meals. It occupies a pleasant old house in downtown Eugen which accommodates only eleven tables. Food is prepared in classic Frenc Cuisine with delicate sauces prepared fresh daily. Service is leisurely with din ners designed to make a special occasion of the evening. Entrée specialties in clude lamb persille, tournedos en croute, fresh Oregon salmon, and local rain bow trout amandine.

Metropol Bakery and Cafe Eugene, Oregon

The Metropol Bakery is located downstairs in the Fifth Street Market. This renovated building now houses many interesting and enjoyable restaurants and shops. The bakery sells a large selection of delicious Viennese pastries, French and variety breads, rolls, and cakes. The Metropol Cafe in downtown Eugene, serves homemade sausage, pate, quiche, soup, and salad.

Pine Tavern Bend, Oregon

Since 1935, the Pine Tavern has been serving three meals a day to the people of the Bend, Oregon area. Located on the Deschutes River, the dining room of the wooden frame building opens onto the river to afford diners a lovely view while they enjoy their meal. Specialties of the tavern are prime rib and steaks as well as fresh fish from the river.

Sunriver Lodge Sunriver, Oregon

Sunriver Lodge, a resort facility near skiing on Mt. Bachelor and trout fishing on the Deschutes River, offers a host of outdoor activities. The resort was designed using natural stone and wood and affords panoramic views of pines and meadows. The food offered in the dining room reflects the taste of the Pacific Northwest with fresh seafood and other hearty meals to satisfy one's hunger after a day outdoors.

Valley River Inn Eugene, Oregon

The Valley River Inn is a contemporary motel complex overlooking the Willamette River. The Left Bank dining room is handsomely decorated to reflect the heritage of Oregon. The specialties of the chef include scampi prepared in a wine-butter-garlic sauce, prime rib and fresh Oregon salmon.

Wolf Creek Tavern Wolf Creek, Oregon

The Wolf Creek Tavern was constructed in the mid 1800s as a roadside inn on the route of the Sacramento to Portland stage coach run. It has been in use as a restaurant for over 100 years. Now a property of the Oregon Department of State Parks, the Inn has been carefully restored, and is listed in the National Register of Historic Places. It offers delightful rooms furnished with antiques, excellent food in the quaint dining room, and the hospitality of a bygone era.

Contents

cover picture by ***Betty R. Stockman***

Historical notes and recipes are indicated in the same manner as this notation. The recipes thus designated have not been tested before inclusion in this cookbook.

MENUS

Terry Maddox

Choosing the Right Wine For That Special Occasion

by

Roger Rutan—Of Grape and Grain

At one time or another, all of us have felt unknowledgeable when selecting a bottle of wine. There are basic guidelines to use in choosing a wine, but you should remember that it is more important to suit your taste. Wine should be chosen to give pleasure to you and your guests.

A frequent suggestion is to serve red wines with red meats and other hearty foods, white wine with fish and fowl, and rosé with either. A full-bodied wine should be served with more flavorful foods while a lighter wine would be better with more delicate tasting foods. If either the wine or the food overpowers the other, only one can be tasted.

A full-bodied red wine like Cabernet Sauvignon is often best to complement lasagne or a charbroiled steak, both with hearty flavors. Pork and lamb, more subtle meats, taste better with lighter red wines such as Gamay Beaujolais or Pinot Noir.

When serving cracked crab, a white wine with some fruitiness, such as a White Riesling, would match well. A wine too dry would clash with the richness of the crab, and a sweet white would overpower the crab flavor. A bottle of 1977 Hillcrest White Riesling served with cracked Dungeness crab—this is Northwest wine and food at its best. Another excellent combination would be the White Riesling with broiled fillet of sole. However, a slightly drier wine, such as a Chenin Blanc, would be better if the sole were done in a creamy sauce. With a spicy sauce on the sole, a dry wine like Chardonnay would be a more complementary choice.

Another suggestion for choosing wines applies when serving several wines at dinner: serve dry before sweet and white before red. A dry white may be suggested for hors d'oevres, a semi-dry white with the soup course, a fruity white with the fish course, and a full-bodied red with the steak, and so on. In addition, most white wines are enjoyed when they are young and fresh, while younger red wines may have to be decanted and allowed to "breathe" to ease some of their youthful sharpness.

The key to matching wine with food is simple. Wine should complement your menu. Wine will add to the enjoyment of any food if it is balanced with that food. While keeping in mind your own individual preferences, these guidelines will help you match your menus with the best wine partners.

Timber Country Breakfast

Fresh Oregon Berries
with cream and sugar

Slices of Summer Baked Ham, p. 206

Willamette Valley Waffles, p. 133
with Blueberry Topping, p. 81

Tea and Coffee

Rhododendron Brunch

Assorted Oregon Cheeses
with Sliced Hood River Apples and Crackers

Ham with Asparagus, p. 208

Raspberry Salad, p. 102
on lettuce leaf

Whole Wheat Muffins, p. 144

Norwegian Lace Cookies, p. 284
Pecan Petite Bars, p. 279

Bel Canto Punch, p. 47

Tea and Coffee

Jogger's Salad Bar

Salmon Salad, p. 108
Curried Spinach Salad, p. 86
Tomato Aspic Salad, p. 100

Sunflower Whole Wheat Bread, p. 154

Strawberries in Almond Yogurt, p. 315

Bottled Mineral Water

Tea and Coffee

Pendleton Round-Up Lunch

Mexican Avocado Dip, p. 25
with corn chips

Barbeque Beef, p. 189
on Sourdough Rolls

Fresh Corn in the Husk, p. 335

Layered Green Salad, p. 90

Hood River Apple Cake, p. 286

Beer
Soft Drinks

A typical pioneer breakfast would often include hot mush with brown sugar and cream, homemade buns or light-bread, fried pork, ham or venison, eggs and milk (canned or fresh) and coffee or tea.

Oregon Coast Picnic

Greenleaf Vegetable Dip, p. 27
with Fresh Vegetables

Suggested Wine:
1978 Adelsheim Washington Semillon

Cheese-Crisp Baked Chicken, p. 233
Coleslaw Salad, p. 93
Baked Beans, p. 119

Suggested Wine:
1979 Sokol Blosser White Riesling, Yamhill County

Jeanie's Chocolate Lover's Brownies, p. 273
Danish Apple Bars, p. 276

Garden Harvest

Italian Vegetable Dip, p. 26
with Raw Fresh Vegetables

Garden Soup, p. 59

Zucchini Frittata, p. 129

Fresh Beefsteak Tomatoes
with Parsley Dressing, p. 113

Granary Bread, p. 151

Rhubarb Custard Pie, p. 301

Fresh Apple Juice

An Hors d'Oeuvre Happening

Smoked Almonds, p. 44

Uncle Will's Pickled Asparagus, p. 45

Teriyaki Appetizers, p. 37

Speedy Spinach Mushroom Caps, p. 33

Salmon Mousse, p. 41
with Assorted Crackers

Chutney Cheese Spread, p. 30
with Fresh Fruit

Suggested First Wine:
1979 Parducci Chenin Blanc

Suggested Second Wine:
1979 Hinman Vineyards, Oregon Riesling

Homecoming Tailgate

Martinis for a Crowd, p. 48
or
Gin Fizz, p. 51

Bacon and Sour Cream Dip, p. 28
with Fresh Raw Vegetables

Pastry Cheese Ball, p. 31
with crackers

After-Game Ham Sandwich, p. 209

Pineapple-Cabbage Salad, p. 100

3-Layer Fudge Brownies, p. 273
Egg Nog Sugar Cookies, p. 283

Rose Festival Buffet

Champagne Punch, p. 47

Gougere Cheese Pastry Ring, p. 36
Cocktail Meatballs, p. 38
Marinated Mushrooms, p. 33

Whole Stuffed Salmon, p. 241

Molded Avocado Salad, p. 101

Spinach Salad, p. 85

French Rice, p. 171

Glazed Carrots, p. 334

Leila's Feather Rolls, p. 149

Suggested Wine:
1977 Firestone Vineyards Chardonnay

Quick Cheese Cakes, p. 296

Mt. Bachelor Bash

Pepper Jelly, p. 46
with Cream Cheese and Crackers

Beer Cheese Soup, p. 65

Easy Spinach Salad, p. 87

Rolled French Bread, p. 150

Suggested Wine:
1976 Rodet Macon-Villages

Lemon Lush, p. 310

Suggested Wine:
1978 Hillcrest White Riesling, Late Harvest

McKenzie River Catch

Trout with Pecans, p. 239

Rice-Broccoli Bake, p. 170

Summer Salad, p. 91

Rosemary Bread, p. 157

Suggested Wine:
1977 Chateau Ste. Michelle Chardonnay

Gooey Chocolate Cake, p. 290

Suggested Wine:
1975 Chateau Filhot, Sauterne

Pioneer Supper

Old Fashioned Brunswick Stew, p. 265

Oregano Salad, p. 89

Potato Rolls, p. 149
with butter

Grandmother's Pound Cake, p. 292

Orange Spice Tea, p. 53

Historical Thanksgiving Dinner

Oysters on the Halfshell
Cream of Chicken Soup
Fried Fish   Baked Salmon
Roast Wild Turkey
Homemade Cranberry Sauce
Mashed Potatoes   Baked Squash
Boiled Onions   Parsnip Fritters
Venison Pastry
Pumpkin Pie   Mincemeat Pie
Apple Pie   Almond Ice Cream
Lemon Jelly   Hickory Nut Cake
Cheese   Fresh Fruits
Coffee

Shakespearean Feast

Mushroom Tarts, p. 32
Happy's Scalloped Oysters, p. 255

Suggested Wine:
1978 Chateau de Montfort Vouvray

Fish Chowder, p. 70

Dressed Roast Pheasant, p. 265

Venison in Red Wine, p. 261

Green Rice, p. 171

Candied Carrots, p. 121

Curried Baked Fruit, p. 317

Beer Wheat Bread, p. 155

Suggested Wine:
1978 Jadot Beaujolais-Villages

Pioneer Plum Pudding, p. 318

After Theatre Dessert

Chocolate Covered Fruit, p. 317

Strawberry Cream Cheese Pie, p. 302

Macadamia Nut Bars, p. 278

Sour Cream Lemon Pie, p. 303

Bacardi Rum Cake, p. 294

Suggested Wine:
Calissano Asti Spumante
1978 Long Vineyards Johannisberg Riesling

or

Kahlua Liqueur, p. 51

Coffee

Microwave Meal

Rondele Mushrooms, p. 331
Hot Crab Dip, p. 331
with Crackers

Suggested Wine:
1977 Vernaccia Di San Gimignano

Herb Chicken Breasts, p. 339

Tossed Salad with French Salad Dressing, p. 113

Seasoned Rice, p. 336

Tangy Cheese Cauliflower, p. 335

Suggested Wine:
1978 Robert Mondavi Fume Blanc

Baked Apples, p. 344

Suggested Wine:
1976 Chateau Bellevue, Sauterne

Rainy Day Children's Afternoon

Refreshments

Almost Orange Julius, p. 52
or
Frozen Fruit Treats, p. 354

Cracker Jacks, p. 354
or
Monster Cookies, p. 282

Activities

Crayon Meltings, p. 357
or
Finger Painting, p. 357

Playdough, p. 356
or
Dough Art, p. 356

APPETIZERS AND BEVERAGES

Elizabeth F. Gough

Mexican Avocado Dip

6-8 avocados
1 medium onion, finely chopped
1-2 tomatoes, finely chopped
½ head lettuce, shredded
1 7-ounce can green chili salsa
Dash garlic salt
½ cup Cheddar cheese, grated
Taco chips

Peel and mash avocados on large platter. Then add onion, tomatoes, lettuce, and chili salsa, mixing well after adding each item. Add dash of garlic salt. Garnish with cheddar cheese over top, serve with taco chips.

YIELD: 5 cups

NOTE: To prevent discoloration, place the avocado seeds in avocado dip until ready to serve. Then remove the seeds.

Bean Dip Caliente

1 16-ounce can stewed tomatoes
1 30-ounce can refried beans
1 garlic clove, minced
1 medium onion, chopped fine
2-4 Tablespoons chili powder to taste
Salt and pepper to taste
½ teaspoon dry oregano
¾ pound medium sharp Cheddar cheese, grated

Mix together all ingredients except cheese. Simmer on lowest heat on stove top for 3 hours, stirring occasionally. Add cheese and blend in just until cheese melts. Do *not* boil. Serve immediately in chafing dish.

YIELD: 1 quart

Aunt Dorothy's Dip

¾ cup mayonnaise
¾ cup sour cream
1 Tablespoon minced onion
1 teaspoon dill
1 Tablespoon chopped parsley
1 teaspoon beau monde
Lettuce
Assorted fresh vegetables

Combine all ingredients except lettuce and assorted vegetables. Blend well, and place in a lettuce-lined bowl. Cover and refrigerate for 3 hours. Arrange fresh vegetables on a serving platter with a bowl of dip in the center.

YIELD: 1½ cups

VARIATION: Serve with potato chips.

Spinach Dip

1 10-ounce package frozen chopped spinach or 1 pound blanched fresh spinach
½ cup fresh parsley
½ cup green onion
½ teaspoon dill seed
1 cup mayonnaise (home made is best)
1 cup sour cream
1 teaspoon seasoned salt (Lawry's)
1 Tablespoon fresh lemon juice
Fresh vegetables or crackers

Place partially thawed spinach in a bowl. Chop parsley and onion and add with all other ingredients. Mix well. Place in refrigerator (the flavor improves after 24 hours). Serve spinach dip with fresh vegetables or crackers.

SERVES 8-10

Taheeni Dip

1 cup mashed cooked eggplant
3 Tablespoons lemon juice
3 Tablespoons olive oil
1 large garlic clove
1 teaspoon salt
2 Tablespoons sesame seeds, toasted
2 Tablespoons chopped parsley
Raw vegetables or toast-type crackers

In blender on high combine the eggplant, lemon juice, olive oil, garlic, and salt. Blend one minute or until creamy. Place mixture in a serving bowl and garnish with sesame seeds and chopped parsley. Cover and refrigerate several hours. Serve with raw vegetables or toast-type crackers.

YIELD: 1½ cups

Italian Vegetable Dip

1 pint sour cream
2 .7-ounce packages Italian Dressing mix
1 medium avocado, peeled and chopped fine
1 medium tomato, peeled and chopped
2 Tablespoons mayonnaise
2 teaspoons lemon juice
Dash Tabasco
Chilled fresh vegetables

Blend all ingredients. Cover and refrigerate overnight. Serve with chilled fresh vegetables.

SERVES 12-14

Greenleaf Vegetable Dip

½ envelope dry onion soup mix
3 hard-boiled egg yolks
½ cup sour cream
¼ cup mayonnaise
1 Tablespoon horseradish
1 large cucumber, peeled and cubed
1 medium avocado
1 teaspoon lemon juice
Tabasco sauce
Salt
Lettuce
Raw vegetables

In a medium-size mixing bowl or blender add soup mix, egg yolks, sour cream, mayonnaise, horseradish, and cucumber. Mix thoroughly. Peel and pit avocado. Dice avocado, add lemon juice, Tabasco, and salt to taste; add to mayonnaise mixture. Place mixture on a bed of lettuce in a serving bowl. Cover and chill 2 hours. Serve with raw vegetables.

YIELD: 1½ cups

NOTE: Nice summertime dip.

Chili Con Queso

1 large onion, minced
1 small garlic clove, minced
4 Tablespoons butter, divided
1 13-ounce can tomatoes
1 4-ounce can chopped green chiles
2 Tablespoons flour
1 cup cream or evaporated milk
Tabasco sauce to taste
Salt to taste
½ pound Cheddar or Monterey Jack cheese, grated
Tortilla chips

Cook onion and garlic in 2 Tablespoons butter until soft. Add tomatoes and simmer until thickened. Break tomatoes into small pieces. Add chiles. Make sauce with remaining 2 Tablespoons butter, flour, and cream. Cook until thick. Add to tomatoes, season with Tabasco and salt. Add cheese 3-4 minutes before serving. When all the ingredients are thoroughly blended, place in a chafing dish, keeping the chafing dish temperature low enough to prevent the cheese mixture from boiling or burning. Serve with tortilla chips.

SERVES 10-12

Bacon and Sour Cream Dip

¾ pound bacon
1 cup sour cream
2 green onions, minced
Dash garlic salt
Dash Tabasco
Lettuce

Cook bacon and crumble into small pieces. Blend together bacon, sour cream, green onions, garlic salt, and Tabasco. Cover and store in refrigerator. Serve on a bed of lettuce. Good with fresh garden vegetables.

YIELD: 3 cups

Chipped Beef Dip

2 8-ounce packages cream cheese
4 Tablespoons milk
5 ounces chipped beef, rinsed
1 medium onion, chopped
1 teaspoon garlic salt
¼ teaspoon pepper
1 cup sour cream
½ cup pecans

Mix together cream cheese, milk, chipped beef, onion, garlic salt, pepper; fold in sour cream. Place in 1-quart casserole, arranging pecans on top. Bake at 350°F for 20 minutes. Serve warm with crackers.

YIELD: 3 cups

Hot Crabmeat Dip

3 8-ounce packages cream cheese
1 cup mayonnaise
2 7-ounce cans crabmeat or ½ pound fresh
¼ cup sherry
1 teaspoon powdered sugar
1 teaspoon grated onion
1 Tablespoon prepared mustard
½ teaspoon salt
Crackers or small rye bread rounds

Melt cream cheese over double boiler. Add mayonnaise, crabmeat, sherry, powdered sugar, grated onion, mustard, and salt. Stir until creamy and hot. Serve in a chafing dish with crackers or rye bread.

SERVES 20

NOTE: This is excellent reheated as an open-face sandwich on rye bread.

Hot Crab and Cheese Dip

2 3-ounce packages cream cheese
1 Tablespoon minced onion
2 Tablespoons milk
¼ teaspoon horseradish
¼ cup crabmeat
Dash garlic powder
Parmesan cheese to taste
Crackers or chips

Combine all ingredients in order listed, except cheese. Bake in 400°F for 20 minutes. Sprinkle Parmesan cheese on top before serving. Serve with crackers or chips.

SERVES 4-6

Crab Dip

1 8 ounce package cream cheese (room temperature)
3-4 Tablespoons mayonnaise
4 teaspoons Worcestershire sauce
2-3 Tablespoons ketchup
Garlic salt to taste
8-10 ounces crabmeat, fresh or canned
Chips or crackers

Blend the cream cheese and mayonnaise until smooth. Add Worcestershire sauce, ketchup, and garlic salt. Fold in shredded crab meat. Serve cold with chips or crackers.

YIELD: 2½ cups

Pink Shrimp Dip

2 5-ounce jars Kraft pimiento cheese spread
10 ounces mayonnaise
2 Tablespoons grated onion
¾ teaspoon horseradish
2 4½-ounce cans shrimp, drained
Tabasco to taste
Garlic salt to taste
Fresh vegetables or crackers

Blend cheese, mayonnaise, onion, horseradish, and shrimp. Add Tabasco and garlic salt to taste. Chill for 2 hours. Serve with fresh vegetables or crackers.

YIELD: 2 cups

Clam Dip

1 8-ounce package cream cheese
8 ounces canned minced clams (reserve clam juice)
1 Tablespoon mayonnaise
¼ teaspoon garlic salt
1 Tablespoon Worcestershire sauce
¼ teaspoon monosodium glutamate
Crackers or chips

Mix all ingredients in order listed. Use reserved clam juice to obtain the right consistency. Refrigerate for at least 4-7 days before serving. Serve with crackers or chips.

YIELD: 1½ cups

Columbia Clam Dip

1 pint small curd cottage cheese
½ 2.7-ounce jar poppy seeds
1 Tablespoon sesame seeds
Dash celery seeds
½ 2.7-ounce jar toasted onion
1 pint sour cream
Garlic powder to taste
Dash seasoned salt
1½ 8-ounce cans chopped clams, drained
Lettuce
Paprika
Crackers

Fold together cottage cheese, all seeds, and onion. Add sour cream and mix gently. Stir in garlic powder and seasoned salt. Add chopped clams and mix well. Cover and refrigerate for at least 2 hours. Serve with crackers. Serve on lettuce with dash of paprika for color.

YIELD: 3 cups

Chutney Cheese Spread

1½ cups shredded sharp Cheddar cheese (6-8 ounces)
8 ounces cream cheese, softened
2½ Tablespoons dry sherry
½ teaspoon curry powder
¼ teaspoon salt
⅓ cup finely chopped chutney
1 Tablespoon snipped chives (optional)
Crackers (optional)
Fresh fruit (optional)

Combine first five ingredients and blend well. Stir in chutney. Turn into serving dish. Top with chives if for appetizer and serve with crackers. If served as dessert, serve with fresh fruit to dip into mixture.

YIELD: 2 cups

Sombrero Spread

½ pound ground beef
¾ cup chopped onion, divided
¼ cup extra-hot ketchup
1½ teaspoons chili powder
½ teaspoon salt
1 8-ounce can kidney beans undrained
½ cup shredded sharp Cheddar cheese
¼ cup chopped stuffed green olives
Corn chips

Brown meat and ¼ cup chopped onion in a skillet or chafing dish. Stir in ketchup, chili powder, and salt. Add beans, including liquid, and mash to mix thoroughly with other ingredients. Heat and garnish with shredded cheese, remaining ½ cup chopped onion, and olives. Serve with corn chips.

YIELD: 3 cups

Pastry Cheese Ball

2 Pepperidge Farm patty shells
1 7-ounce ball Gouda cheese
1 egg, beaten

Thaw patti shells and roll into an 8-inch circle. Remove wax coating on cheese. Cover cheese with pastry and seal edges well. Refrigerate for several hours. Glaze with beaten egg. Bake at 400°F for 10 minutes; reduce to 350°F and bake for 10 minutes more. Remove from oven and let sit for 30 minutes. Serve with crackers.

YIELD: 1 ball

NOTE: This looks and tastes elegant.

Cathy's Cheese Ball

2 8-ounce packages cream cheese
1 .7-ounce package Good Seasons Italian Dressing Mix or Good Seasons Cheese Garlic Dressing Mix
¾ cup nuts or paprika and parsley

Combine cheese and dry dressing mix thoroughly. Form into ball, roll in nuts or paprika and parsley flakes. Chill until ready to serve. Serve with crackers.

YIELD: 1 large cheese ball

NOTE: Quick and easy.

Mushroom Tarts

3 3-ounce packages cream cheese
½ cup butter
1½ cups sifted flour
¾ pound mushrooms, minced
1½ large onions, finely chopped
3 Tablespoons butter
1½ teaspoons salt
½ teaspoon thyme
2 Tablespoons flour
¼ cup sour cream
1 egg, beaten

Beat cream cheese, ½ cup butter, and 1½ cups flour until soft dough forms. Wrap dough in wax paper, refrigerate about 1 hour. Meanwhile, cook mushrooms and onions in 3 Tablespoons butter until tender. Stir in salt, thyme, and 2 Tablespoons flour until blended. Stir in sour cream. Divide chilled dough in half. Roll out first half of dough thinly on a floured board. Cut into circles with a 3-inch cookie cutter or use open end of a glass. Place 1 Tablespoon mushroom mixture on each circle. Brush edges with beaten egg and fold top edge over to meet bottom edge. Press edges together. Prick tops in 3 places. Place on ungreased cookie sheet, brush with beaten egg. Repeat with second half of dough and filling. Bake at 450°F for 12-15 minutes or until golden.

SERVES 6-8

NOTE: Make these ahead of time and freeze.

Stuffed Mushrooms

24 medium mushrooms
½ cup butter
1 envelope onion soup mix
¾ cup dry bread crumbs
⅓ cup sherry
2 Tablespoons butter
½ cup Parmesan cheese
Parsley sprigs

Remove stems from mushrooms and chop, reserving whole caps. In a large pan melt ½ cup butter and add chopped mushroom stems; cook until tender. Remove pan from heat, add onion soup mix, bread crumbs, and sherry. Mix well. Fill the mushroom caps with the mixture, mounding it high. Brush with 2 Tablespoons of butter and sprinkle the mushroom caps with Parmesan cheese. Place on a greased cookie sheet and broil for 5 minutes. Serve on a platter garnished with parsley.

YIELD: 24

Mushroom Appetizer

4 slices cooked bacon, crumbled
¼ cup drained chopped ripe olives
½ cup grated Parmesan cheese
1 Tablespoon Worcestershire sauce
1 small onion, grated
32 cleaned mushrooms (stems removed)

In medium-size bowl mix bacon, olives, Parmesan cheese, Worcestershire, and onion. Stuff mushrooms with mixture. Bake at 350°F for 15 minutes. Then broil mushrooms 5 more minutes, until done.

YIELD: 32

SUGGESTION: This could be served with steak or roast beef.

Speedy Spinach Mushroom Caps

1 pound fresh mushrooms
1 12-ounce package Stouffer's Spinach Soufflé (thawed)
½ cup melted butter
⅓ cup grated fresh Parmesan cheese

Cut stems off mushrooms and chop, reserving mushroom caps; mix chopped stems into thawed spinach. Dip whole mushroom caps into melted butter; shake off excess. Place 1 teaspoon of spinach mixture into each cap. Sprinkle each mushroom with Parmesan cheese. Bake at 350°F for 15-20 minutes, until puffy and lightly browned.

SERVES 10-12

Marinated Mushrooms

1 pound fresh mushrooms (small buttons)
¾ cup salad oil
⅓ cup red wine vinegar
3 Tablespoons chopped chives
½ teaspon granulated sugar
2 Tablespoons lemon juice
1 teaspoon tarragon
1 small garlic clove, chopped
1 teaspoon salt

Wash mushrooms thoroughly. Combine remaining ingredients to make marinade. Add mushrooms and refrigerate for several days. Serve with toothpicks. If mushrooms will be sitting out for 5 or 6 hours, leave them in the marinade, if not, drain them before serving.

SERVES 10-12

Artichoke Fritata

2 6-ounce jars marinated artichoke hearts, chopped (reserve liquid)
3 green onions, chopped
1 garlic clove, mashed
4 eggs
6 soda crackers, crumbled
Salt and pepper to taste
½ pound sharp Cheddar cheese, grated
2 Tablespoon chopped parsley

Drain marinade from the artichokes into a skillet. Chop the artichokes and set aside. Add onions and garlic to skillet. Sauté until onions are limp. In a bowl, beat eggs with wire whisk. Add soda crackers, salt and pepper. Stir in cheese, parsley, artichokes, and onion mixture. Pour mixture into a buttered 8×8-inch pan. Bake at 325°F 35-40 minutes until set. Let cool in pan, then cut into bite-size squares. Can be served warm or cold.

SERVES 8

Chile Rellenos

2 4-ounce cans whole green chile peppers
¾ pound Monterey Jack cheese, shredded
¾ pound Cheddar cheese, shredded
9¾ ounces evaporated milk
6 eggs, beaten slightly

Wash, seed, and slit open chiles. Place on bottom of an 8 × 10-inch baking dish. Layer with Jack cheese and Cheddar cheese. Mix milk and eggs together and pour over cheeses. Bake at 350°F for 40 minutes. Allow to cool 10 minutes before cutting.

SERVES 8-10

Sweet & Sour Water Chestnuts

1 pound bacon
2 8-ounce cans water chestnuts
1½ cups ketchup
⅔-1 cup granulated sugar
Juice of ½ lemon

Cut bacon into thirds and wrap 1 piece around each water chestnut. (If water chestnuts are large, cut in half.) Secure the bacon and chestnuts with toothpicks. Bake at 350°F for 30 minutes. Do not over cook. Drain fat. Make sauce by combining ketchup, sugar and lemon juice and pour over baked bacon and chestnuts; bake for additional 30-45 minutes. Serve hot.

SERVES 8-10

Party Tomatoes

1 basket cherry tomatoes
1 8-ounce package cream cheese
1 6½-ounce can shrimp, drained (reserve small amount of liquid)
Garlic salt
Pepper
Dash Worcestershire sauce
2 Tablespoons finely chopped green onion

Cut tomatoes in half. Scoop out and discard insides (seeds). Mix together cream cheese and small amount of liquid from shrimp. Blend until creamy, add shrimp. Add garlic salt, pepper, Worchestershire sauce, to taste, and onion. Blend gently. Stuff tomato halves with mixture. Chill until ready to serve.

YIELD: 4 servings

Spinach-Filo Rolls

1 medium onion, diced
4 Tablespoons butter
3-4 pounds fresh spinach, washed, boiled 5 minutes and drained, or 4 10-ounce packages frozen chopped spinach, thawed and drained
½ teaspoon dill (optional)
2 cups cottage cheese
1 cup grated fresh Parmesan cheese
8 eggs, beaten
Salt and pepper to taste
1½-2½ cubes butter
1 16-ounce package phyllo leaves (follow directions inside package for thawing)

Sauté onion in 4 Tablespoons butter until golden. Add spinach and optional dill and sauté for 5-10 minutes. Put in large mixing bowl and let cool. Add cheeses and eggs; salt and pepper to taste. Melt 1½-2½ cubes butter. Place one leaf of phyllo on flat surface and brush with butter. Place another leaf on top of the first and brush with butter. Continue until there are five layers of dough in stack. Spread 1-1½ cups spinach/cheese mixture on phyllo stack. Roll up beginning with a short side. Place in buttered baking dish. Repeat process with remaining phyllo and filling. Bake at 350°F for 50-60 minutes, until golden brown. Slice to serve. (May be frozen before baked.)

YIELD: 4-6 rolls

NOTE: This is time consuming to make, but worth the extra work.

Gougere Cheese Pastry Ring

1 cup milk
½ cup butter
Pinch salt
1 cup sifted all purpose flour
Pinch nutmeg
3 eggs
¼ pound Swiss cheese
1 egg beaten

Preheat oven to 400°F. Put the milk, butter and a pinch of salt into a saucepan. Bring slowly to a boil, stirring constantly. When the liquid boils, immediately pour in the flour and stir briskly with a wooden spoon. Continue to cook over low heat for a few minutes, beating well until the mixture has thickened. Remove the pan from the heat and beat for a minute or two. Add the nutmeg and the 3 whole eggs, one by one, beating constantly after each addition. Cut the Swiss cheese into small, very thin slices and add it to mixture. Thoroughly grease and flour a flat baking sheet. Spoon the dough onto it in the shape of a ring. Glaze with the beaten egg. Place in the center of the pre heated oven and bake for about 20 minutes. Cut the baked gougere in slices and serve hot. May be served as a first course or with cocktails. Recipe may be doubled, filling center of "ring" with batter to form a pizza shape.

SERVES 6-8

Cheese Bread Cubes

Unsliced loaf sandwich bread
¾ pound butter
¾ pound medium Cheddar cheese, grated
½ teaspoon Worcestershire sauce
½ teaspoon dry mustard
1 teaspoon salt
2 egg whites

Remove crusts from bread and cut into 1¼-inch slices, then in fourths, or into 1-inch cubes. In the top of a double boiler, melt the butter and cheese. Stir until melted. Blend in Worcestershire, mustard, and salt. With electric mixer beat in egg whites. Remove pan from heat. Dip bread cubes into mixture. Place on cookie sheet and freeze. After the cubes are frozen, store in an air-tight bag. When ready to serve, bake on cookie sheet in pre heated 325°F oven for 10-15 minutes. Serve at once.

YIELD: 2 dozen

NOTE: These are nice to have in the freezer for drop-in guests.

Biscuit Quiche

4 ounces refrigerator buttermilk biscuits
9 ounces Swiss cheese, shredded
2 Tablespoons flour
1 cup whipping cream
3 eggs, beaten
2 teaspoons nutmeg
¼ teaspoon pepper
1 teaspoon salt
¼ pound fresh mushrooms, diced
1 onion, chopped
2 Tablespoons butter
1 10-ounce package frozen chopped spinach

Press biscuits into bottom of ungreased pie pan, to form crust. Toss cheese with flour, and combine with cream, eggs, and seasonings. Sauté mushrooms and onion in butter. Add to above mixture. Add thawed and drained spinach. Mix well. Pour over crust. Bake at 350°F for 45 minutes.

SERVES 8-10

The Spanish named a native Oregon aromatic, mint-like vine "yerba buena." This "good herb" was popularly dried and used to brew tea and became known as "Oregon tea" by the early settlers.

Teriyaki Appetizers

1 pound beef sirloin tip
1 teaspoon ginger
⅓ cup soy sauce
¼ cup honey
1 garlic clove, minced
1 teaspoon grated onion
3 Tablespoons oil
½ cup water

Cut sirloin in strips 2 × ½ × ¼-inch pieces. Blend ginger and next four ingredients in a bowl. Add meat strips and marinate about 1 hour. Remove meat, reserving marinade, and brown quickly on all sides in the hot oil in a skillet. Blend water into the reserved marinade in a saucepan. Bring to a rapid boil and cook 2-3 minutes, stirring constantly. Add meat to thickened marinade to glaze; remove and drain on wire rack. Insert a wooden pick into each meat strip and serve with the sauce.

YIELD: 24

Chili Sauce Meatballs

2 pounds ground round
2 teaspoons salt
1 teaspoon pepper
2 teaspoons paprika
1½ teaspoons Worcestershire sauce
1 cup cornflakes, crushed
2 eggs

SAUCE:
1 12-ounce bottle chili sauce
1 12-ounce jar grape jelly
2 Tablespoons lemon juice

Combine ground round with seasonings, cornflakes, and eggs. Roll into small-size balls. Bake 15 minutes on cookie sheets in 350°F oven. Combine sauce ingredients in chafing dish. Add meatballs and simmer 45 minutes. Serve with toothpicks.

SERVES 15-20

Cocktail Meatballs

1 .7-ounce package dry Italian dressing mix
3 pounds ground beef
Oil
2 cups mayonnaise or salad dressing
¾ cup prepared horseradish
½ teaspoon monosodium glutamate
2 teaspoons dry mustard
2 teaspoons lemon juice
½ teaspoon salt

Add package Italian salad dressing mix to ground beef and form into bite-size balls. Brown meatballs evenly on all sides in oil. Combine mayonnaise horseradish, MSG, mustard, lemon juice, and salt in chafing dish and heat until hot. Add meat balls. Serve with toothpicks. If made ahead and frozen, freeze the sauce separately from meatballs.

SERVES 15-20

NOTE: Men love this recipe.

Nachos

1 pound ground beef
1 pound cherizo sausage
1 onion, chopped
1-2 8-ounce cans refried beans
12 ounces Monterey Jack or mild Cheddar cheese, grated
1 8-ounce jar taco sauce
1 medium avocado, chopped
1 medium tomato, chopped
1 2¼-ounce can chopped ripe olives
½ cup sour cream
Taco chips

In a large pan brown meat; add onion, and cook until onion is transparent. Drain off fat. Spread the refried beans in a 3-quart casserole; add meat mixture. Cover with cheese. Pour taco sauce over the cheese. (At this point may cover and chill.) Bake at 400°F for 25-30 minutes. Garnish with chopped avocado, tomato, olives, and sour cream. Serve hot with taco chips.

YIELD: 8 cups

Sausage and Cheese Logs

16 pork or beef sausage links
16 slices white bread
2 Tablespoons butter
2½ cups shredded sharp Cheddar cheese

Cook sausage links until done. Allow to drain on paper towel. Cut crusts from bread. Place bread on wax paper and roll flat with rolling pin. Combine butter and cheese, heat in double boiler until all is melted. (Don't allow water to touch bottom of pan.) Cover your work surface with a piece of wax paper; on this spread both sides of flattened bread with cheese mixture. Place 1 sausage on each cheesed bread and roll up. Place seam side down on well-greased cookie sheet or jelly roll pan. (Can be frozen at this point.) Bake at 400°F 10-12 minutes. Slice each roll into 4-6 pieces. Insert toothpick in each slice; serve.

YIELD: approximately 60 pieces

Indians used many wild roots and barks as cures for common aches and ills. Wild poppy roots were used to relieve toothaches. A tea was made from the bark of dogwood to cure colds and fevers. Wild hops and witch hazel applied to sprains and swellings eased the pain.

Paté Stuffed Bread

1 large loaf crusty French bread
2 8-ounce packages cream cheese, softened
¼ cup beer
¼ cup chopped parsley
¼ cup chopped onion
¼ cup chopped radishes
1 Tablespoon dry mustard
½ pound liverwurst, cut into small cubes

Cut loaf of bread vertically into 3 pieces. Slice off ends; discard. Pull out as much of the bread's insides as possible, leaving about ¼ inch crusty shell. Crumble the bread which has been removed from shell and toast on cookie sheet in 350°F oven for about 15 minutes. Stir cream cheese until smooth and soft; stir in beer, parsley, onion, radishes, and mustard. Gently fold in liverwurst cubes and toasted bread. Pack into bread shells. Reassemble and wrap in foil. Refrigerate at least 4 hours, or overnight. To serve, unwrap and slice as thinly as possible.

SERVES 8-10

Braunschweiger Glacé

1 ¼-ounce package unflavored gelatin
½ cup cold water
1 10½-ounce can beef consommé
½ pound braunschweiger
3 Tablespoons mayonnaise
1 Tablespoon lemon juice
1 Tablespoon grated onion
Parsley
Crackers

Dissolve gelatin in cold water. Heat consommé to boiling. Stir in gelatin mixture and pour into 2-cup mold. Chill until firm. Meanwhile mix braunschweiger, mayonnaise, lemon juce, and onion. When chilled, spoon out jellied consommé to ½ inch on all sides. Fill with braunschweiger mixture. Reheat scooped out consommé and pour over filled mold. Chill until ready to serve or freeze for later use. Invert on serving plate, decorate with parsley and serve with crackers as a spread.

YIELD: 2 cups

Delicious Chicken Wings

60 chicken wings

MARINADE:
¾ cup soy sauce
1 2-pound jar apricot, peach, or pineapple jam
5 Tablespoons granulated sugar
4 Tablespoons fresh lemon juice
2 teaspoons ground ginger
1 teaspoon cinnamon
1 teaspoon nutmeg
½ teaspoon allspice
¼ teaspoon thyme
¼ teaspoon garlic salt
¾ teaspoon monosodium glutamate

Cut chicken wings in 3 pieces at joints; discard tip. Combine marinade ingredients and brush over drumstick wings. Roast in pan at 350°F approximately 2 hours. Baste frequently. If made day before, save out a little of the marinade to use as a basting sauce when you reheat them, or serve cold.

SERVES 10-15

Salmon Mousse

4 shallots, sliced
¼ pound butter
1 15½-ounce can salmon
Juice of ½ lemon
Capers to taste
1-2 anchovy fillets (optional)
10 green olives, sliced
Lettuce
Crackers

Sauté shallots in butter and set aside. Combine in food processor or blender the shallot/butter mixture, salmon, lemon juice, capers, and anchovies.Process for one second in processor or ten seconds in blender. Decorate bottom of mold with sliced olives; add salmon mixture. Chill 1-2 hours. When ready to serve invert mold on a bed of lettuce and serve with crackers.

YIELD: 2 cups

VARIATION: Garnish with cucumber slices, greek olives and pimiento. Also delicious stuffed into hollowed out half cucumber.

Filled Crab Rolls

1 pound American cheese, grated
2 green peppers, chopped
½ pint stuffed olives, chopped
1 cup butter melted
½ pound crabmeat
1 cup tomato hot sauce
48 rolls, (poppy seed, hard or potato)

Combine ingredients and fill scooped-out rolls. Wrap individually in foil, twisting ends. Let stand in refrigerator overnight. When ready to use, put into covered pan and heat ½ hour at 350°F.

YIELD: 4 dozen

Crabbies

½ cup butter or margarine, softened
1 5-ounce jar Kraft Old English Cheese Spread
2 teaspoons Miracle Whip or more to taste
½ teaspoon garlic salt
½ teaspoon seasoned salt
1 6½-ounce can crabmeat, drained
6 English muffins, split

Mix first six ingredients and spread on English muffin halves.
TO FREEZE: Freeze muffins on cookie sheet. When frozen, stack and wrap. When ready to use, remove from freezer, cut in fourths, and heat thoroughly in 350°F oven for 10 minutes.
TO USE IMMEDIATELY: Cut each muffin in fourths. Heat thoroughly in 350°F oven.

YIELD: 48

Clams Casino

1 6½-ounce can minced or chopped clams, undrained
1 10½-ounce can white clam spaghetti sauce (Progresso)
1 cup seasoned bread crumbs (Progresso Italian style)
4 strips bacon

Mix clams, spaghetti sauce, and bread crumbs. Pack into small scallop or porcelain shells. Top each with ⅓ slice uncooked bacon. Bake at 400°F until bacon is done, approximately 20 minutes.

SERVES 6-1

Marinated Shrimp

2 pounds shrimp
Salted water
Ice water
2 Tablespoons water
1 garlic clove
½ medium onion, cut up
1 stalk celery, cut up
1 cup mayonnaise
¼ cup salad oil
3 Tablespoons chili sauce
1 teaspoon celery seed
Dill seed

Boil shrimp in salted water for 3 minutes and then plunge into ice water. Put 2 Tablespoons water, garlic, onion, and celery in blender. Mix all together. Add mayonnaise, oil, chili sauce, and celery seed. Put shrimp in this sauce and marinate overnight. When serving, put about 5 shrimp in scallop shell and sprinkle with dill seed. Serve as a first course or appetizer in the living room before going to the table.

SERVES 8-10

NOTE: This could also be served with picks for cocktails, serving more people.

Shrimp Mousse

1 10½-ounce can tomato soup
1 8 ounce package cream cheese
1 ¼-ounce envelope Knox gelatin
¼ cup water
½ cup finely chopped onion
½ cup finely chopped celery
½ cup finely chopped green pepper
1 cup mayonnaise
1 6½-ounce can shrimp, mashed (may use tuna or salmon)
Parsley
Crackers

Heat undiluted soup. Beat in softened cream cheese. Soak gelatin in water until dissolved. Add to soup mixture and let cool. Add onion, celery, and green pepper. Add in the mayonnaise and shrimp; mix well. Grease mold and pour in mixture. Chill until firm. Remove from mold and garnish with fresh parsley. Serve with crackers.

YIELD: 4 cups

Shrimp Cheese Balls

2 3-ounce packages cream cheese
1½ teaspoons prepared mustard
1 teaspoon grated onion
1 teaspoon lemon juice
Salt and cayenne pepper to taste
1 4½-ounce can shrimp or ¾ cup cooked shrimp
⅔ cup chopped salted nuts

Soften cream cheese. Blend in mustard, onion, lemon juice, salt and cayenne pepper. Mix well. Drain shrimp, break into pieces, and add to cheese mixture Chill. Form into ½-inch balls and roll in chopped nuts.

YIELD: 3½ dozen

Smoked Almonds

½ teaspoon liquid smoke
2 teaspoons water
1 cup almonds
1 Tablespoon oil
Salt

Mix smoke and water. Then add almonds and mix well. Let stand overnight Drain almonds and place in shallow pan. Add oil and toss until well coated Roast in 300°F oven for 25 minutes, stirring frequently. When golden, remove and sprinkle with salt.

YIELD: 1 cup

Nuts and Bolts

½ cup margarine
¼ cup salad oil
¼ cup bacon fat
½ cup Worcestershire sauce
2 teaspoons garlic salt
4 teaspoons celery salt
4 cups unblanched almonds (or mixed nuts)
4 cups Wheat Chex or other small shredded wheat squares
4 cups Rice Chex
2 cups Cheerios
2 cups thin pretzels
1 8-10-ounce package Cheese Flings or similar cracker snack

Melt the margarine, oil, and bacon fat. Stir in Worcestershire sauce. Add salts Remove from heat and let stand a few minutes. In large roasting pan combine nuts, cereals, pretzels, and Cheese Flings. Pour sauce over this and toss to blend. Bake uncovered in slow oven (200°F) for 2 hours, stirring every 30 minutes.

YIELD: 5 quarts

Dill Pickles

FOR 1 QUART PICKLES:
10-14 small pickling cucumbers
1½ Tablespoons pickling salt
2-3 medium-size garlic cloves
3-4 flowers of dill (1 flower defined as top of 1 stem)
1 cup apple cider vinegar
Water

FOR 40 QUARTS PICKLES:
2 lug boxes cucumbers
1 5-pound bag pickling salt (1½ Tablespoons per quart)
½ pound garlic
2 large bunches dill
2 gallons cider vinegar
Water

Stuff jar or jars with cucumbers. Add the salt. Add the garlic. Stuff dill down between the cucumbers. Add vinegar and then fill remainder of jar with water. Close jar and shake to dissolve salt. Check jar the next day. If there is a residue of salt on bottom of jar, shake and tighten lid twice a day for 3 days. Open after 8 weeks.

YIELD: 1 or 40 quarts

Uncle Will's Pickled Asparagus

1½ quarts water
1 quart white vinegar
5 Tablespoon plain salt (non-iodized)
2 Tablespoons pickling spice
7 pounds fresh asparagus
Garlic cloves (1 per quart jar)
Hot chili peppers (1 per quart jar)

Bring to boil the water, vinegar, and salt. Boil for 15 minutes. Remove all cloves from pickling spice or as many as possible. Wrap remaining spice in cheese cloth or tea holder and hang in vinegar mixture. Break off ends of asparagus and blanch for 1-1½ minutes, then plunge into ice water. Place in each jar 1 clove garlic and one hot chile pepper. Pack asparagus in jars standing on end, then pour brine into jars, making sure it is very hot at time to insure a good seal on jars. Store in pantry for 2½-3 months before opening jars.

YIELD: 4 quarts

Sauerkraut was a standby for almost every pioneer family. Without refrigeration, pickling was one of the few methods to preserve vegetables, and it was the only way to preserve cabbage. It was not until about 60 years ago that nutritionists discovered that sauerkraut was also an excellent source of vitamin C, as were the cucumber pickles that filled a large portion of every fruit cellar from New England to the Pacific.

Honey Jelly

2½ cups honey
¾ cup water
½ cup Certo pectin

Bring to a boil the honey and water and then add Certo. Bring to a boil again. Remove from heat, skim, bottle, and top with paraffin.

YIELD: 4 jelly glasses

Pepper Jelly

1½ cups finely chopped green pepper
1½ cups cider vinegar
6½ cups granulated sugar
25 shakes tabasco
1 6-ounce package liquid pectin
5 drops green food coloring
Paraffin

Combine chopped green pepper, vinegar, sugar, and tabasco in 3-quart saucepan. Bring mixture to a boil over medium heat and boil for 5 minutes. Remove from heat and add pectin and food coloring. Return pan to medium heat; bring mixture to boil. Boil for 2 minutes and pour immediately into hot, sterilized pint-size jars. Seal with paraffin. Jelly may be stored in a cool dry place for up to 12 months.

YIELD: 7 cups

NOTE: Serve with cream cheese and crackers. Nice as a gift.

Racco Hoo

"A beverage, to be used in the same way as tea or coffee. Mix together one pound of grated chocolate, one pound of pulverized sugar, one pound of rice flour, and four tablespoons of arrowroot. When used, boil one pint of milk and then add three tablespoons of the above mixed with a little water."

Peterson's Magazine, 1858, Tillamook County Pioneer Museum

Banana Daiquiri

2 ripe bananas
1 cup water
1 cup rum
1 Tablespoon granulated sugar
½ cup prepared daiquiri mix
½ cup Orange liqueur (Triple Sec)
Ice (optional)

Put all ingredients in blender; mix. If frozen daiquiri is desired, add enough ice to fill one third of blender, then add all ingredients.

YIELD: 4-6 glasses

VARIATION: Use other fresh fruit such as 3 fresh peaches or 2 cups strawberries.

Bel Canto Punch

½ gallon riesling wine
2 28-ounce bottles ginger ale
1 quart cranberry juice cocktail
1 cup galliano liqueur
1 12-ounce can frozen orange juice concentrate, undiluted
3 trays ice cubes

Chill wine, ginger ale, cranberry juice, and galliano. When ready to serve, blend chilled liquids in punch bowl with frozen orange juice. Add ice cubes.

YIELD: 4½ quarts

Champagne Punch

2 fifths champagne
1-2 quarts ginger ale
6 ounces brandy or cointreau
Strawberries, orange slices, lemon slices (optional)

In a punch bowl add champagne, ginger ale, and brandy. Add lots of ice. Garnish with fruit.

YIELD: 3 or 4 quarts

NOTE: This is the *best* champagne punch you will ever taste!

Frosty Punch

1 fifth Bacardi White Rum
4 6-ounce cans frozen limeade
6 12-ounce bottles 7-up
4 limeade cans water

Mix the above together and freeze until frosted, not frozen hard. When ready to serve, place in punch bowl.

YIELD: 6 quarts

Father's Fish House Mix

1 cup water
2 cups granulated sugar
1 cup lime juice
1½ bottles Jamaica rum (fifth)
1 fifth American brandy
1 cup peach brandy
3 quarts champagne

Three days prior to serving, heat water and sugar to boiling; cook to syrup. Combine syrup, lime juice, rum and brandy. Store. When ready to serve, add champagne to mixture.

YIELD: 6 quarts

VARIATION: This is a punch with impact!! The impact can be softened by adding plain soda instead of the champagne.

Galliano

2 cups granulated sugar
1 cup water
6 drops pineapple extract
3 teaspoons vanilla extract
1½ teaspoons banana extract
½ teaspoon pure anise extract
1 quart 100-proof vodka
5 drops yellow food coloring

Combine sugar and water in large pan. Boil gently 5 minutes, stirring occasionally. Remove from heat and measure out 2 cups syrup, discarding any syrup left over. Pour syrup into large container and let cool. Add all extracts, vodka and food coloring. Stir until well blended. Ready to serve immediately.

YIELD: 1½ quart

Ginn Fizz

Crushed ice
jigger lime or lemon juice
jiggers simple syrup
jiggers gin
egg
cup whipping cream
Dash of orange flower water

SIMPLE SYRUP:
1 cup water
2 cups granulated sugar

Make ahead the simple syrup by boiling the water and sugar; cook to syrup consistency. Fill blender one third full with crushed ice. Combine all ingredients as listed. Blend until frothy.

YIELD: 4-6 glasses

Hot Buttered Rum

quart French vanilla ice cream, slightly thawed
pound butter, softened
pound brown sugar
pound powdered sugar
2 teaspoons cinnamon
2 teaspoons nutmeg
Rum
Boiling water
Nutmeg

Mix ice cream, butter, sugars, cinnamon, and 2 teaspoons nutmeg, in order listed, in large bowl with electric mixer. Mix thoroughly. Store in freezer. To use, mix 2-3 Tablespoons of batter to 1 jigger of rum. Fill cup with 8 ounces boiling water. Top with nutmeg.

YIELD: 1½ quarts batter

Kahlua

4 cups granulated sugar
3 ounces instant coffee
1 quart boiling water
2-3 cups vodka
4 teaspoons *real* vanilla

Mix sugar and coffee; add the boiling water, vodka and vanilla. Store in 1-gallon container and shake periodically for 30 days. You might want to sample for that proverbial "quality control"!

YIELD: ½ gallon

Kahlua Liqueur

4 cups granulated sugar
3 cups water
1 ounce Antiqua Coffee
1 quart vodka
1 vanilla bean

Boil sugar and water together for 5 minutes. Let cool. Take 1 cup of syrup and add 1 ounce of Antiqua coffee. Mix well and add to the rest of the syrup. Add vodka. Divide equally into three bottles. Divide the vanilla bean into thirds and put one third into each bottle. Cork and let set at least one month.

YIELD: 1½ quarts

NOTE: Really a nice gift idea.

Margaritas for a Crowd

2 quarts LaPaz Margarita Mix
1 quart Mr. and Mrs. T. Sweet Sour Mix
1 quart Tequila (this is more than a fifth.)
1 pint Triple Sec
½ cup lime juice
3 limes quartered
Margarita salt

Mix all the liquid ingredients and freeze in large plastic containers. For each serving, mix ½ cup mixture on high speed in blender for a few seconds. Rim glasses with lime, then margarita salt. Pour mixture into glasses.

YIELD: 35 glasses

NOTE: Great for a large Mexican dinner party.

Martinis for a Crowd

1 fifth Gin
6 ounces dry Vermouth
10 ounces water

Combine gin, vermouth, and water. Store indefinitely in the freezer. Serve on the stem—without ice in the glass.

YIELD: 5 cups

NOTE: Beware! These are so smooth that they will get you.

Sparkling Punch

3 cups water
3 cups granulated sugar
3 cups boiling water
¼ cup tea leaves
3 cups orange juice
1 cup lemon juice
3 cups pineapple juice
2 quarts ginger ale
Sliced fruit (oranges lemons, strawberries)

Combine 3 cups water and sugar. Heat until sugar is dissolved, then boil 7 minutes. Cool and refrigerate. Combine 3 cups boiling water and tea leaves. Steep 5 minutes, then strain tea and cool. When ready to serve, combine fruit juices, syrup mixture, and tea in punch bowl. Add ginger ale and garnish with fruit.

YIELD: 3½ quarts punch

NOTE: To keep from diluting punch, freeze an additional 1 quart ginger ale in a mold.

Tom and Jerrys

6 eggs, divided
2 cups fine granulated sugar, divided
Dash of salt
½ teaspoon vanilla
½ teaspoon baking powder
¼ teaspoon baking soda
1 teaspoon lemon juice
Bourbon
Boiling water
Nutmeg

Beat the 6 egg whites until dry. Gradually add 1 cup *fine* granulated sugar. Beat. Add salt, vanilla, and baking powder. In a separate bowl, beat until creamy the 6 egg yolks. Add remaining 1 cup *fine* granulated sugar. Beat. Add baking soda and lemon juice. Beat. Fold the two mixtures together. To serve mix 1 ounce bourbon, 1 cup boiling water, and 1 teaspoon batter in cup. Float 1 more teaspoon batter on top. Sprinkle with nutmeg. Use more or less batter according to taste.

YIELD: 1½ quarts batter

SUGGESTION: This makes an excellent gift around the holidays.

In pioneer days coffee was often scarce. Peas that had been sun dried and ground finely were a suitable substitute when "real coffee" could not be obtained.

Almost Orange Julius

1 6-ounce can frozen orange juice
1½ cups milk
½ cup water
1 teaspoon vanilla
½ cup granulated sugar
1 tray ice cubes

Blend all ingredients in blender until mushy. Serve immediately.

SERVES 3-

NOTE: Kids love this as an after school snack.

Grape Juice

1 cup concord grapes
1 cup granulated sugar
Boiling water

Wash and stem grapes. Put grapes into a quart jar. Add sugar. Fill jar with boi ing water and seal. Invert the jar for 2 hours. Juice is ready in 6 weeks.

YIELD: 1 qua

NOTE: This is such a snap, it's worth making many quarts at the same time.

Fruit Punch

1 cup granulated sugar
3 cups water, divided
1 cup prepared tea
1 pint strawberry syrup
1 6-ounce can orange juice, undiluted
1 16-ounce can crushed pineapple
Juice from 3 lemons
2 pints raspberry sherbert
1 quart soda water

Combine sugar and 1 cup water in a sauce pan. Boil to syrup; let cool. punch bowl add prepared tea, strawberry syrup, orange juice, crushed pin apple, remaining 2 cups water, and lemon juice. When ready to serve ad raspberry sherbert and soda water.

YIELD: 3 quar

NOTE: Great for a summer party!

Hot Spiced Nectar

3 cups apricot nectar
2 cups orange juice
1 cup water
2 Tablespoons lime juice
¼ cups plus 2 Tablespoons brown sugar
6-inch stick cinnamon
½ teaspoon whole cloves

In large saucepan combine nectar, orange juice, water, lime juice, and sugar. Tie cinnamon and cloves in cheese cloth bag and add to juice mixture. Bring to boil, reduce heat and simmer uncovered 15 minutes. Discard spice bag and serve hot in punch cups.

YIELD: 1½ quarts

Orange Spice Tea

3 large navel oranges
8 ounces loose tea
3-inch cinnamon stick, chopped and broken
2 Tablespoons whole cloves

Remove thin layers of peel from the oranges and cut peel into thin strips. (Fruit itself is not used in this recipe.) Heat in 250°F oven for 10 minutes or until just dry. Toss together the orange peel, tea, cinnamon stick, and cloves. Cover and store in dark place for one week to develop flavor.

YIELD: 2 cups

Russian Tea Mix

1 cup instant tea mix (hot variety)
1 18-ounce jar Tang
2 cups granulated sugar
1 6.2-ounce package dry unsweetened lemonade mix
1 teaspoon ground cloves
1 teaspoon cinnamon

In a large bowl, mix all ingredients thoroughly. Store in tightly covered containers. To serve, add 2 teaspoons of mix to 8 ounces of boiling water. Stir.

YIELD: 6 cups

SUGGESTION: Packaged in a pretty jar, this makes a nice gift for a neighbor at Christmas.

SOUPS AND SAUCES

Betty R. Stockman

Potage Bonvalet

½ pound white beans
Water
1 onion, chopped
½ cup butter
1 parsnip, peeled and diced
2 potatoes, peeled and diced
1 quart beef stock
½ pint whipping cream
Salt and pepper to taste
Sour cream

Place beans in a large pot. Cover them with water and soak overnight. Next day, sauté onion in butter. Add parsnip and potatoes to drained beans. Stir in beef stock. Cook 1 hour or until beans are tender. Blend in blender or food processor and then add whipping cream. Season to taste. Serve piping hot with dollop of sour cream.

SERVES 6-8

A hearty, rich soup.

Prospector's Soup

"Put 2 tablespoons of bacon fat and 3 tablespoons of flour into a saucepan and stir over a medium fire until the flour is golden brown. Then add 1 quart of boiling water and half a can of milk, stirring in slowly until smooth, and season with salt and pepper to taste. An onion may be added to improve the flavor."

Oregon: End of the Trail, 1951

Curried Bean Soup

2 10-ounce packages frozen green or lima beans or equivalent fresh
5 Tablespoons butter
⅔ cup sliced green onions
1½ teaspoons curry powder
¾ teaspoon salt
¼ teaspoon pepper
¾ teaspoon dry rubbed tarragon
8-10 sprigs parsley, finely chopped
1 cup cream
3½ cups chicken broth or 2 13½-ounce cans
Chopped chives

Cook together the beans, butter, onion, and curry powder until very tender and soft. Place mixture into food processor or blender and add remaining ingredients except chicken broth and chives. Blend until smooth. Empty into a saucepan, place over simmering water and add chicken broth. Heat well and serve garnished with chopped chives.

SERVES 6

Corn Chowder

4-5 slices bacon, diced
¼ cup chopped onion
1½-2 cups corn frozen or canned
1 pint tomatoes or 4-5 fresh
2½-3 cups diced potatoes
1 Tablespoon granulated sugar
1½-2 teaspoons salt
½ teaspoon paprika
2½-3 cups boiling water

Fry bacon until crisp; add onion and stir and cook approxiamtely 5 minutes. Drain. Add corn and tomatoes with liquid. Stir in potatoes. Sprinkle with seasonings. Add enough boiling water to create consistency desired. Cook slowly until potatoes are tender, approximately 20-25 minutes.

SERVES 6-8

The daughter of an Oregon Pioneer describes their food supply: "We raised everything; lots of potatoes, vegetables, cows and pigs. Folks would go to the store and buy flour, salt and sugar and that's about all."

Seasons of Harvest: Recollections of Lane County, 1975

Spanish Gazpacho

1 46-ounce can V-8 juice
1 10½-ounce can condensed consommé (not bouillon)
4 Tablespoons red wine vinegar
4 Tablespoons olive oil
¾ teaspoon cuminos
1 plus teaspoon crushed oregano
1 teaspoon salt
1 teaspoon pepper
1 large sweet onion, chopped
1 large green pepper, cut into large chunks
½ large cauliflower, cut into flowerettes
1 medium cucumber, skinned and cut into chunks
3 medium tomatoes, cut into chunks
2 Tablespoons capers, with some juices
1 6-ounce can whole pitted black olives
Avocado slices
Sour cream

Mix all ingredients except avocado and sour cream. Chill for 24 hours, covered. Serve with avocado slices and dollop of sour cream!

SERVES 10

Gazpacho

- 3 cups tomato juice
- 2 Tablespoons olive or salad oil
- 2 Tablespoons wine vinegar
- 1 garlic clove
- 2 tomatoes, peeled and quartered
- 1 small cucumber, peeled and cut in pieces
- 1 small green pepper, seeded and cut in pieces
- 3 stalks celery
- ¼ medium onion, cut up
- 4 sprigs parsley
- 1 teaspoon salt
- ¼ teaspoon pepper
- Croutons

In blender container, put 1 cup tomato juice, oil, vinegar, and garlic. Blend until garlic is finely chopped. Add half each of the tomatoes, cucumber, green pepper, celery, onion, parsley, salt, and pepper to blender container. Blend until vegetables are puréed. Transfer to a 2-quart container. Repeat with remaining tomato juice, vegetables, and seasonings. Combine blended ingredients; cover and chill thoroughly in refrigerator. Serve chilled and garnished with croutons.

SERVES 6

Garden Soup

- 1 large onion, diced (1 cup)
- ¼ cup olive oil
- 1½ quarts water
- 4 large tomatoes, peeled, seeded and diced (3 cups) or 1 28-ounce can
- ½ pound green beans, diced
- 1 medium zucchini, diced
- 1 potato, diced
- 1 cup diced leeks
- 1 cup diced celery
- ¼ pound spinach, chopped, or ½ 10-ounce box frozen
- 3 cloves garlic, minced
- 2 Tablespoons salt
- 2 teaspoons fine herbs
- Dash pepper
- 5 ounces vermicelli
- 1 15-ounce can white or pinto beans
- ½ pound Swiss cheese, grated

Sauté onion in oil until tender. Add water and all vegetables except canned beans. Add garlic and seasonings. Bring to a boil, reduce heat and simmer covered ½ hour. Add vermicelli and beans. Cook until vermicelli is tender, about 5 minutes. Ladle into bowls and top with grated cheese.

YIELD: 12 cups

Lentil Soup

3 ounces salad oil
3 ounces bacon, diced
¾ cup diced carrots
1 onion, diced
¾ cup diced celery
¾ cup flour
3½ quarts water
1 cup lentils
1 teaspoon salt
2 teaspoons Lawry's Seasoning Salt
2 teaspoons monosodium glutamate
4 Tablespoons beef base or 4 cubes beef bouillon
Dash nutmeg
Dash white pepper
¾ cup diced potatoes

In a large soup kettle heat salad oil. Add bacon, carrots, onions, and celery. Sauté until onion and celery are transparent. Add flour, stirring constantly. When flour is blended, slowly add water. Stir until blended. Then add lentils, salt, seasoning salt, MSG, beef base, nutmeg, pepper, and potatoes. Simmer for 3 hours or more.

SERVES 6-8

Dutch Green Pea Soup

2 pounds fresh ham hock
3-4 quarts water
1 pound pre-soaked green split peas
8 leeks, finely chopped
1 celery root, peeled and diced
3 cups chopped celery leaves
1 bay leaf
½-¾ teaspoon thyme, rubbed
⅛ teaspoon dry mustard
2 dashes cumin
2 teaspoons salt
1 teaspoon ground pepper
2-3 cups chicken broth (optional)
Croutons

The day before serving, place the ham hock and water in a large soup kettle. Bring to a boil and then simmer until meat is very tender (2½ hours). Cool and skim off fat. Remove meat and add to liquid the remaining ingredients except meat and chicken broth. Dice meat and return to kettle. Simmer 3 hours. If soup is too thick, chicken broth can be added. Refrigerate; serve the next day as this soup is best after the first day and is excellent garnished with Parmesan or Parmesan and garlic croutons.

SERVES 8-10

Cream of Fresh Mushroom Soup

¼ cup butter or margarine
2 Tablespoons chopped onion
½ cup all purpose flour
½ teaspoon salt
½ teaspoon monosodium glutamate
⅛ teaspoon pepper
Few grains cayenne pepper
3 cups chicken broth
8 ounces fresh mushrooms, sliced lengthwise
2 cups milk, scalded
2 Tablespoons dry sherry
Parsley

Heat butter in saucepan. Add onion and cook until crisp-tender. Blend flour, salt, MSG, and peppers; stir into onion mixture. Add the chicken broth gradually, stirring constantly. Continuing to stir, bring to boiling and cook 1 minute. Stir in the mushrooms. Cook covered over low heat for 30 minutes, stirring occasionally. Remove cover and add scalded milk. Cook uncovered over low heat 5-10 minutes. Just before serving, stir in sherry. Garnish with parsley.

SERVES 6

French Onion Soup

5 cups sliced onions
3 Tablespoons butter
1 Tablespoon vegetable oil
1 teaspoon salt
¼ teaspoon granulated sugar
2 10½-ounce cans beef broth
1 soup can water
3 Tablespoons flour
½ cup dry white wine
Salt and pepper to taste
Grated Parmesan cheese

Cook onions slowly with butter and oil in heavy, covered 4-quart saucepan for 15 minutes. Stir in salt and sugar; cook uncovered 35-40 minutes, stirring often. Heat broth and water to boiling. Sprinkle onions with flour and cook additional 3 minutes, stirring constantly as it thickens. Remove from heat and add the boiling broth. Blend well. Refrigerate at this point if serving later. If using immediately, add wine, season to taste, and simmer partly covered about 35 minutes longer. If refrigerated, 35-40 minutes before serving add wine and seasonings; simmer. Add Parmesan cheese to each bowl before serving.

SERVES 8

NOTE: To speed up cooking time, onions may be prepared in microwave— excellent.

Cream of Potato Soup

6 potatoes, peeled
1 Tablespoon butter
2 leeks, chopped
4 green onions, chopped
2½ Tablespoons flour
3 Tablespoons butter
4 10½-ounce cans Campbell's chicken broth, fresh chicken broth, or bouillon and water
5 ounces potato water (saved from boiling potatoes)
8 ounces sour cream
1¼ cups half and half
Salt and white pepper to taste
⅛ teaspoon monosodium glutamate (optional)
½ cup fresh grated Cheddar cheese

Cut peeled potatoes in thirds and boil. Drain, saving 5-6 ounces of potato water; set potatoes aside. Melt 1 Tablespoon butter in soup kettle, add leeks and onions; cook just until tender, not brown. Mix flour with 3 Tablespoons butter, forming paste. Add chicken broth to leeks and onions in kettle. Stir flour/ butter paste into mixture with wire whisk. Mash the reserved drained potatoes manually. Do not use an electric mixer. Add potatoes to kettle. Add potato water. Simmer 10 minutes. Add sour cream, half and half, salt and pepper, and MSG. Heat, but do not boil. Serve garnished with grated cheese.

SERVES 10

VARIATION: For Vichyssoise, cool before adding sour cream and half and half. Chill. Garnish with chopped parsley.

Cock-A-Leekie Soup

1½ bunches leeks, diced
2 onions, diced
3 stalks celery, diced
¼ pound butter
4 cups chicken stock
2 pounds potatoes, diced
Half and half
Salt and pepper to taste

Sauté vegetables in butter until soft. Add chicken stock and diced potatoes; sim mer for 1½ hours. Put mixture into blender or food processor and blenc Before serving, reheat mixture to boiling point and add half and half until cor sistency of a thick cream soup. Do not boil. Salt and pepper to taste.

SERVES

Vichyssoise Aunt Bonaparte

1 medium white sweet onion, chopped
4-6 leeks, sliced, using white part only
¼ plus cup butter
6 medium potatoes, peeled and thinly sliced
1 quart chicken broth
2 plus teaspoons salt
3 cups milk
1 pint heavy cream
Snipped chives and parsley

In large pan, brown the onions and leeks in butter until transparent. Add potatoes, broth, and salt. Boil 30-40 minutes or until *tender.* Place in processor and blend or purée. Return mixture to large pan, adding the milk and 1 cup of the cream. Bring to boil. Cool and rub through a sieve; correct seasoning if necessary. Chill. Add remaining cream. Chill thoroughly, garnish with chives and parsley, and serve!

SERVES 6-8

Hearty Pumpkin Soup

1 large onion, chopped
¼ cup margarine or butter
½-¾ teaspoon curry powder
2 cups canned pumpkin (Santiam)
2½ cups rich chicken stock
½ teaspoon salt
¼ teaspoon white pepper
2 cups heavy cream
Sour cream
Fresh chopped parsley

Sauté onion in butter in a large soup kettle or saucepan until soft. Sprinkle with curry powder and sauté a few more minutes. Place onion mixture and canned pumpkin in a blender and blend for 1 minute, or blend in a food processor for about 20 seconds. Place pumpkin purée back into the soup kettle and add chicken stock, heating slowly. Blend in salt, pepper, and cream. Do *not* boil soup after cream has been added. Garnish with sour cream and a sprinkle of fresh parsley.

SERVES 4-6

NOTE: A nice beginning to a holiday meal.

Winter Tomato Soup

1 cube butter
2 Tablespoons olive oil
1 large onion, thinly sliced (about 2 cups)
1 teaspoon thyme
1 teaspoon basil
Salt and pepper to taste
1 2-pound, 3-ounce can Italian tomatoes (Progresso)
3 Tablespoons tomato paste
3¾ cups chicken broth, divided
4 Tablespoons flour
1 teaspoon granulated sugar
1 cup cream (heavy or half and half)

In saucepan melt butter and add olive oil, onion, thyme, basil, and salt and pepper. Cook, stirring, until onions wilt. Add tomatoes and tomato paste. Simmer 10 minutes. Blend together 5 Tablespoons of the chicken broth with the flour. Add this to soup, stir, then add rest of broth. Simmer 30 minutes, stirring often to prevent burning. Purée soup in blender. Return to heat. Add sugar and cream. Simmer 5 more minutes.

SERVES 8

Cream of Zucchini Soup

6 cups sliced zucchini
1 cup water
2 Tablespoons minced onion
1 teaspoon seasoned salt
1 teaspoon parsley flakes
2 teaspoons chicken broth
4 Tablespoons butter
4 Tablespoons flour
4 shakes white pepper
¼ teaspoon monosodium glutamate
½ teaspoon Beau Monde
2 teaspoons chicken broth
2 cups milk
1 cup half and half cream
Paprika

Combine and cook zucchini, water, onion, salt, parsley, and 2 teaspoons chicken broth. When tender and only a little water is left, put through a sieve. Reserve. (This may be frozen.) When ready to serve, melt butter, stir in flour, pepper, MSG, and Beau Monde, and remaining 2 teaspoons chicken broth. Blend. Add milk and cream and simmer until thickened. Stir in reserved zucchini juice. If too thick, add more milk. Top with sprinkle of paprika.

SERVES 8

Zucchini Soup

4 slices bacon, chopped
6 cups cubed zucchini
4 cups beef stock
1 teaspoon basil
1 teaspoon salt
¼ teaspoon pepper
1 teaspoon seasoning salt
2 small onions
2 small garlic cloves
4 Tablespoons chopped fresh parsley
Parmesan cheese

In a 3 to 4-quart saucepan sauté bacon. Add zucchini, beef stock, basil, salt, pepper, and seasoning salt. Using a food processor or blender chop onion and garlic. Add to zucchini mixture. Add parsley. Cook until zucchini is tender. Pour cooked mixture into processor or blender and blend until smooth. Reheat and check seasoning. Garnish with Parmesan cheese.

SERVES 4-6

Beer Cheese Soup

½ cup butter
½ cup finely diced carrots
½ cup finely diced celery
½ cup finely diced onion
½ cup flour
Salt to taste
½ teaspoon dry mustard
5 cups chicken broth
1 Tablespoon grated Parmesan cheese
8 ounces sharp Cheddar cheese, shredded
11 ounces flat beer

Have all the ingredients ready for mixing before starting to cook. Melt butter in large kettle; let butter "froth" but not brown. Add vegetables and sauté until tender. Gradually blend in flour, turning heat down slightly. Add salt and dry mustard, rolling it between your fingers to avoid lumps. Cook mixture until it begins to brown. Add chicken broth; return heat to high. Add cheeses, blend and stir constantly. Add beer. Bring to a boil for only a moment, reduce heat and serve.

SERVES 4-6

NOTE: To reheat, place in oven and warm slowly (275°F) so cheese won't curdle. Do not use direct heat.

Creamy Chicken Noodle Soup

3 Tablespoons butter
1 cup sliced onion
1 cup sliced celery
1 cup sliced fresh mushrooms
½ teaspoon poultry seasoning
1 cup diced cooked chicken
2 cups partially cooked noodles (just softened)
Water
1 10½-ounce can cream of chicken soup
2 cubes chicken bouillon
Salt and pepper to taste

Melt butter in 3-quart saucepan. Sauté onions, celery, and mushrooms in butter along with poultry seasoning until onions are just tender. Add chicken and noodles. Cover with water and add soup and bouillon cubes. Bring to boil and reduce heat. Simmer until noodles are tender. Correct seasoning by adding salt and pepper to taste.

SERVES 8

"Remove all grease from soup by throwing a lettuce leaf into the pot. This will absorb all the grease and may be removed as soon as it has served its purpose."

Klamath County Museum

Cream of Chicken Soup

1 3-pound chicken
Water to cover
2 Tablespoons salt
4 celery stalks, chopped
4 carrots, chopped
1 large onion, chopped
½ pound butter
1 cup flour
½ cup chopped pimientoes
½ cup blanched, chopped green pepper
1 teaspoon monosodium glutamate
½ teaspoon white pepper

Boil chicken in water with salt and vegetables until tender. Strain off 8 cups stock and place in another kettle. Bone and chop the chicken; set aside. Make roux by melting butter and adding flour. Bring strained chicken stock to a very low boil, slowly adding roux. Simmer 10-15 minutes until soup takes on a glaze. Add pimientoes, green pepper, and the chopped chicken. Add MSG and white pepper. Stir occasionally.

SERVES 8-10

NOTE: Good served with cheese bread.

Chicken Bisque Soup

from the Gables, Corvallis, Oregon

3-pound stewing hen
6 cups water
Tablespoons salt
½ cup melted butter
cup flour
½ cup chopped chicken (taken from above)
½ cup chopped pimientos
½ cup blanched peppers
1 teaspoon monosodium glutamate
½ teaspoon pepper
3-4 drops yellow food coloring

Boil the stewing hen in water with salt until tender. Strain off 8 cups of stock. Make a roux of the butter and flour. Add strained stock and simmer 15 minutes. Carve ½ cup chicken from carcass and add to mixture. Add remaining ingredients, stiring constantly until heated. Serve at once.

SERVES 6-8

Mom's Borsch

1 2-pound piece lean rump roast
3 quarts beef stock
1-2 large onions, chopped
2 stalks celery, cut into 2-inch pieces
3-4 carrots, quartered
3 small leeks, chopped
2 white turnips, peeled and diced
2 parsnips, peeled and diced
3 sprigs parsley
2 bay leaves
6 peppercorns, slightly mashed in mortar and pestal
6 large beets, cut julienne
1 cabbage, cut into small wedges
3 Tablespoons tomato paste
Salt and fresh ground pepper to taste
2 Tablespoons red wine vinegar
1 Tablespoon granulated sugar
1 small raw beet
1 Tablespoon chopped dill
½ pint sour cream

Combine first 11 ingredients in large kettle, bring to a boil, then simmer for 2½ hours. Remove and reserve beef; remove and discard bay leaves and peppercorns. Blend stock mixture in processor until smooth. Return stock to kettle with next 4 ingredients and simmer for 1 hour. Add vinegar and sugar. Cut reserved beef into bite-size pieces. Return to kettle and simmer 10 minutes. Grate raw beet, strain juice, and add to soup at last minute. Sprinkle with dill. Serve with sour cream.

SERVES 6-8

Winter Soup

1 cup dried lentils, washed
2 quarts water
¼ cup tomato sauce
2 teaspoons salt
1 teaspoon oregano
½-1 teaspoon basil
½ teaspoon thyme
Fresh ground pepper
1 clove garlic, minced
2 stalks celery, sliced
1 onion, sliced
3 carrots, sliced
6 mushrooms, sliced
1 baking potato, unpeeled and cut in chunks
⅓ cup *fresh* parsley
1-2 16-ounce cans tomatoes drained
4 ounces pork sausage, browned and well-drained
1 Tablespoon butter
Lots of *fresh* grated Parmesan cheese

Combine all ingredients except tomatoes, sausage, butter, and Parmesan cheese. Cover and simmer for 1 hour. Add tomatoes and browned sausage: simmer 15-30 minutes longer. Add butter, blending into soup. Sprinkle each serving with Parmesan cheese.

SERVES 5-6

OPTIONAL: May use liquid drained from tomatoes as part of required 2 quarts of water.

Steak Soup

1 pound ground chuck
1 cup flour
½ pound margarine
8 cups water
1-1½ cups canned tomatoes
4 Tablespoons beef flavor base
1 carrot, grated
1 onion, grated
1 stalk celery, chopped
Pepper (no salt)
Other seasonings such as herb mix may be used
Fresh mixed vegetables (optional)

Cook and crumble ground chuck until browned. Meanwhile make a roux with the flour and margarine. When thickened and smooth, gradually add water to roux and blend. then add remainder of ingredients, including well-drained meat, and simmer for 1½ hours. Stir occasionally. When reheating you may have to add a bit more water.

SERVES 8

VARIATION: Fresh, skinned tomatoes may be used in place of canned tomatoes. Place in blender with enough juice or water to make equivalent.

Vegetable Beef Soup

3 pounds beef short ribs, and/or soup bone
1 pint tomato juice
Water (approximately 6 cups)
2 teaspoons salt
6 peppercorns
1 cup chopped celery
⅓ cup chopped onion
2 teaspoons salt
2 teaspoons Worcestershire sauce
¼ teaspoon chili powder
2 bay leaves
2 15-ounce cans tomatoes
4 Tablespoons barley (optional)

Place meat and tomato juice in a large soup kettle. Add enough water to cover meat. Add salt and peppercorns; bring to a boil. Cover and simmer for 2 hours. Strain and cool overnight or until fat solidifies on top. Remove fat and discard. Remove meat from bones and return meat to broth; add the remaining ingredients except barley. Simmer 1 hour. At this time barley may be added and cooked until tender.

SERVES 6-8

Hawaiian Portuguese Soup

1 pound garbanzo, pinto or red kidney beans
Water
2 onions, chopped
2 beef shin bones
1 ham hock
1 Tablespoon salt
2 stalks celery, chopped
2 carrots, sliced
2 potatoes, cubed
¼ cup minced fresh parsley
1 small cabbage, cored and cubed
1 8-ounce can tomato sauce
1 2-pound can stewed tomatoes
2 garlic cloves, chopped
3 Linguisa (Portuguese) sausages, sliced, or hot, spicy pork or beef sausage
½ teaspoon ground anise
¼ teaspoon ground cinnamon
¼ teaspoon ground cloves
¼ teaspoon fresh ground pepper

Place beans in large kettle. Fill kettle with water 3 inches above the level of beans. Bring to a boil. Remove from heat. Cover and let beans soak for 1 hour. Add onions, shin bones, ham hock, and salt. Bring to a boil. Reduce heat. Partially cover and simmer for 2-3 hours. Remove meats. Discard fat and bone and return meat to pot. Add celery, carrots, potatoes, parsley, cabbage, tomato sauce, tomatoes, garlic, and sausages. Season soup with remaining spices. Simmer soup for 1 hour and serve hot with lots of crusty bread.

YIELD: 5-6 quarts

Fish Chowder

4 large potatoes
4 medium onions
1 cup chopped celery
6 cloves
2 garlic cloves, minced
2 cups milk or half and half
1 Tablespoon salt
2-3 small bay leaves
½ teaspoon peppercorns
2½-3 cups stock, water or court bouillon
2 pounds fish chunks, boned (any firm fish is good)
1 cup white wine
½ cup butter

Wash, peel, and cut potatoes into medium cubes. Slice onions. Combir vegetables with spices in large saucepan. Cover with stock. Boil un vegetables are done, approximately 25 minutes. Remove cloves and ba leaves. Add fish, milk, wine, and butter. Simmer 10-15 minutes, or until fish fully cooked. Serve hot.

SERVES

NOTE: If court bouillon is used, reduce remaining wine in recipe to ½ cu Cooked fish may be used, but be sure to remove all bones.

Fish Soup Creole Gumbo

1 large onion, chopped
2 slices ham or bacon, chopped
2 garlic cloves, chopped
1 10½-ounce can tomato soup
4 cups water
1 15-ounce can okra, undrained
2 green peppers, chopped
1 8-ounce can oysters (optional)
1 pint fresh or canned crab
1 6½-ounce can clams, undrained
1 cup any leftover fish, cooked or uncooked (sole, red snapper, salmon, etc.)
½ teaspoon thyme
Dash of cayenne
Salt and pepper to taste
Fresh parsley, chopped

Simmer onions and ham together until onions are cooked. Add rest of ing dients and simmer about 1 hour.

SERVES

Seafood Bisque

Biederbeck's

4 Tablespoons butter
Small onion, chopped fine
½ cup chopped celery
2 Tablespoons chopped parsley
1 teaspoon dry mustard
2 bay leaves
½ teaspoon paprika
½ teaspoon oregano
½ teaspoon tarragon
1 teaspoon thyme
1 teaspoon basil
½ cup flour
2 cups clam nectar
½ cup white wine
1 cup chili sauce
1 cup tomato purée
1½ cups sour cream
2 cups half and half
½ lemon with rind
Dash Tabasco
Dash Lea & Perrins
4 ounces clams
6 ounces baby shrimp
2 ounces scallops
8 ounces white fish
(sole, perch, cod, etc.)
2 ounces crabmeat

Melt the butter and sauté onion, celery, parsley, and next 7 spices. Set aside. Make a roux of the flour, clam nectar, and white wine. Cook down briefly, and then combine the roux and sautéed ingredients. Add the next 7 ingredients. Stir to blend. Add remaining seafood, and heat briefly to cook all seafood.

SERVES 6

NOTE: This recipe can be widely varied, and one need not be concerned if all ingredients are not available. Just follow the general cooking procedure.

"Bernhardt's Skin Tonic:

½ pint alcohol
2 ounces spirits of camphor
2 ounces spirits of ammonia
5 ounces sea salt
Boiling water sufficient
to make 1 quart

Put all in a bottle and agitate thoroughly. Rub into the skin with the hands. Always shake before using. Takes the fatigue from one's muscles after a long walk or much exercise."

I. Armstrong, Some More Good Things to Eat, 1907

Shrimp and Crab Bouillabaisse

¼ cup salad oil
3 Tablespoons butter
1 teaspoon garlic powder
3 medium onions, sliced
3 medium green peppers, chopped
1 cup sliced celery
2 medium leeks, chopped
1 Tablespoon salt
¼ teaspoon pepper
1 Tablespoon thyme, crushed
Pinch saffron powder
1 medium bay leaf
1 cup dry white wine
3 pounds white fish chunks (haddock, cod, etc.)
1 1-pound can tomatoes
1 10-ounce can tomato sauce
1 7-ounce can king crabmeat
½ pound deveined cooked shrimp
Fresh parsley, chopped

Heat oil and butter over medium heat. Sauté garlic, onions, peppers, celery and leeks until vegetables are just tender, 5-10 minutes. Add seasonings, wine fish meat, (except crab and shrimp), tomatoes with juice, and tomato sauce Simmer over low heat for 15-20 minutes. Remove any cartilage from crab Drain. Rinse shrimp in cold water and drain. Add crab and shrimp to soup Simmer covered, stirring occasionally, 15 minutes. If soup seems too thick, add more wine. Garnish with parsley.

SERVES 6-8

Seafood Soup

1 6½-ounce can tuna
1 6½-ounce can shrimp
1 4-ounce can clams
1 16-ounce can tomatoes or stewed tomatoes
1 16-ounce can green beans
1 medium onion, chopped
2 cloves garlic, minced
1 teaspoon basil
1 teaspoon oregano
Salt and pepper to taste
1 4-ounce can chopped mushrooms (optional)
1 4-ounce can hot peppers (optional)
1 16-ounce can wax beans (optional)
1 46-ounce can tomato juice

Mix all ingredients together except tomato juice and simmer for 1 hour. Ad tomato juice and heat thoroughly.

SERVES 6-

Senegalese Soup

3 Tablespoons butter
3 teaspoons curry powder
3 Tablespoons flour
4½ cups chicken broth
1 cup finely chopped shrimp
1½ cups whipping cream or milk
Salt and pepper to taste
1 Tablespoon chopped chives

Melt butter. Add curry powder and cook 1 minute. Stir in flour and cook until bubbly. Pour in broth and cook until thickened, stirring with whisk, then add the shrimp. Add cream, salt and pepper, and heat. Do not boil. Garnish with nipped chives.

SERVES 4

NOTE: Good with an Indonesian or Greek menu!

Indian Clam Chowder

"The Indian method of making clam chowder was to soak the clams overnight in a fresh-water stream, and then throw them into a hollowed log containing water heated to the boiling point by hot stones. After they had opened, the clams were scraped from their shells and replaced in the water, together with chunks of jerked or smoked venison, dried wild onions, and wapato roots that the squaws had gathered in dry lake beds."

Oregon: End of the Trail, 1951

Clam Chowder

pound bacon, diced
½ pound ham, cubed
cups chopped onion
¼ cup flour
2 cups diced potatoes
6 cups clams, undrained and minced
7 cups milk
Salt and pepper to taste
Butter or margarine

Sauté the bacon and ham, drain off most of the bacon drippings, and save. Add the onion to bacon and ham mixture; sauté until the onion is limp. Stir in the flour. Pour enough bacon drippings back into the pan to fry the potatoes. Add the potatoes and fry, stirring constantly, about 15 minutes or until the potatoes are soft. Add the clams with liquid and cook 5 more minutes. Add milk; season with salt and pepper to taste. Dot with butter or margarine when serving.

SERVES 12-16

Oyster Stew

The Oyster Bar

3 gallon pot of whole milk
1 rounded soupspoonful salt
1 rounded babyspoonful pepper
3 heaping teaspoons Schilling's Savor Salt
⅕ pound butter
1-2 quarts oyster meat
Butter, garnish

Heat milk in double boiler until it is as hot as possible. Add salt, pepper, and savor salt. Then add butter. When all are combined thoroughly, add oyster meat. Simmer ½ hour or until oysters surface. Skim off oysters and portion into serving bowls. Let milk mixture simmer 15-30 minutes longer, then ladle over oysters. Top each serving with butter patty.

Mushroom-Oyster Stew

1 pint (12-ounce jar fresh petite oysters
3 Tablespoons butter
1 teaspoon beau monde
Dash of clove
Dash of nutmeg
Dash of ginger
Dash of cinnamon
1 teaspoon powdered mushrooms
1 teaspoon chicken stock base
1 cup hot water
1 cup light cream
1 teaspoon brandy or cognac

Drain oysters and reserve liquid. Melt butter and add oysters and seasonings Cook oysters until plump and edges curl. Add powdered mushrooms, stock and hot water. Heat to simmer, stirring occasionally. Add cream and reserved oyster liquid. When soup again simmers, add brandy. Serve at once!

SERVES

In 1861 native oysters were discovered in Oregon waters. Captain R. Hillye entered Yaquina Bay in 1864 for the purpose of gathering the oysters. By 188 two towns had been established around the burgeoning oyster business, Oysterville to the north and Oyster City to the south of the bay.

Blender Hollandaise Sauce

1 cup butter
4 egg yolks
2 Tablespoons lemon juice
Pinch salt
¼ teaspoon Tabasco

Heat butter in small saucepan until very hot (not browned). Place last 4 ingredients in blender, cover, and blend at low speed. With blender still on, immediately pour the hot butter in a steady stream into the blender. When all butter has been added, turn off motor. Serve immediately or keep warm by setting blender container in warm water. If sauce becomes too thick, add 1 Tablespoon hot water and blend a short time.

YIELD: 1¼ cups

NOTE: This one has never curdled, thus far!

Quick Béarnaise Sauce

2 egg yolks
1 Tablespoon lemon juice
1 teaspoon tarragon vinegar
1 teaspoon tarragon
¾ cup hot, melted butter
2 Tablespoons chopped parsley

Place egg yolks, lemon juice, vinegar, and tarragon in blender or food processor. With blender or processor at high speed add melted butter very slowly. Pour sauce into bowl. Fold in parsley.

YIELD: 1 cup

Sweet and Sour Wine Sauce

1 cup granulated sugar
1 cup vinegar
½ cup Madeira wine, divided
½ cup Oriental bean threads (optional)
1 green pepper
2 Tablespoons soy sauce
2 Tablespoons cornstarch
1 Tablespoon preserved ginger
½ cup pineapple chunks
¼ cup chopped sweet pickles

Combine sugar, vinegar, and ¼ cup wine in a saucepan. (If bean threads are used, soak according to package directions.) Remove seeds and membranes from green pepper and cut into very fine strips. Add green pepper, bean threads, and soy sauce to liquids; bring to a boil. Dissolve cornstarch in remaining ¼ cup wine and stir into boiling liquids. Cook, stirring constantly, until mixture turns clear and thickens. Add remaining ingredients and heat thoroughly. Serve over deep-fried chicken or pork.

YIELD: 2½ cups

Indian Sauce

Using the basic recipe from the Indians, this conserve was used by the pioneers to perk up winter meals.

"12 apples
19 small onions
½ teaspoon salt
1 teaspoon dry mustard
12 ripe tomatoes
1 pint vinegar
3 cups sugar
1 teaspoon celery seeds

Cook together until apples and onions are done. Seal in sterile jars. To be used on meat."

Tillamook County Museum

Salsa

1 medium onion
2 Tablespoons vinegar
3 medium-size tomatoes
1 4-ounce can whole green chiles, deveined, seeds removed, and diced
1 Tablespoon vegetable oil
Salt and pepper to taste

Chop onion and soak in vinegar. In a separate bowl mix tomatoes, which have been cut into bite-size pieces, and diced chiles. Drain onion and add to tomato mixture. Blend in oil and salt and pepper. Let set at least 4 hours in refrigerator.

YIELD: 1½-2 cups

Perfect B-B-Q Sauce

1 cup ketchup
1 cup water
¼ cup dehydrated minced onion
¼ cup packed brown sugar
2 Tablespoons Lea & Perrins Worcestershire sauce
½ teaspoon salt

Combine all ingredients, stirring until the sugar is dissolved. Store covered in the refrigerator. Uses: (1) Baste for chicken, pork or beef. (2) Pour over meat and cook over medium heat until the meat is tender and sauce is reduced by one half. (3) Use as a marinade for meat to be cooked over charcoal. Baste with sauce while meat is broiling. (4) Combine with cooked shredded chicken, pork or beef. Heat through and serve meat over toasted English muffins or hamburger buns.

YIELD: 2½ cups sauce

Best Barbecue Sauce

- 2 8-ounce cans tomato sauce
- 1 medium onion, chopped and sautéed in butter
- ⅛ teaspoon garlic salt
- Tablespoon Worcestershire sauce
- 2-3 squirts Tabasco sauce
- 1 cup packed brown sugar
- ¼ cup wine vinegar
- 1 Tablespoon parsley flakes

Mix all the ingredients together in a saucepan and bring to boil, simmering 15 minutes. Use on ribs, chicken or hamburger.

YIELD: 3-4 cups

Sweet and Sour Mustard

- ounces Coleman's dry mustard
- cup malt or regular vinegar
- 1¼ cups granulated sugar
- 6 eggs

Soak mustard in vinegar for several hours. Stir in sugar. Add eggs one at a time, beating with wire whisk as you add. Place over cold water in a double boiler. Heat and stir the mixture until it becomes thick.

YIELD: 2 pints

Piquant Mustard

- 1 cup dry mustard
- ⅓ cup dry white wine
- ⅓ cup tarragon vinegar
- ⅓ cup honey
- 2 Tablespoons water
- 1 .9-ounce package garlic salad dressing mix
- 1½ teaspoons salt
- ½ teaspoon garlic powder
- 2 eggs, slightly beaten

Mix all ingredients, except eggs, in top of double boiler. Cover and let stand -6 hours at room temperature. Stir eggs into mustard mixture. Cook over simmering water, stirring constantly, until mixture thickens. Pour into sterilized jars. Cool slightly and cover. Refrigerate at least 24 hours and use within 3 months.

YIELD: 2 cups

SUGGESTION: Tasty and unusual gift. Also excellent with homemade picnic salami.

Piquant Cocktail Sauce

1½ cups Heinz Chili Sauce (12-ounce bottle)
1½ Tablespoons fresh lemon juice
2 teaspoons finely minced chives or spring onion
½ cup finely minced celery
1 teaspoon Worcestershire sauce
1½ Tablespoons horseradish
⅛-¼ teaspoon curry
¾ teaspoon dry mustard
2 teaspoons sweet relish
½ teaspoon salt
½ teaspoon pepper
Dash Tabasco

Mix all ingredients and allow to sit 12 hours before using. Great with fresh cracked crab. It's spicy!

YIELD: 2 cups

Tartar Sauce

1 cup mayonnaise
6 Tablespoons finely chopped dill pickles
1 Tablespoon white wine vinegar
1 Tablespoon dill weed
1 teaspoon parsley
½ teaspoon Worcestershire sauce
⅛ teaspoon salt
⅛ teaspoon dry mustard
Dash cayenne pepper

Mix all ingredients and refrigerate. Good on any fish or French fries.

YIELD: 1 cup

Teriyaki Marinade

½ cup soy sauce
⅔ cup vegetable oil
¼ cup granulated sugar
2 Tablespoons lemon juice or sherry
½ teaspoon monosodium glutamate
1 clove garlic, minced

Mix together all ingredients. Pour over chicken or beef and marinate for hours.

YIELD: 1½ cup

Teriyaki Sauce

¾ cup soy sauce
¼ cup granulated sugar
¼ cup saké or dry sherry
2 teaspoons ginger
⅛ teaspoon garlic powder

Blend together all ingredients. Brush over chicken or flank steak and broil. Keeps indefinitely in refrigerator.

YIELD: 1 cup

Marilyn's Meat Marinade

½ cup A-1 sauce
1 8-ounce can tomato sauce
2 Tablespoons white vinegar
½ cup packed brown sugar

Combine all ingredients in a saucepan. Simmer 5 minutes. Marinate flank steak overnight; other steaks, 4 hours.

YIELD: 2 cups

Lamb Marinade

3 medium onions, minced
1 piece (1 × 3-inch) fresh ginger, chopped and peeled
7 cloves fresh garlic, pressed
½ cup red wine vinegar
¼ cup granulated sugar
⅔ cup lemon juice
1 Tablespoon ground coriander
1 teaspoon cuminos (cumin)
1 teaspoon garam marsala (optional)
1 teaspoon ground turmeric
¼ teaspoon ground mace
¼ teaspoon nutmeg
¼ teaspoon cinnamon
¼ teaspoon ground cloves
1 teaspoon rosemary
1 cup olive oil
2½ teaspoons salt
¼ teaspoon pepper
½-1 teaspoon cayenne pepper
½ teaspoon orange food coloring

To prepare marinade, mix together all of the ingredients; pour over the lamb and marinate for 24 hours, turning frequently. Barbecue and baste with leftover juices.

YIELD: 2½-3 cups marinade

NOTE: Enough for 1 9-10 pound butterflied leg of lamb.

Cranberry Orange Sauce

2 pounds fresh or frozen cranberries
2 oranges
4 cups granulated sugar
1 cup white wine

Wash and pick over berries, removing any that are soft. Dice whole oranges, removing any seeds. Combine all ingredients in a large kettle. Bring to a full boil. Reduce heat and continue cooking until cranberries pop open and mixture is thickening. Pack into hot sterilized jars and seal as for jelly. For best flavor, let stand several days before using.

YIELD: 4 pints

Cranberry Relish

1 pound whole cranberries
2 lemons
1½ cups granulated sugar
1 cup walnuts, coarsely broken
¼-½ cup orange juice
Fresh parsley

Break cranberries into pieces. Chop lemons, including peel; remove and discard pits. Combine all ingredients except parsley and mix well. Store in refrigerator overnight. Garnish with parsley.

SERVES 6

Cranberry Chutney

1 cup fresh whole cranberries
1 small onion, chopped
1 cup peeled and chopped apple
½ green pepper, chopped
½ cup packed brown sugar
½ cup dark corn syrup
¾ cup vinegar
1½ teaspoons ginger
1½ teaspoons mustard seed
1 teaspoon salt
1½ teaspoons lemon juice
¼ teaspoon grated lemon rind
2½ cups raisins

Combine all ingredients in large kettle saucepan. Bring to a boil, stirring constantly. Reduce heat and continue to cook and stir for approximately 1 hour, or until mixture thickens. Store in sterilized jars in refrigerator, or seal as in canning.

YIELD: 1½ pints

Brandied Cranberries

1 pound cranberries
2 generous cups granulated sugar
Brandy

Wash and drain cranberries. Place in a jelly-roll pan or on a cookie sheet with sides. Sprinkle with sugar until berries are covered. Broil, stirring several times for first few minutes, 6-8 inches below burner. (Stirring prevents sugar from crystallizing.) Continue broiling until berries have popped, this takes several minutes. Pour into a storage container and add generous amount of brandy. Stir lightly, cover and refrigerate. Will keep indefinitely in refrigerator. Good with turkey or chicken.

YIELD: 6 cups

Marshmallow Sauce

1 cup granulated sugar
⅔ cup light corn syrup
½ cup hot water
2 egg whites
¼ teaspoon vanilla
Dash of salt
¼ cup mayonnaise
1 Tablespoon grated orange rind

Combine sugar, corn syrup, and hot water. Heat, stirring until sugar dissolves. Then boil without stirring to firm ball stage (244-248°F) on candy thermometer. (In humid weather cook to 248°F.) Beat egg whites until stiff. Slowly add hot syrup, beating at high speed until thick and fluffy. Add vanilla and salt. Gently fold in mayonnaise and orange rind. If thicker than desired, fold in 1-2 Tablespoons more mayonnaise, or 1-2 teaspoons water.

YIELD: 3 cups

NOTE: Great with fresh pineapple spears served over ice cream. This sauce can be thinned with more mayonnaise and some orange juice for a salad dressing for fresh fruit.

Blueberry Topping

1-2cups fresh or frozen blueberries
Powdered sugar to taste

Place blueberries in blender with powdered sugar. Blend until smooth and fluffy. Serve on waffles, pancakes, or ice cream.

YIELD: 1-2 cups

SALADS AND DRESSINGS

Darlene M. Kosoff

Quick Spinach Salad

1 bunch fresh spinach
1 3-ounce can French fried onion rings
2 Tablespoons grated Parmesan cheese
1 0.7-ounce package Good Seasons Cheese Garlic salad dressing, prepared as directed on package

Wash, dry and tear spinach leaves into bite-size pieces, discarding stems. Place spinach in large salad bowl and add canned onion rings. Just before serving, add grated cheese and salad dressing to taste. Toss and serve.

SERVES 6-8

Wilted Spinach Salad

1½ pounds fresh young spinach
10 strips bacon
4 Tablespoons olive oil
6 Tablespoons red wine vinegar
2 teaspoons herb mixture (rosemary, tarragon, oregano)
2 teaspoons Worcestershire sauce
2 teaspoons Dijon prepared mustard
4 teaspoons granulated sugar
Fresh ground pepper to taste

Tear, wash, and dry spinach into bite-size pieces and put in salad bowl. Cut bacon in 1-inch pieces and sauté until crisp. Drain off drippings, remove bacon, crumble and set aside. In the same pan, mix olive oil, vinegar, herbs, Worcestershire sauce, mustard, and sugar. Mix well and heat through. Add fresh ground pepper and pour over spinach. Cover bowl with a lid and let steam 15 seconds. Toss salad and serve on large salad plates. Spoon any excess dressing onto salads and sprinkle bacon over top.

SERVES 4

Creamy Spinach Salad

1 bunch spinach, stemmed
1 small red onion, cut into rings
½ pound bacon, cooked crisp and drained

DRESSING:
½ cup mayonnaise
2 Tablespoons granulated sugar
2 Tablespoons white wine vinegar

Mix dressing and let sit at least 1 hour before putting on salad. Clean and dry spinach leaves. Tear into bite-size pieces and place in salad bowl. Spread onion rings over top of spinach. Crumble bacon and put over top. Toss with dressing and serve.

SERVES 4

Korean Spinach Salad

1½ pounds fresh spinach
8 ounces fresh bean sprouts
1 8½-ounce can water chestnuts, drained and sliced
5 slices bacon
Salt and pepper to taste
2 hard-cooked eggs, sliced

DRESSING:
⅔ cup salad oil
⅓ cup granulated sugar
⅓ cup ketchup
⅓ cup white wine vinegar
⅓ cup finely chopped green onion
2 teaspoons Worcestershire sauce

Trim and discard tough spinach stems. Rinse leaves and pat dry. Tear into bite-sized pieces. Combine spinach, sprouts, and water chestnuts in bowl. Fry bacon, drain and crumble into spinach. Cover and refrigerate. In jar, combine oil, sugar, ketchup, vinegar, onion, and Worcestershire sauce. Stir and chill. Just before serving, pour dressing over and toss. Sprinkle with salt and pepper. Garnish with eggs.

SERVES 8

Curried Spinach Salad

2 pounds fresh spinach
3 golden delicious apples
⅔ cup dry roasted Spanish peanuts
½ cup raisins
⅓ cup thinly sliced green onion
2 Tablespoons toasted sesame seeds

DRESSING:
½ cup white wine vinegar
⅔ cup salad oil
1 Tablespoon finely chopped Major Grey's chutney
1 teaspoon each curry powder, salt, and dry mustard
¼ teaspoon liquid hot pepper

Prepare dressing and let stand 2 hours at room temperature to blend flavors. Rinse and trim spinach leaves, pat dry. Tear into bite-size pieces. Wrap well and chill until serving time. To serve, core and dice apples, then in a large bowl, combine spinach, apples, peanuts, raisins, onion, and sesame seeds. Shake the dressing before serving and pour over salad. Toss lightly.

SERVES 6-8

"When washing spinach, a pinch or two of salt added to the water will help make the sand sink to the bottom of the pan."

Klamath County Museum

Easy Spinach Salad

2-3 bunches spinach
2 Tablespoons butter
½-1 teaspoon garlic juice
1 cup walnut pieces
1 orange

DRESSING: (Makes 1¾ cups)
⅓ cup granulated sugar
1 teaspoon salt
1 teaspoon paprika
¼ cup orange juice
2½ Tablespoons lemon juice
1 Tablespoon vinegar
1 teaspoon finely chopped onion
1 cup salad oil

Wash and dry spinach, tear into pieces, chill. Combine butter and garlic juice over medium heat, add walnuts and brown, stirring continuously so walnuts won't burn. Drain walnuts. Peel and slice orange. Toss orange and walnuts with spinach. To make dressing, combine ingredients in jar and shake well or blend in blender. Pour enough dressing to cover salad but not make it soggy.

SERVES 6-8

NOTE: Dressing is also good with fruit salad.

Green and White Salad

½ medium cauliflower
½ pound fresh spinach
¼ pound sliced fresh mushrooms
½ cup pine nuts or slivered almonds
1 firm ripe avocado, peeled, pitted, and sliced

DRESSING:
6 Tablespoons salad oil
3 Tablespoons white wine vinegar
1 large garlic clove, minced
½ teaspoon salt
½ teaspoon dry mustard
½ teaspoon basil
¼ teaspoon pepper
Dash nutmeg

Rinse, drain and coarsely chop the cauliflower (3 cups yield). Wash and pat dry spinach. Stack leaves and slice crosswise into ¼-inch wide strips. Place in salad bowl with the cauliflower; cover and refrigerate if made ahead. In a jar, combine oil, vinegar, and all of the spices. Just before serving salad, add mushrooms. Pour dressing over all and add nuts which have been baked in a shallow pan at 350°F for 7 minutes. Mix gently. Garnish with avocado.

SERVES 6

NOTE: Good for potlucks—different type of salad and it doesn't wilt easily.

Romanian Tossed Salad

½ head romaine lettuce
½ head iceberg lettuce
1 small head cauliflower
1 avocado, peeled
1 8½-ounce can sliced water chestnuts
1 2-ounce package sliced almonds, toasted

DRESSING:
1 garlic clove, minced
1-2 teaspoons salt
2 Tablespoons lemon juice
¼ teaspoon dry mustard
¼ teaspoon celery seed
¼ teaspoon granulated sugar
¼ teaspoon pepper
5 Tablespoons oil

Tear lettuce into bite-size pieces. Cut up cauliflower and avocado into bite-size pieces. Combine lettuce, cauliflower, water chestnuts, and avocado. When ready to eat add toasted almonds. To make dressing, combine all ingredients in jar and shake. Pour dressing over salad and toss.

SERVES 8-10

Romaine with Hot Bacon Dressing

½ head romaine lettuce (2 quarts prepared)
⅓ cup thinly sliced green onion
6 slices bacon

DRESSING:
2 Tablespoons granulated sugar
3 Tablespoons vinegar
1 egg, well beaten
3 Tablespoons reserved bacon drippings
Salt and pepper to taste

Wash the romaine leaves well, pat dry and break into bite-size pieces. Place the romaine and green onion in a bowl, cover, and refrigerate. In a frying pan, cook the bacon over medium heat until crisp; remove it from the pan, drain, crumble, and set aside. Discard all but 3 Tablespoons of the drippings. (May be done ahead to this point.) Just before serving, combine the sugar, vinegar, and egg, mixing a little at a time with the reserved bacon drippings. Cook over medium-low heat, stirring, until heated and thickened; do not boil. Remove from heat, season with salt and pepper to taste, and pour over the romaine and onions. Sprinkle in the crumbled bacon and mix well. Serve immediately.

SERVES 6

Oregano Salad

1 head romaine lettuce (4 quarts prepared)
⅔ cup grated Parmesan cheese

DRESSING:
6 Tablespoons salad oil
3 Tablespoons red wine vinegar
¼ cup water
½ teaspoon oregano
½ teaspoon garlic powder
½ teaspoon onion powder
½ teaspoon monosodium glutamate or salt
1 teaspoon Worcestershire sauce
1½ teaspoons garlic salt
1½ teaspoons granulated sugar
¼ teaspoon pepper

Rinse and pat dry the lettuce, then put it in a large salad bowl and sprinkle Parmesan cheese on top. To make the dressing, mix salad oil, vinegar, water and seasonings in a covered jar. Shake well to blend. Add enough oregano dressing to the lettuce and cheese to moisten. Toss and serve.

SERVES 6-8

Artichoke Caesar Salad

2 heads romaine lettuce
2 6-ounce jars marinated artichoke hearts, reserve marinade
¼ cup grated Parmesan cheese
1 cup hot toasted sourdough bread croutons
8 rolled anchovy fillets with capers (optional)

DRESSING:
Marinade from artichoke hearts
⅓ cup olive oil
3 Tablespoons lemon juice
1 raw egg yolk
½ teaspoon Dijon prepared mustard
½ teaspoon garlic salt
¼ cup grated Parmesan cheese

To make the dressing, drain the marinade off the artichokes into a small bowl. (Set the artichokes aside.) To the marinade add oil, lemon juice, egg yolk, mustard, garlic salt, and Parmesan cheese. Set aside. Tear the lettuce into bite-size pieces and put in a salad bowl. Beat the dressing mixture with a whisk or put in blender and blend until smooth. Pour the dressing over lettuce and toss until coated. Add artichoke hearts (cut if too big) then sprinkle with Parmesan cheese and croutons. Garnish with anchovy fillets if desired.

SERVES 4

NOTE: Pepper lovers can top with fresh ground pepper before serving!

Layered Green Salad

1 head of lettuce
4 hard-boiled eggs, sliced
½ green pepper, diced (optional)
8 slices bacon, fried and diced
1 cup diced celery
1 10-ounce package frozen peas, uncooked
1 sweet onion, sliced thin
2 Tablespoons granulated sugar
2 cups mayonnaise
4 ounces Cheddar cheese, grated

Tear lettuce into bite-size pieces and place in large bowl or 9 × 12-inch dish. Layer eggs, vegetables, and bacon in order given. Add the sugar to the mayonnaise and spread over all. *Do not stir.* Top with grated cheese and cover. Refrigerate 12 to 24 hours.

SERVES 10-12

Roquefort Salad

1 head lettuce
1 garlic clove, peeled and cut in half
1 cup walnuts, chopped
¼-½ pound Roquefort cheese, crumbled
½ cup whipping cream
Juice of 1 lemon
6 Tablespoons peanut oil

Wash the lettuce under cold running water; strip off the leaves by hand, one by one, and dry well. Rub the inside of a salad bowl with the garlic and discard the clove. Place the walnuts in the bowl; add the Roquefort cheese, and blend them together. Gradually mix in the cream and the lemon juice. Add the oil, mixing thoroughly with a wooden spoon or beating lightly with a whisk. Break the lettuce leaves into the bowl and mix until they are thoroughly coated with the salad dressing.

SERVES 4

Summer Salad

6-8 cups lettuce, torn into bite-size pieces
1 cucumber, peeled and thinly sliced
1 11-ounce can mandarin oranges, drained
3 Tablespoons sliced green onion or ½ sweet onion, sliced in thin rings
1 ripe avocado, seeded, peeled, and thinly sliced

DRESSING:
¾ teaspoon grated orange peel
½ teaspoon grated lemon peel
¼-⅓ cup orange juice concentrate
½ cup salad oil
2½ Tablespoons granulated sugar
2 plus Tablespoons red wine vinegar
1 Tablespoon lemon juice
¼ teaspoon salt
Dash pepper

Several hours before serving, combine dressing ingredients in a screw-top jar and *shake*. To serve, combine lettuce and remaining ingredients in a large salad bowl, pour dressing over all, and toss lightly.

SERVES 8

Hot Mushroom Salad

1 head butter lettuce torn for salad and stored in refrigerator to chill
¼ pound Monterey Jack cheese, shredded
½ pound mushrooms, sautéd in butter

DRESSING:
½ cup olive oil
¼ cup tarragon vinegar
2 Tablespoons Dijon prepared mustard
3 garlic cloves, minced
Salt and pepper

Put salad plates in freezer 1 hour before serving. Make the salad dressing by combining all ingredients and blending. Set aside. To serve, mix lettuce, cheese and dressing, and put on individual plates. Sauté the mushrooms just before serving and pour over salads so hot mushrooms will slightly melt the cheese.

SERVES 4-6

NOTE: Good with plain meat dinners.

Metropol Café Potato Salad

2 pounds red-skinned potatoes
Salted water
1 cup chopped parsley
1 cup finely sliced green onion
⅓ cup chopped ripe olives
½ cup olive oil (approximately)
½ cup red wine vinegar (or more)
Salt and pepper to taste
Fresh or dried basil to taste
Metropol Café Mayonnaise

Boil the potatoes in salted water, until tender. Cool. Chop them into pieces 1 × ¼-inch. Toss potatoes into a bowl with the parsley, green onion, and olives, adding olive oil, vinegar, and seasonings until everything is coated and seasoned. Prepare several hours before serving to allow the flavors to mingle. Check seasoning just before serving (add more vinegar for sharpness, if necessary). Serve with homemade Metropol Café Mayonnaise (below).

SERVES 6-8

Metropol Café Mayonnaise

1 egg yolk
¼ teaspoon grey poupon Dijon prepared mustard
Pinch white pepper
⅓ teaspoon salt
1 Tablespoon red wine vinegar
⅓ cup plus 2 Tablespoons olive oil
⅓ cup plus 2 Tablespoons salad oil

Place egg yolk, spices, and vinegar in bowl or electric mixer bowl. At high speed, whip for a few seconds. Then, begin adding the oil first in droplets, then a slow stream while continuously whipping. You may add a bit more vinegar to season it, or alternate with vinegar and oil, but don't add too much vinegar. When all the oil has been added, check the seasoning and serve.

YIELD: 1 cup

NOTE: Use within 3 days. Best to prepare with electric mixer.

Hot German Potato Salad

6 medium-size red potatoes, boiled in jackets (about 2 pounds)
6 slices bacon
¾ cup chopped onion
2 Tablespoons flour
1-2 Tablespoons granulated sugar
1½ teaspoons salt
½ teaspoon celery seed
Dash pepper
¾ cup water
⅓ cup vinegar

Peel and cube potatoes, set aside. Fry bacon slowly; drain on paper, crumble, and set aside. Sauté onion in bacon fat until golden brown. Blend in flour, sugar, salt, celery seed, and pepper. Cook over low heat stirring until smooth and bubbly. Remove from heat. Stir in water and vinegar. Heat to boiling, stirring constantly. Boil 1 minute. Carefully stir in the potatoes and bacon. Remove from heat. Cover and let stand until ready to serve. Reheats well.

SERVES 6-8

Coleslaw Salad

2 pounds green cabbage, finely shredded

DRESSING:
1½ cups sour cream
2 egg yolks
2 Tablespoons lemon juice
3 teaspoons horseradish
¼ teaspoon paprika
¼ teaspoon pepper
1½-2 teaspoons prepared mustard
3 teaspoons granulated sugar
1 teaspoon salt or to taste
½ cup shredded carrots
½ cup crushed pineapple, drained

Prepare cabbage, place in bowl, and set aside. Combine sour cream and egg yolks until well blended. Mix in all remaining dressing ingredients. Pour dressing over cabbage; toss until cabbage is well coated. Refrigerate for 30 minutes before serving.

SERVES 6-8

Tabbouleh

2 cups water
½ cup uncooked bulgar
3 medium tomatoes, finely chopped
1 cup finely chopped parsely
1 cup finely chopped onion
⅓ cup fresh lemon juice
2 teaspoons salt
⅓ cup oil
2 Tablespoons finely chopped mint (optional)
Fresh ground pepper

Boil water and pour over bulgar. Let sit 10 minutes and drain off water. Add tomatoes, parsley, and onion. Mix together lemon juice, salt, oil, optional mint, and ground pepper. Pour over the bulgar mixture. Refrigerate until ready to serve.

SERVES 4-6

"A small piece of camphor ice in the drawer with silver will prevent tarnish."
Klamath County Museum

Ensalada Esmeralda
(Emerald Salad)

1 pound zucchini, whole, blanched
1 3-ounce package cream cheese
2 Tablespoons chopped onion
1 avocado, pared and cubed
2 green chiles, peeled and cut in strips
Oil, vinegar, salt and pepper or Italian dressing
Romaine Lettuce, chopped
Pimiento-stuffed olives

Cut zucchini in thick slices. Break cheese in pieces. Combine with onion, avocado, and chiles. Add oil, vinegar, salt and pepper (or Italian dressing). Refrigerate for 20-25 minutes. Serve on bed of lettuce and garnish with olives.

SERVES 4-6

Fire and Ice

6 large firm, ripe tomatoes
1 large green pepper, seeded
1 red onion
1 cucumber

DRESSING:
¾ cup vinegar
1½ teaspoons celery salt
1½ teaspoons mustard seed
⅛ teaspoon black pepper
½ teaspoon salt
4½ teaspoons granulated sugar
⅛ teaspoon red pepper
¼ cup cold water

Skin and cut each tomato into 4 or 8 parts. Slice green pepper into strips. Slice red onion into rings. Place in a bowl. Heat mixture of vinegar, seasonings, and water. Bring to boil and boil furiously for 1 minute. While hot, pour over tomatoes, green pepper, and onion. Chill. Stir occasionally. Just before serving, add a peeled and sliced cucumber. (The tomatoes will keep for days in the refrigerator. Fresh cucumbers need to be added—they will get soft.)

SERVES 8

NOTE: The tomatoes are very hot and are the "fire," while the cucumber is the "ice." Spicy and tangy. A colorful Christmas salad.

Broccoli Salad

1 pound broccoli, cut into bite-size pieces
2 medium-size ripe tomatoes
2 Tablespoons thinly sliced green onion
½ cup mayonnaise
½ teaspoon salt
¼ teaspoon pepper
1 Tablespoon lemon juice
Sliced hard-boiled eggs (optional)

Cook broccoli just until crisp (5-10 minutes). Drain and cool. Dice tomatoes and combine with green onion, mayonnaise, salt, pepper, and lemon juice. Toss gently with broccoli. Chill and serve. If desired, garnish with eggs.

SERVES 4-6

NOTE: Good with any roasted meat.

Mushroom, Cheese, and Watercress Salad

1 cup fresh mushrooms
1 cup diced Gruyere cheese
½ cup bias-sliced celery
2 cups washed fresh watercress
½ cup fresh alfalfa sprouts (optional)

DRESSING:
¼ cup wine vinegar
½ cup olive oil
1 Tablespoon Italian Seasoning
Dash salt
Freshly ground pepper

Toss mushrooms, cheese, celery, and watercress in salad bowl. Just before serving, combine vinegar, oil, and seasonings. Pour over salad. Toss lightly again. Sprinkle top with sprouts, if desired.

SERVES 4

Layered Vegetable Platter

1 pound fresh green beans
2 large tomatoes, peeled and sliced
1 medium-size red onion, sliced
1 cup cut up artichoke hearts
1½ cups sliced fresh mushrooms

DRESSING:
½ cup wine vinegar (white or red)
¼ cup olive oil
2 garlic cloves, minced or pressed
1 teaspoon basil
½ teaspoon oregano
Salt and pepper

Snap beans into 2-inch lengths. Cook only until blanched, 5 minutes or less. Drain. Plunge into cold water. Drain. Arrange salad vegetables on serving platter in layers beginning with tomatoes, then onion, artichoke hearts, mushrooms, and last, the beans. Combine dressing ingredients and pour over salad. Cover and refrigerate for 4 hours. Baste several times with dressing which can be drained off at edges.

SERVES 8

NOTE: Good with barbecued meat. An easy Greek salad variation; add feta cheese and Greek olives.

Layered Vegetable Salad

¾ cup bottled Italian dressing
½ teaspoon garlic salt
½ teaspoon salt
¼ teaspoon pepper
10 mushrooms, thinly sliced
4 green onions, sliced
2 medium cucumbers, peeled and thinly sliced
½ cup chopped parsley
1 medium green pepper, seeds removed, and cut into thin strips
3 large tomatoes, cut into thin wedges
6 ounces Swiss cheese, cut into thin strips
4 hard-boiled eggs, sliced

In bottom of salad bowl, combine salad dressing, garlic salt, salt, and pepper. Add mushrooms and green onions, and mix into dressing. On top of this mixture layer the cucumbers, parsley, green pepper, tomatoes, and Swiss cheese. *Do not mix salad.* Cover and refrigerate 3-4 hours. Just before serving, mix together and garnish with egg slices.

SERVES 8

NOTE: Good make-ahead salad.

Bean-Beet Salad

⅔ cup granulated sugar
⅔ cup vinegar
1 teaspoon salt
1 16-ounce can shoestring beets
1 16-ounce can sliced green beans
⅓ cup chopped green onion
½ cup mayonnaise
2-3 hard-boiled eggs, chopped
Chopped green onion

Make marinade of sugar, vinegar, and salt. Drain beets and beans. Put into separate containers and divide the marinade between the two. Refrigerate overnight. The next day, drain the beets and beans thoroughly. Put beets on bottom of 6 × 10-inch Pyrex dish. Add green onion, then the green beans. Mix together mayonnaise, eggs, and a few green onions, and spread over beans and beets for topping.

SERVES 8

Mixed Salad

1 medium cucumber, pared
1 avocado, peeled, pitted and sliced
2 large bananas, sliced
1 large green pepper, cut in thin strips
1 medium-size red pepper, cut in thin strips
½ small onion, very thinly sliced and separated

DRESSING:
⅓ cup vinegar
¼ cup salad oil or olive oil
½ teaspoon salt
¼ teaspoon bottled hot pepper sauce (Tabasco)

Halve the cucumber lengthwise, remove seeds, and slice crosswise. Arrange cucumber, avocado, bananas, green pepper, red pepper, and onion in a salad bowl. Make dressing by combining ingredients in a jar. Pour dressing over salad and marinate 1-2 hours.

SERVES 8

NOTE: The bananas make this salad unique!

Salt was scarce in the early days of the Oregon country, especially in the less accessible areas. It was often traded for its weight in gold.

Sauerkraut Salad

1 16-ounce can sauerkraut
1 cup granulated sugar
1 green pepper, chopped
1 4¼-ounce can chopped ripe olives
1 cup chopped carrots
1 cup chopped celery

Drain, rinse, drain again, and chop sauerkraut. Add sugar and mix well. Add remaining ingredients. Refrigerate at least 2 hours.

SERVES 4

NOTE: Easy, unusual salad.

Marinated Vegetable Salad

3 6-ounce jars marinated artichoke hearts plus marinade
1 14½-ounce can asparagus, drained (optional) or fresh, steamed and cooled
1 16-ounce can green beans, drained or fresh, steamed and cooled
1 head cauliflower, cut into cauliflowerettes
2 zucchini, sliced with peel left on
1 pound whole mushrooms (slice larger ones)
1 cup sliced celery
Few broccoli flowerettes (optional)
2 0.7-ounce packages Good Seasons Italian dressing mix, prepared as directed on package

Combine all ingredients and chill at least two hours, preferably overnight. (If overnight, stir once or twice to mix the marinade throughout.) Drain and serve.

SERVES 8-10

Molded Spinach Salad

1 3-ounce package lime jello
1 cup boiling water
1 10-ounce package frozen chopped spinach, thawed and drained
¼ cup cold water
½ cup mayonnaise
2 Tablespoons vinegar
¾ cup cottage cheese
1 Tablespoon minced onion
⅓ cup chopped celery
Lettuce
Louis-type dressing

Dissolve jello in 1 cup boiling water. Add spinach, cold water, mayonnaise, vinegar, cottage cheese, onion, and celery. Pour into rectangular pan. Serve on a bed of lettuce and top with shrimp. Serve with Louis-type dressing.

SERVES 6

Jellied Vegetable Salad

1 3-ounce package lemon gelatin
¾ cup boiling water
3 Tablespoons lemon juice
½ cup mayonnaise
½ cup sour cream
1 Tablespoon prepared mustard
½ teaspoon salt
1¼ cups shredded cabbage
¼ cup diced celery
¼ cup sliced radishes
¼ cup sliced carrots
2 Tablespoons diced green onion
2 Tablespoons diced green pepper

Dissolve gelatin in boiling water and set aside. Cool. Mix together lemon juice, mayonnaise, sour cream, mustard, and salt. Add to gelatin. Fold in cabbage, celery, radishes, carrots, green onion, and green pepper. Refrigerate in salad molds.

SERVES 6

Tomato Aspic Salad

1 3-ounce package lemon jello
1 cup boiling water
1 8-ounce can tomato sauce
3 Tablespoons lemon juice
1 Tablespoon Worcestershire sauce
6 drops Tabasco
¼ cup chopped celery
¼ cup chopped onion
¼ cup chopped green pepper
¼ cup sliced green olives
½ pound shrimp (canned or cooked fresh)
Lettuce

Combine lemon jello and water. Add tomato sauce, lemon juice, Worcestershire, and Tabasco. Chill until slightly jelled; then add the remaining ingredients, except lettuce. Chill until jelled; then turn out on a bed of lettuce.

SERVES 6-8

Pineapple-Cabbage Salad

1 3-ounce package lime jello
1 cup water
1 cup miniature marshmallows
1 cup well-drained crushed pineapple
1 cup chopped nuts
1 cup chopped cabbage
1 cup mayonnaise
1 cup whipped cream

Cook jello, water, and marshmallows over low heat until they dissolve. Add the pineapple, nuts, and cabbage, and let set up until fairly firm. Fold in the mayonnaise and whipped cream and let set up until firm.

SERVES 8

Molded Avocado Salad

1 3-ounce package lime jello
1 cup boiling water
1 teaspoon salt
3 Tablespoons chopped celery
1 Tablespoon chopped onion
2 ripe avocados, peeled and mashed
½ cup mayonnaise
½ cup whipped cream

Dissolve jello in boiling water. Set aside to cool until thick, then whip until light. Fold in remaining ingredients. Pour into mold, and let set up.

SERVES 8

Cranberries have long grown wild in the peat-bog land found along the Oregon coastal region. In 1879 commercial cultivation began in the Coos Bay area. Charles Dexter McFarlen imported a variety that was particularly suited to the soil in this area. He gave his family name to the strain of berries, and now 75 percent of all the cranberries grown in the Pacific Northwest are of this variety.

Molded Blueberry Salad

FIRST LAYER:
1 3-ounce package strawberry jello
1 cup hot water
1 cup cold water

SECOND LAYER:
½ cup cold water
1 ¼-ounce envelope Knox Gelatine
1 cup whipping cream, unwhipped
1 cup granulated sugar
1 8-ounce package cream cheese
1 teaspoon vanilla
½ cup chopped nuts

THIRD LAYER:
1 3-ounce package strawberry jello
1½ cups hot water
2 cups blueberries

This is a 3-layered salad; allow time for each layer to set.
FIRST LAYER: Dissolve strawberry jello with hot water. Add cold water and pour into 9 × 13-inch Pyrex dish. Let set up until firm.
SECOND LAYER: Mix cold water with gelatine. Heat until gelatine dissolves. Add whipping cream and sugar. Using a blender, blend cream cheese until soft, then add the whipping cream mixture to it. Add vanilla. Blend until thick and frothy. Stir in chopped nuts and pour over first layer. Let set until firm.
THIRD LAYER: Mix strawberry jello and hot water. Add blueberries. Pour over second layer and allow to set until firm.

SERVES 12-15

Raspberry Salad

1 6-ounce package raspberry jello
2 cups boiling water
2 10-ounce packages frozen raspberries
1½ cups applesauce
2 cups sour cream
2 cups miniature marshmallows

Dissolve jello in hot water and cool to lukewarm. Add frozen berries and applesauce. Mix and pour into pan, approximately 7 × 11 inches, until set firm (or overnight). Mix sour cream and marshmallows. Spread over salad and let set several additional hours. Cut in 2 - 3-inch squres and serve on greens.

SERVES 8

NOTE: Excellent with poultry.

Strawberry Salad Supreme

1 6-ounce package strawberry jello
1½ cups boiling water
2 10-ounce packages frozen strawberries, undrained
1 13½-ounce can crushed pineapple, undrained
¼ teaspoon salt
1 8-ounce package Philadelphia cream cheese, softened
½ cup sour cream

Dissolve jello in boiling water. Add strawberries, pineapple, juice from both and salt. Pour ½ of jello mixture in mold and refrigerate until set. Beat cream cheese into sour cream. Spread cheese mixture on top of molded jello after it is set. Pour remaining jello on top of cream cheese. Refrigerate to completely set up.

SERVES 8-10

NOTE: Good with seafood or poultry.

Avocado Melon Salad

¼ cup sour cream
2 Tablespoons apricot preserves
1 Tablespoon mayonnaise
1 small cantaloup, pared
1 small avocado, pared
Leaf lettuce

Mix sour cream, apricot preserves, and mayonnaise together; cover and refrigerate. Cut cantaloup into 4 wedges. Cut avocado lengthwise in half and then cut each half into 4 slices. Arrange lettuce, cantaloup, and avocado on serving platter. Pour dressing over top.

SERVES 4

Cranberry Arctic Frost Salad

1 cup whipping cream
1 cup chopped nuts
1 cup drained, crushed pineapple
1 16-ounce can whole cranberries or whole-berry cranberry sauce, drained
2 Tablespoons mayonnaise
2 Tablespoons granulated sugar
1 8-ounce package cream cheese

Whip cream. Fold in nuts and pineapple. Liquify cranberries in blender. Add mayonnaise, sugar, and cream cheese to berries in blender and mix together. Fold cranberry mixture into cream mixture and freeze in oblong Pyrex dish. About 15 minutes before serving, take the salad out of the freezer. Slice and serve.

SERVES 6-8

Mother's Cranberry Christmas Salad

1 1-pound package of cranberries
1 cup granulated sugar
1 cup drained, crushed pineapple
4 cups miniature marshmallows
1 cup whipped cream

Grind cranberries. Add sugar, then pineapple. Add marshmallows. Let this set in refrigerator overnight. Add whipped cream just before serving.

SERVES 6-8

Cranberry Velvet Salad

1 6-ounce package raspberry jello
1¼ cups hot water
1 cup cold water
2 cups sour cream
2 15-ounce cans jellied (no pulp) cranberry sauce
1 cup chopped walnuts

Dissolve jello in hot water. Add cold water. Chill until thick. Blend the sour cream and cranberry sauce together with a beater. Add to jello mixture and then add the chopped nuts. Pour into mold.

SERVES 12

NOTE:Good holiday dish with turkey and chicken. Can be made the night before using.

Jellied Cranberry-Cheese Salad

1 cup water
¼ cup red cinnamon candies
1 3-ounce package lemon jello
1 16-ounce can whole cranberry sauce
½ cup diced celery
1 3-ounce package cream cheese, softened
¼ cup mayonnaise
1 Tablespoon lemon juice
¼ teaspoon grated lemon peel

In saucepan, heat water and candies until candies dissolve. Add jello. Stir until dissolved. Remove from heat and beat in cranberry sauce. Chill until partially set. Stir in celery. Pour half the mixture into a 4-cup mold. (Save the other half for the top layer.) Chill. Blend cream cheese, mayonnaise, lemon juice, and lemon peel. Carefully spread over gelatin mixture in mold. Spoon remaining gelatin mixture over cheese mixture. Chill.

SERVES 6

NOTE: Excellent with holiday dishes; turkey and ham.

Fruited Cheese Salad

3 cups cream-style cottage cheese
1 8-ounce container Cool Whip
1 6-ounce package orange jello
1 13½-ounce can pineapple tidbits or crushed pineapple, well drained
1 11-ounce can mandarin oranges, drained

Blend cottage cheese and Cool Whip. Stir in dry jello. Fold in pineapple tidbits and mandarin oranges. Press into mold. Let set for 3-4 hours.

SERVES 12-15

VARIATION: For pink salad, use raspberry or strawberry jello and delete the mandarin oranges.

Fruit Salad

1 8-ounce container Cool Whip
1 3-ounce package instant pistachio pudding mix
1 20-ounce can crushed pineapple and juice
1 cup miniature marshmallows
½ cup finely chopped nuts (walnuts, filberts, or almonds)

Mix all ingredients together and let set for 2 hours or overnight in the refrigerator.

SERVES 6-8

A Tropical Fruit Salad

2 pineapples
1 papaya, peeled, seeded and diced
2 bananas, peeled and diced
4 kiwi fruit, peeled and sliced
Few strawberries, if available, for color
4 chicken breasts, skinned, poached, boned, and cut into bite-size pieces
Pine nuts
4 sprigs mint

DRESSING:
½ pint cream, whipped
1 8-ounce package cream cheese
4 ounces fresh orange juice
2 ounces Grand Marnier

Cut pineapples in half. Hollow out the fruit and dice the pineapple into chunks. Place pineapple chunks in bowl. Invert and drain the pineapple shells and place them in refrigerator. (The shells will be used later to hold the fruit and chicken.) Add the other fruit and chicken to the pineapple chunks. Combine all the ingredients for the dressing and blend together. Dressing will be slightly thick. Pour the dressing over the salad and toss. Fill the pineapple shells with the salad. Sprinkle pine nuts over the fruit and decorate with sprigs of mint.

SERVES 4

VARIATION: Don't mix dressing with fruit; serve separately. Serve fruit mixture on a bed of leafy lettuce for an attractive salad platter instead of the pineapple shells.

Hot Chicken Salad

4 cups cooked diced chicken or turkey
2 cups diced celery
2 Tablespoons lemon juice
¼ cup diced pimientos
½ teaspoon salt
1 4¼-ounce can chopped ripe olives
4 hard-boiled eggs, diced
⅔ cup chopped almonds
1½ cups mayonnaise
1 Tablespoon chopped onion
1½ cups grated cheese
1½ cups crushed potato chips

Mix all ingredients except cheese and potato chips. Put in 9 × 13-inch Pyrex dish. Cover with cheese and chips, and bake at 350°F for 25 minutes.

SERVES 6-8

"When you find a crack in your favorite dish or plate, boil it in a pan of milk for 45 minutes. This should make the crack disappear and actually make the dish stronger."

Oregon Historical Society

Chinese Noodle Salad

1 10-ounce package frozen peas
1 head lettuce
4 celery stalks, sliced
2 cups diced cooked chicken, 2 6½-ounce cans tuna or shrimp, or 2 cups fresh shrimp
1 5-ounce can Chinese noodles

DRESSING:
1 cup mayonnaise
⅓ cup soy sauce
Dash garlic powder

Cook peas as directed on package. Set aside to cool. Tear lettuce into bite-size pieces. Mix with the celery, and add the chicken. Make dressing by mixing all the ingredients. When ready to serve, add noodles to salad. Pour dressing over salad and toss.

SERVES 6-8

Taco Salad and Dressing

1 head iceberg lettuce
1 onion, chopped
4 tomatoes, chopped
1 avocado, peeled and sliced (optional)
½ pound Cheddar cheese, shredded
1 pound ground beef, cooked
1 15-ounce can kidney beans
1 9-ounce bag Doritos chips, crushed

DRESSING:
1 10½-ounce can tomato soup
¾ cup vinegar
2 Tablespoons chopped onion
1 teaspoon Worcestershire sauce
1 teaspoon celery salt
1 teaspoon paprika
1 cup salad oil
¾ cup granulated sugar

Tear lettuce into bite-size pieces and put in large bowl. Add onion, tomatoes, avocado, cheese, hamburger, and kidney beans. Combine all the dressing ingredients and blend in blender. Pour half of the dressing over salad to lightly coat. Add more to taste. Toss. Top with crushed Doritos.

SERVES 10-12

Molded Crab Salad

2 Tablespoons plain gelatin
½ cup cold water
1 cup chili sauce
1 cup mayonnaise
1 cup heavy cream, whipped
1½ cups fresh crabmeat or canned crab
½ cup chopped celery (optional)

Soften gelatin in cold water for 5 minutes. Add chili sauce and stir well. Heat chili sauce mixture in double boiler. Stir until smooth. Cool chili sauce by replacing the hot water in bottom of double boiler with cold or ice water. Let stand until mixture is cool, but not stiff. Put mayonnaise in a bowl and slowly add whipped cream, stirring constantly mix well. Add chili sauce mixture, crab meat, and celery (optional). Pour into a 5-cup mold and refrigerate.

SERVES 6

Salmon Salad

1-pound piece of salmon
1 cup sour cream
½ cup chili sauce
1 Tablespoon lemon juice
4 teaspoons horseradish
1-2 tomatoes
1 avocado
1 cucumber
Lettuce
¾ cup shredded Cheddar cheese

Poach salmon, drain and chill. Combine sour cream, chili sauce, lemon juice, and horseradish. Refrigerate. Peel and slice tomatoes, avocado, and cucumber. (If preparing avocado ahead, sprinkle it with lemon juice and salt to prevent discoloration.) At serving time, tear lettuce into small pieces and put in bowl. Flake salmon into the bowl and add the tomatoes, avocado, cucumber, and cheese. Add the sour cream mixture and toss.

SERVES 4

Guacamole Salad

1 bunch salad greens
2 4-ounce packages alfalfa sprouts
3 ripe avocados, peeled and pitted and cut into eighths
¾ onion, cut up
1 Tablespoon lemon juice
1½ teaspoons salt
⅜ teaspoon freshly ground black pepper
½ green pepper, sliced into 4 rounds
½ pound cooked shrimp
Frito corn chips

Cover 4 dinner plates with salad greens, then with alfalfa sprouts. Place avocado, onion, lemon juice, salt, and pepper in food processor bowl and process with metal blade until smooth. Spread on top of alfalfa sprouts. Put a round of green pepper on each plate; place shrimp in center of round. Garnish each salad with handful of crushed Fritos.

SERVES 4

NOTE: This recipe works well with a blender if a food processor is not available. A great luncheon salad served with white wine.

Shrimp-Topped Salad

2 3-ounce packages lemon jello
2 cups boiling water
1 8-ounce package cream cheese, softened
½ cup half and half or milk
1 cup sliced celery
1 cup chopped black ripe olives
1 cup cream, whipped
Lettuce

TOPPING:
1 Tablespoon lemon juice
1 cup mayonnaise
1 teaspoon grated onion
4 teaspoons chopped green pepper
2 6½-ounce cans shrimp, drained

Dissolve jello in boiling water. Cool until it starts to set. Blend cream cheese and half and half until smooth. Then add to jello. Add celery and olives and fold in whipped cream. Refrigerate in small molds or in a 9 × 9-inch pan until firm. To make topping, blend lemon juice and mayonnaise; add onion and green pepper; fold in shrimp. To serve, place slice of molded salad on lettuce leaf. Divide topping among servings by pouring on top of each piece.

SERVES 8-9

Curried Artichoke Shrimp Salad

1 8-ounce package Chicken Rice-a-Roni
1 6-ounce jar marinated artichoke hearts
1 4¼-ounce can shrimp
2 green onions, chopped
3 ripe olives, sliced
Lemon slices, parsley

DRESSING:
Marinade from artichoke hearts
⅓ cup mayonnaise
½ teaspoon curry powder

Cook Rice-a-Roni according to directions on box, except use only 1 Tablespoon of butter or margarine to brown rice. Remove from heat and let cool to room temperature. Drain artichoke hearts (reserving marinade for dressing), chop, and mix with the shrimp, green onion, and olives into the rice. Make the dressing by combining the artichoke marinade, mayonnaise, and curry powder. Mix dressing into rice mixture and refrigerate overnight. Just before serving, garnish with lemon slices on top of rice.

SERVES 6

Macaroni Shrimp Salad

2 cups cooked small elbow or shell macaroni
1 cup cooked salad shrimp
½ cup diced celery
1 8½-ounce can water chestnuts, diced
1 8½-ounce can crushed pineapple, well drained
½ cup broken pecans or walnuts
Lettuce
½ cup grated Montery Jack cheese (optional)

DRESSING
½ cup mayonnaise
1½ Tablespoons lemon juice
1 teaspoon granulated sugar
Salt and pepper to taste

Combine cooked macaroni, shrimp, celery, water chestnuts, pineapple, and nuts. Make salad dressing by combining ingredients and mixing well. Pour over salad and stir to combine thoroughly. Serve on a bed of lettuce. Top with sprinkling of cheese, if desired.

SERVES 4

Shrimp or Bacon Stuffed Avocado Salad

4 avocados, unpeeled
Lemon juice
8 slices bacon, fried crisp, drained and crumbled or 8 ounces cooked shrimp, chilled and washed
Lettuce

SAUCE:
½ cup butter
¼ cup granulated sugar
¼ cup ketchup
¼ cup wine vinegar
2 Tablespoons soy sauce

Cut avocados in half, leaving skin on. Rub with lemon juice. Fill avocado halves with bacon and place on 8 lettuce-lined plates. Combine sauce ingredients in pan and cook over low heat until hot. Pour sauce over avocado and lettuce; serve immediately.

SERVES 8

Frozen Pea Salad

2 10-ounce packages frozen peas, thawed but not cooked
1 8½-ounce can water chestnuts, sliced
1 6¼-ounce can cashews
½ pound bacon, fried crisp, drained, and crumbled
1 cup sliced green onion
1 pint sour cream

Combine and mix all ingredients. Refrigerate before serving.

SERVES 8

Salad Nicoise

STEP ONE:
2 cups olive oil
½ cups tarragon vinegar
¼ cup fresh lemon juice
2 garlic cloves, crushed
1 Tablespoon dry mustard
1 teaspoon granulated sugar
1 Tablespoon salt
Freshly ground black pepper

STEP TWO:
2 pounds new potatoes, boiled (just cooked) and sliced
2 cups green beans (just cooked)
1 14-ounce can artichoke hearts, drained

STEP THREE:
Salad greens
3 7-ounce cans tuna, drained and marinated in 1 Tablespoon lemon juice
1 pint cherry tomatoes
1 cup pitted ripe olives (optional)
6 hard-boiled eggs, quartered
½ cup canned or bottled red pepper strips
1 large green pepper, cut in rings (optional)
1 2-ounce can achovies (optional)
2 Tablespoons capers
¼ cup parsley

STEP ONE: Blend olive oil, vinegar, and the next six ingredients in blender.
STEP TWO: Combine potatoes, beans, and artichoke hearts. Marinate with dressing for at least 2 hours. Stir occasionally.
STEP THREE: When ready to serve, line a salad bowl with salad greens. Drain marinated vegetables and keep the dressing for later use. Place the drained vegetables on the greens. Put the tuna in the middle of the bowl and arrange the tomatoes, olives, eggs, red and green pepper, anchovies, and capers around it. Sprinkle a little of the salad dressing over the salad and garnish with the parsley. Pass the salad dressing at the table if more is needed.

SERVES 6-8

NOTE: Allow time for marinating the vegetables.

Long before commercial fruits and nuts were introduced to Oregon, the Indians seasonally harvested many wild native fruits. Crab apples, Pacific plums, Oregon grape, bird cherry, and wild currant grew in the forests. Hickory nuts, Chinquapins, hazelnuts, acorns, and walnuts were gathered to store for the long winter months. Sugarpine nuts had an interesting flavor and were a popular addition to the winter stock pile.

Easy Nicoise Salad

1 0.7-ounce package Good Seasons Italian dressing
4-5 small potatoes
1 head leafy green lettuce
1 16-ounce can whole green beans, drained
1 16-ounce can kidney beans, drained
1 16-ounce can waxed beans, drained
2 7-ounce cans tuna, drained, and broken in chunks
2 tomatoes, peeled and cut in wedges
2 hard-boiled eggs, sliced
1 Tablespoon snipped parsley

Prepare salad dressing according to package directions. Boil potatoes, cookin until tender. Cut in chunks, leaving skins on, and mix with ½ of dressing. Cool Tear lettuce and arrange on large platter. Sprinkle some salad dressing on let tuce. Attractively arrange potatoes, green beans, kidney beans, waxed beans and tuna in separate mounds on lettuce. Sprinkle more salad dressing ove everything. Top with tomatoes and eggs. Sprinkle with remaining salad dress ing. Garnish with parsley. Chill at least 2 hours.

SERVES

Red Salad Dressing

(French)

1 cup granulated sugar
1 cup vinegar
1 cup oil
1 cup ketchup
Salt, pepper, and/or other seasonings to taste

Mix sugar, vinegar, oil and ketchup in blender or mixer. Add salt, pepper, an other seasonings, if desired. Refrigerate.

YIELD: 3½ cup

NOTE: This recipe may be easily cut in half or otherwise reduced.

French Salad Dressing

1 Tablespoon Dijon prepared mustard
1 Tablespoon chopped shallots
3 Tablespoons cider vinegar or white wine vinegar
½ cup olive oil

Mix all ingredients and pour over assorted greens. Allow 1 Tablespoon dressing for each cup of greens.

SERVES 4-6

Spinach Salad Dressing

⅔ cup salad oil
¼ cup wine vinegar
2 Tablespoons white wine
2 teaspoons soy sauce
1 teaspoon granulated sugar
1 teaspoon dry mustard
¼-1 teaspoon curry powder
½ teaspoon salt
½ teaspoon garlic powder
1 teaspoon pepper

Combine all ingredients in covered jar. Shake before using. Refrigerate.

YIELD: enough for 2 large salads

NOTE: Good with curry dishes.
VARIATION: Add crumbled bacon and hard boiled egg slices to spinach before topping with dressing.

Parsley Dressing for Fresh Tomatoes

2 cups chopped fresh parsley
½ cup chopped chives
1 cup drained and chopped sweet pickles
2 garlic cloves, minced
Salt and pepper to taste
¼ cup oil
½ cup red wine vinegar
¼ cup tarragon vinegar

Mix all ingredients together and let stand at room temperature for a day. Then, refrigerate in covered jar. Keeps for 2 weeks. Use over fresh tomatoes or a combination of tomatoes, cucumbers and Bermuda onions.

YIELD: 1 pint

Parmesan Salad Dressing

6 Tablespoons olive oil
2 Tablespoons tarragon vinegar
1 Tablespoon fresh lemon juice
1 teaspoon salt
1 teaspoon granulated sugar
⅛ teaspoon freshly ground pepper
½ cup grated Parmesan cheese
1 egg

Combine all ingredients in a blender and whirl until blended. Store in glass jar in the refrigerator. Good on any tossed or mixed lettuce salad.

YIELD: ¾ cup

Creamy Onion Dressing

1 cup Wesson oil
½ cup white vinegar
1 cup granulated sugar
1 teaspoon dry mustard
½ teaspoon salt
1 teaspoon celery seed
1 small white salad onion

Put everything but the onion in the blender and whirl for 8-10 minutes. Add onion, cut into chunks, and blend 1-2 minutes longer. Keep in refrigerator tightly covered.

YIELD: 2½ cups

Nora's Roquefort Dressing

1 quart Best Foods mayonnaise
1 3-ounce brick Roquefort cheese
1 8-ounce package cream cheese
1-1½ cups buttermilk, depending on thickness desired
Juice of 2 garlic cloves

All ingredients must be at room temperature for best results. Combine and mix all ingredients well. *Do not beat.* Dressing will have chunks of cheese in it that you will not be able (or want) to cream out. Refrigerate.

YIELD: 1½ quarts

NOTE: Makes a big batch; can be packaged into small jars for gifts.

Roquefort Dressing

1 pint mayonnaise
¼ cup wine vinegar
½ teaspoon dry mustard
½ cup parsley flakes (or chopped parsley)
2-4 ounces blue cheese
½ pint sour cream
1 clove garlic, crushed
½ teaspoon salt
¼ teaspoon pepper (optional)

Mix all ingredients together in blender and store in refrigerator.

YIELD: 3 cups

Buttermilk Dressing

1 cup buttermilk
1 cup mayonnaise
1 Tablespoon lemon juice
¼ teaspoon onion powder
½ teaspoon salt
½ teaspoon monosodium glutamate
1 teaspoon dried parsley flakes, ground

Combine all ingredients and refrigerate. This is best if made several hours ahead of serving time. It keeps very well in refrigerator.

YIELD: 2 cups

Croutons

2 cups bread cubes with crusts removed
2 Tablespoons butter or margarine, melted
½ teaspoon paprika
½ teaspoon onion salt

Mix all ingredients together in 2-quart utility dish. Microwave 3-4 minutes or until croutons are dry. Stir once during heating. Croutons will become crisper as they cool.

YIELD: 1½ cups

VEGETABLES

Terry Maddox

Fresh Asparagus in Butter Sauce

2 dozen fresh, thin asparagus spears
1 cup butter
2 fresh garlic cloves
2 teaspoons lemon juice
1 teaspon parsley flakes
½ teaspoon grated lemon rind
Parsley sprigs

Wash spears and snap off white ends. Cut spears into bias-sliced chunks about 2 inches long. In a wok or frying pan melt butter. Press garlic through a press and add with lemon juice and parsley flakes to butter. Heat over medium-high heat. Add asparagus and stir constantly until vegetables are crisp-tender. Remove asparagus to warm serving dish. Add lemon rind to butter sauce in pan. Heat until bubbly and pour over asparagus. Garnish with parsley sprigs and serve immediately.

SERVES 4

Asparagus Casserole

2 10-ounce packages frozen asparagus spears, thawed
4 hard-boiled eggs, sliced
Salt and pepper
½ cup grated sharp Cheddar cheese
1 cup medium white sauce, or cream of mushroom soup or cream of asparagus soup
½ cup buttered bread crumbs

Put half the asparagus in bottom of greased 1½-quart casserole dish. Top with half of the sliced eggs, salt, pepper, and half of cheese. Spoon on half of the sauce. Repeat layers, using remaining halves. Top with bread crumbs. Bake at 350°F for 30 minutes.

SERVES 6

Baked Beans

2-3 slices bacon, diced
1 19-ounce can B&M baked beans
2-3 cooking apples
2 Tablespoons butter or margarine
¼ cup packed brown sugar

Partially fry bacon; drain. Place beans in a 1 to 1½-quart casserole. Pare, slice and grate the apples; sprinkle over top of beans. Dot with butter. Sprinkle with brown sugar. Top with the drained bacon bits. Bake at 350°F for 30 minutes.

SERVES 8-10

Mother's Baked Beans

½ teaspoon pepper
4 Tablespoons packed brown sugar
1 cup ketchup
4 Tablespoons vinegar
2 Tablespoons Worcestershire sauce
Oil
2 onions, sliced
1 green pepper, chopped
2-3 pork chops
1 3-pound can pork and beans

In a small pan mix and simmer the pepper, brown sugar, ketchup, vinegar, and Worcestershire sauce. In a frying pan with a little oil sauté the onions and green pepper. Remove from pan and set aside. Brown 2 or 3 pork chops in the same frying pan. Meanwhile, put pork and beans into pot, then add the onion and green pepper. Pour in the sauce and lay the browned pork chops on top. Bake covered at 325°F for 2-2½ hours.

SERVES 15

NOTE: You may want to remove the bones from the pork chops before serving, but don't use pork loin or steak because bones add flavor.

Cool Carrots

2 large bunches carrots
Salted water
1 green pepper, chopped
1 10¾-ounce can tomato soup
½ cup salad oil
¾ cup vinegar
1 5-ounce jar cocktail onions or cocktail pickled onions, drained
1 cup granulated sugar
1 teaspoon dry mustard

Peel and dice carrots. Cook in salted water until tender; drain. Combine remaining ingredients in saucepan and bring to a boil, stirring occasionally. When mixture comes to a boil, pour over carrots. Cool, then chill. Marinate for at least 1 day before eating.

SERVES 4

NOTE: Can be kept several weeks in refrigerator.

Candied Carrots

- **2 10-ounce packages frozen whole baby carrots**
- **½ cup butter**
- **½ cup packed brown sugar**
- **½ cup honey**
- **¼ teaspoon salt**

Defrost carrots. Place butter and brown sugar in saucepan. Heat until butter melts and sugar dissolves. Add honey and salt. Add carrots, stirring well to coat. Cook over low heat until carrots are tender and glaze is thickened, coating all the carrots.

SERVES 4

Broccoli Casserole

- **2 10-ounce packages chopped frozen broccoli**
- **1 10½-ounce can mushroom soup**
- **2 eggs, well beaten**
- **1 cup grated sharp Cheddar cheese**
- **1 cup mayonnaise**
- **2 Tablespoons minced onion**
- **Salt and pepper to taste**
- **1 cup Ritz cracker crumbs**

Cook broccoli according to directions on package; drain and set aside. Make sauce by mixing soup, eggs, cheese, mayonnaise, onion, and salt and pepper. Thoroughly mix drained broccoli into sauce. Place in greased baking dish and top with cracker crumbs. Bake 45 minutes at 350°F or until bubbling and brown.

SERVES 6-8

Creamy Broccoli Casserole

- **1 pound broccoli**
- **1-1½ cups frozen pearl onions**
- **4 Tablespoons butter**
- **2 Tablespoons flour**
- **1 cup milk**
- **1 3-ounce package cream cheese**
- **2 ounces sharp Cheddar cheese, shredded**
- **½ cup buttered, browned bread crumbs**

Cook broccoli until tender. Lay flat in 8-inch square casserole and sprinkle onions over top. Make sauce by melting butter in saucepan; add flour, stir, and add milk, cooking until thick. Add cheeses; stir until melted. Pour sauce over broccoli and onions; sprinkle bread crumbs on top. Bake at 350°F for 30 minutes.

SERVES 8-9

Broccoli Pudding

1 10-ounce package frozen chopped broccoli
2 teaspoons butter
2 teaspoons flour
½ cup milk
2 Tablespoons dry sherry
½ cup mayonnaise
3 eggs, well beaten
Grated onion
Salt and pepper to taste
Parmesan cheese
Paprika

Cook broccoli and drain; set aside. Melt butter and stir in flour. Add milk an cook, stirring until mixture thickens and boils. Remove from heat. Blend i sherry and mayonnaise. Add eggs and combine mixture with the broccol Season with onion, salt and pepper. Turn into greased 9-inch pie plate. Sprinkl with Parmesan cheese and paprika. Bake in 350°F oven for 30-40 minutes checking with knife after 30 minutes, until firm and set like a custard.

SERVES

Mexican Eggplant

1 large eggplant
Oil
6 ounces chile peppers, seeded and diced
1 6-ounce can pitted ripe olives, sliced
1 29-ounce can tomato sauce
4 teaspoons chopped green scallion
2 cups grated sharp Cheddar cheese
Sour cream

Slice unpeeled eggplant into ½ to ¾-inch slices. Place on cookie sheet and d with oil. Place in 425°F oven for 25 minutes, or until soft. Meanwhile simm chile peppers, olives, tomato sauce, and scallion. In a casserole dish layer o half the eggplant, sauce, and cheese; repeat. Bake uncovered in 350°F oven f 25 minutes. Serve immediately, garnished with dollup of sour cream.

SERVES 4

Peas Steamed

"Put the peas in a tin pail, or some other article with an airtight cover, withou water. To every quart put a piece of butter as large as a quarter of a common sized hen's egg; set it in boiling water until the peas are cooked tender. This i said to be superior to any other mode, as they retain their whole flavor."

Tillamook County Pioneer Museum

Onion Pie

33 soda crackers, crushed
¼ cup melted butter
3 eggs, slightly beaten
1½ cups milk
1 teaspoon salt
Pepper to taste
1-2 bunches green onions
1 cup grated sharp Cheddar cheese

Combine the crackers and melted butter; press into 10-inch pie plate. Combine the eggs, milk, salt and pepper, and cook in a saucepan until thickened to a custard. Chop the green onions until fine, then sprinkle both the onions and the cheese over the crust. Pour the custard over the onions and cheese and bake at 350°F (25 degrees less for glass) for 30-40 minutes, or until inserted knife comes out clean.

SERVES 8

Cheese-Stuffed Peppers

6 large green bell peppers
1½ Tablespoons chopped onion
5 Tablespoons butter, divided
2 cups bread crumbs
3 cups grated American cheese, divided
½ teaspoon salt
Pinch of pepper

Slice off the stem end of peppers and remove seeds. Boil for 5 minutes, and drain upside down. Fry onion until just soft in 1 Tablespoon butter. Combine onion and butter mixture with remaining butter, bread crumbs, 2 cups cheese, and seasonings; mix well. Fill peppers with mixture and sprinkle tops with remaining 1 cup cheese. Put in greased baking dish and bake at 375°F for 30 minutes.

SERVES 6

Party Potatoes

⅓ cup butter
4 cups hot mashed potatoes
1 8-ounce package cream cheese
¼ cup sour cream
½ teaspoon salt
¼ teaspoon pepper
Paprika to taste

Stir butter into hot potatoes. Whip cream cheese with sour cream until it is smooth and fluffy. Stir this into mashed potatoes along with salt and pepper. Spoon into buttered casserole. Sprinkle with paprika and bake at 325°F for 30 minutes.

SERVES 8-10

Potato Casserole

4 pounds potatoes, peeled
1 8-ounce package cream cheese
1 cup sour cream
2 teaspoons salt
⅛ teaspoon pepper
1 garlic clove, chopped
¼ cup chopped chives
2 teaspoons butter
½ teaspoon paprika

Boil potatoes until done. Beat with electric beater. Add next five ingredients. Beat until fluffy. Fold in chives. Put in baking dish. Dot with butter and sprinkle with paprika. Bake at 350°F for 30 minutes.

SERVES 8-10

Potato Pudding

"Mix together twelve ounces of boiled mashed potatoes, one ounce of suet, one ounce of milk, and one ounce of cheese. The suet and cheese to be melted or chopped as fine as possible. Add as much hot water as will convert the whole into a tolerably stiff mass; then bake it in a short time in an earthen dish, either in front of the fire or in an oven."

Godey's Magazine, 1872; Tillamook County Pioneer Museum

Sweet Potato Delight

3 cups cooked mashed sweet potatoes
1 cup granulated sugar
2 eggs, well beaten
1 teaspoon vanilla
¼ cup milk
½ cup butter
TOPPING:
1 cup packed brown sugar
⅓ cup flour
1 cup chopped pecans
⅓ cup butter

Mix all ingredients together, except topping, and pour into buttered casserole. Mix topping ingredients together and sprinkle over casserole. Bake at 350°F for 30 minutes.

SERVES 6-8

Spinach Casserole

2 10-ounce packages frozen chopped spinach
1 envelope dry onion soup mix
1 pint sour cream
⅓ cup shredded Parmesan cheese

Thaw frozen spinach, then mix spinach, soup mix, and sour cream together. Place in casserole dish and sprinkle with Parmesan cheese. Bake at 350°F for 45 minutes.

SERVES 6-8

Spinach-Artichoke Casserole

1 6-ounce jar marinated artichoke hearts, undrained
¼ pound mushrooms, thinly sliced
1 garlic clove, pressed
1 onion, chopped
2 10-ounce packages frozen chopped spinach, defrosted and squeezed dry
1 10½-ounce can cream of mushroom soup
½ cup sour cream
2 eggs, beaten
¼ teaspoon oregano leaves
¼ teaspoon ground nutmeg
¼ teaspoon white pepper
1 teaspoon lemon juice
1 cup crushed, seasoned croutons

Drain artichoke hearts, saving marinade. Set artichokes aside. Place marinade in frying pan and sauté mushrooms, garlic, and onion until onion is limp. Stir in spinach, soup, sour cream, eggs, oregano, nutmeg, pepper, and lemon juice until well blended. Spoon half of mixture into greased shallow casserole. Arrange artichokes on top and cover with remaining spinach mixture. Top with croutons and bake at 325°F 35-40 minutes until custard is set. Let stand a few minutes before serving.

SERVES 4-6

The Indians found the camas root to be an onion-like bulb which, when boiled, tasted much like potatoes. When fermented with hot stones in deep underground pits, it developed a sweet molasses taste. The resulting product had a cheese-like consistency and was pressed into cakes and dried in the sun. These cakes kept well all winter.

Pioneer Dried Pumpkin

"When pumpkins are well ripened, peel and cut into 3 inch strips and string on strong twine, using a large strong needle to string the pumpkin. When pumpkin is strung, hang in bright sunlight during the day until it is thoroughly dried. Store in ventilated bags and hang in cool place. When ready to use, cook pumpkin in very little water over low heat until it is tender and well cooked. Drain liquid from pumpkin if there is any left when done. Fry 2 strips bacon for each serving. Remove and put aside. Fry pumpkin in pan where bacon was fried until well seasoned. Remove to serving dish and crumble bacon on top."

Tillamook County Pioneer Museum

Tomatoes Lutece

8 firm, ripe tomatoes
¼ cup chopped parsley
1 garlic clove, crushed
1 teaspoon salt
1 teaspoon granulated sugar
¼ teaspoon pepper
¼ cup olive oil
2 Tablespoons vinegar
2 teaspoons prepared mustard

Slice tomatoes into thick, even slices; set aside. Combine remaining ingredients in small jar; shake well. Layer tomatoes in shallow dish, covering each layer with dressing. Cover lightly. Let stand at room temperature at least 20 minutes. Chill and serve.

SERVES 8-10

Vegetable Casserole

3 cups diagonally cut celery
Salted water
1 10-ounce package frozen peas
1 16-ounce can white onions, drained
Butter
1 8-ounce can sliced water chestnuts, drained
1 2-ounce jar pimiento, drained
1½ 10½-ounce cans cream of chicken soup
1 4-ounce package slivered almonds, toasted
Crumbled stuffing mix
Parmesan cheese

Par boil celery in salted water for 1 minute; drain and set aside. Partially cook the peas; drain and set aside. Brown the onions in butter. Combine all ingredients, except stuffing and cheese in casserole. Cover with crumbled stuffing mix. Sprinkle with Parmesan cheese. Bake at 350°F for 35 minutes.

SERVES 4-6

Mixed Vegetable Casserole

2 large tomatoes, sliced ¼-inch thick
2 large carrots, thinly sliced
1 large green pepper, seeded cut into strips
2 stalks celery, thinly sliced
2 10-ounce packages frozen cut green beans
1 teaspoon salt
½ teaspoon pepper
10 small white onions
¼ cup chopped parsley
½ teaspoon dried minced basil
½ teaspoon dried thyme leaves
¼ cup olive oil
¼ cup dry white wine

Preheat oven to 375°F. Arrange tomato slices in greased 2-quart casserole. Layer carrots, green pepper, celery, and green beans, sprinkling a little salt and pepper in between each layer. Mound onions in the center. Sprinkle parsley, basil, and thyme over vegetables. Pour oil and wine over the top. Bake covered about 45 minutes until vegetables are tender but crisp. Cool about 5 minutes before serving.

SERVES 8-10

Fresh Spring Vegetables

1 pound fresh green beans
1 pound fresh baby carrots
6 small yellow squash
1 pint cherry tomatoes
Hot water
1 16-ounce can small potatoes
Salted water
¼ pound butter
1 teaspoon salt
¼ teaspoon pepper
½ teaspoon parsley

Wash and tip green beans; cut into 3-inch lengths. Peel carrots. Peel squash and cut in half lengthwise, then into 3-inch strips. Drop tomatoes into very hot water for 30 seconds; cool and peel. Drain potatoes. In a large skillet bring salted water to a boil. Place beans in one-third section of the pan, carrots in another third. Simmer 10 minutes. Add squash in last third of pan. Cover and simmer until all vegetables are just tender. Heat 3 Tablespoons of butter in another skillet. Sauté potatoes and tomatoes until potatoes are lightly brown. Remove all vegetables in groups to a platter and keep warm. Melt remaining butter with salt, pepper, and parsley. Pour over vegetables and serve immediately.

SERVES 6-8

Zucchini Bake

3 medium zucchini, cut in ¼-inch slices
Water
¼ cup sour cream
1 Tablespoon butter
1 Tablespoon grated cheese (Cheddar, Jack, and/or Parmesan)
½ teaspoon salt
⅛ teaspoon paprika
1 Tablespoon chopped chives
⅛ cup bread crumbs
½ cup finely grated Parmesan cheese

Simmer zucchini in water until tender, 6-8 minutes; shake the pan to keep from sticking. Remove, strain and pour cold water over zucchini. Set aside. Combine sour cream, butter, 1 Tablespoon grated cheese, salt, and paprika in a small saucepan. Place over low heat until cheese is melted. Remove sour cream mixture from heat and stir in chives; set aside. Place zucchini in a buttered casserole dish. Carefully fold in sour cream mixture. Cover top with bread crumbs and parmesan cheese. Bake at 350°F for 15 minutes, then brown under broiler if desired.

SERVES 6

Zucchini and Corn Delight

3 pounds small zucchini
Boiling water
1 12-ounce can cream style corn
5 eggs, slightly beaten
1¼ teaspoons salt
½ teaspoon pepper
1 medium onion, minced
1 green pepper, seeded and chopped
2 Tablespoons butter, melted
2 cups grated Cheddar cheese, divided
Paprika

Cook zucchini in boiling water until just tender, about 4 minutes. Drain and cut into chunks. Combine with corn, eggs, and salt and pepper. Sauté onion and green pepper in butter; add to other vegetables, along with 1 cup cheese. Pour mixture into greased casserole dish and sprinkle remaining 1 cup cheese on top. Sprinkle paprika over all for appearance. Bake uncovered for 30 minutes at 350°F or until lightly browned and bubbly.

SERVES 4-6

Zucchini Frittata

4 Tablespoons margarine or butter
½ pound mushrooms, thinly sliced
2 medium zucchini, sliced
6-8 eggs
½ teaspoon salt
1 teaspoon thyme leaves
1 teaspoon dry basil
¼ teaspoon liquid hot pepper
½ cup sliced green onion
½ cup shredded Swiss cheese
½ cup shredded Mozzarella cheese
Grated Parmesan as desired

Melt margarine in frying pan over medium-high heat. Add mushrooms and zucchini; cook, stirring until liquid has evaporated. Beat together eggs, salt, thyme, basil, and hot pepper until blended. Stir in vegetables, then transfer mixture to a well-buttered shallow 3-quart baking dish. Top with onion and cheeses. Bake uncovered at 425°F for 20 minutes, or until center barely jiggles. Let stand 5 minutes before serving.

SERVES 6-8

VARIATION: Substitute any vegetable for zucchini.

Zucchini Boats

6 zucchini (5-inches long)
Boiling water
¼ cup chopped onion
1 Tablespoon cooking oil
1 egg, slightly beaten
¾ cup soft bread cubes
¼ pound fresh mushrooms, sliced
¾ teaspoon salt
¼ teaspoon pepper
¼ cup grated Swiss cheese
½ cup grated Mozzarella cheese
1 teaspoon paprika

Cut fresh zucchini lengthwise into halves. Place in small amount of boiling water and cook covered for 10 minutes or until zucchini can be easily pierced with fork. Remove from water and cool zucchini. Scoop out and reserve center pulp of zucchini, leaving shells about ¼-inch thick. Chop zucchini pulp and strain excess liquid. Sauté onion in oil until tender. Combine zucchini pulp, onion, egg, bread cubes, mushrooms, salt, and pepper. Mix well. Arrange zucchini shells in shallow baking pan dish and fill with zucchini pulp mixture. Sprinkle top with cheeses and paprika. Bake in oven at 350°F for 20-25 minutes.

SERVES 6-8

BREADS

Elizabeth F. Gough

Willamette Valley Waffles

½ cup margarine
1 Tablespoon granulated sugar
2 egg yolks
1 cup plus 1 Tablespoon flour
Dash of salt
4 teaspoons baking powder
1 cup buttermilk
2 egg whites
¼ teaspoon almond flavoring
⅔ cup chopped filberts

Cream together the margarine and sugar. Add the egg yolks and blend. In a separate container mix the flour, salt, and baking powder. Using low speed on mixer, alternately add the buttermilk and flour to the egg yolk mixture. Add the almond flavoring. Beat the egg whites until stiff, and fold into the batter. Spoon batter onto a preheated waffle iron, spread out the batter and sprinkle with approximately 2 Tablespoons of nuts. Cook waffles according to directions on waffle iron. Repeat.

YIELD: 6-8 full-size waffles

SUGGESTION: Top waffles with butter and your favorite syrup, or for a special treat, top with sliced peaches and whipped cream.

VARIATION: Use 1 cup milk plus 1 Tablespoon vinegar for buttermilk.

"To keep white table linen from turning yellow, wrap it in a fast-color blue paper."

Klamath County Museum

Buttermilk Waffles

2 eggs
2 cups buttermilk
1 teaspoon baking soda
2 cups sifted flour
2 teaspoons baking powder
½ teaspoon salt
⅓ cup margarine, melted
Syrup, whipped butter or fruit sauce

Beat eggs well. Add the rest of the ingredients and beat until smooth. Batter will be thin. Bake in a waffle iron until golden brown. Serve with your favorite syrup, whipped butter, or fruit sauce.

SERVES 6

Original French Toast with Port Wine Syrup

1 cup half and half
6 eggs
1 Tablespoon vanilla
½ teaspoon cinnamon
6 slices bread
2 Tablespoons butter

SYRUP:
½ cup water
½ cup port wine
1¾ cups granulated sugar

Whip half and half and eggs together. Mix in vanilla and cinnamon. Dip bread in batter and fry in melted butter. To make syrup, combine water and port wine; bring to boil. Pour over sugar and mix well. Syrup can be made ahead and stored in the refrigerator.

SERVES 6

Cottage Cheese Pancakes

4 eggs
1 cup cottage cheese
¼ cup flour
1 teaspoon granulated sugar
¼ teaspoon salt

Put the eggs and cottage cheese in a blender and then add the rest of the ingredients. Blend at high speed until the batter is smooth. Pour the batter onto a griddle heated to 450°F. Make small pancakes.

SERVES 4

French Pancakes

1½ cups flour
¾ teaspoon salt
2 teaspoons baking powder
4 Tablespoons powdered sugar
4 eggs
1⅓ cups milk
⅔ cup water
1 teaspoon vanilla
Sour cream, butter, jam, brown sugar, and fresh fruit
Powdered sugar

Sift together flour, salt, baking powder, and sugar into a large bowl. Beat the eggs. Add milk, water, and vanilla to eggs and beat together. Make a well in the dry ingredients and pour in the liquids. Mix lightly, ignoring lumps. Pour onto a hot griddle for *large, thin* pancakes. Serve with bowls of sour cream, butter, jam, brown sugar, and fresh fruit. Roll pancakes up around these items and sprinkle powdered sugar over them.

SERVES 6

German Pancakes

Henry Thiele's Restaurant

1 cup flour
1 level Tablespoon salt
3 Tablespoons granulated sugar
1 cup cream or milk
9 eggs
Melted butter
Lemon juice
Powdered sugar
Syrup or apricot topping

Mix the flour, salt, and sugar with the cream to form a smooth paste. Beat the eggs into the paste. Fry one third in a large pan until nice and brown, then put in a 400°F oven until pancake bakes through thoroughly. Repeat. When done, put melted butter, lemon juice, and powdered sugar in center of each pancake and make into a roll. Serve with syrup or apricot topping.

YIELD: 3 pancakes

Mush Flannel Cakes

"Mix a pint of corn mush with two of wheat flour, a spoonful of butter or lard, two eggs and half a teacup of yeast. Make it into a batter with water or milk and fry like hotcakes."

Ladies Friend Magazine, 1869; Tillamook County Pioneer Museum

Dutch Babies

⅓ cup butter or margarine
5 large or extra-large eggs
1 cup milk
1 cup flour
Powdered sugar, syrup and fresh lemon wedges

Put butter in a 9 × 13-inch baking dish and set in a 425°F oven to melt. While butter is melting, put the eggs in a blender and blend on high for 1 minute. Gradually add milk, then flour (slowly); blend for 30 seconds. Remove the baking dish from the oven and pour the batter into the hot, melted butter. Return to heated 425°F oven and bake until puffy and nicely browned, approximately 20-25 minutes. Serve immediately with powdered sugar, syrup, and fresh lemon wedges.

SERVES 4

SUGGESTION: Other good sauce accompaniments include fresh strawberries; brown sugar and sour cream; banana or papaya slices sautéed in butter and served with lime wedges; or sautéed appled slices sweetened with cinnamon and sugar and served with sour cream or plain yogurt.

Union Pacific Apple Pancakes

In 1910, the Union Pacific Railroad compiled a cookbook titled, The Union Pacific System: 150 Recipes for Apple Dishes. Oregon apples were readily available to the chefs of the railroad and were frequently a part of the menus. Giant baked apples, apple pies, fried apple rings, and apple pancakes were served on the Union Pacific.

"1 cup flour
¼ teaspoon salt
1½ teaspoons baking powder
1 Tablespoon melted butter
½ cup milk
1 beaten egg
½ teaspoon vanilla
1¼ cups homemade applesauce

Sift flour, salt and baking powder. Combine butter, milk and egg. Stir into flour. Add vanilla and applesauce. Beat well. Spoon batter into a hot, well greased griddle, allowing enough batter to make 4" cakes. When edges are lightly browned, turn and cook on second side. Serve hot with maple syrup or apple jelly and lots of butter."

The Union Pacific System: 150 Recipes for Apple Dishes, 1910; Eugene Register-Guard

Cinnamon Raisin Coffee Cake

1½ cups flour
3 teaspoons baking powder
¾ cup granulated sugar
½ teaspoon salt
¼ cup soft shortening
½ cup milk
1 egg
1 teaspoon vanilla

FILLING:
2 Tablespoons margarine, melted
½ cup light brown sugar
2 Tablespoons flour
2 teaspoons cinnamon
½ cup raisins or chopped walnuts

Combine flour, baking powder, sugar, and salt in a large bowl; then cut in shortening. Beat milk, egg, and vanilla together and combine thoroughly with dry ingredients. Combine filling ingredients. Place about ⅔ of cake mixture in a 9-inch round greased and floured cake pan. Top with filling and add remaining cake mixture. Bake at 375°F for 30 minutes.

SERVES 10-12

Sour Cream Coffee Cake

cups granulated sugar
½ cubes butter
eggs
cup sour cream
teaspoon vanilla
cups flour
½ teaspoon salt
1 teaspoon baking powder

TOPPING:
½ teaspoon cinnamon
3 Tablespoons brown sugar
½ cup chopped nuts

Cream together the sugar, butter, and eggs. Add the sour cream, vanilla, flour, salt, and baking powder; mix together. Combine topping ingredients. Pour half the batter into a greased tube pan. Cover with half the topping. Add the rest of the batter and top with the remainder of the topping. Bake at 350°F for 1 hour. Cover with foil for the last 15-20 minutes to prevent the top from getting too brown.

SERVES 16-20

Chocolate Chip Coffee Cake

½ cup butter or margarine
cup granulated sugar
eggs
teaspoon vanilla
cups flour
teaspoon baking soda
teaspoon baking powder
½ teaspoon salt
1 cup sour cream

TOPPING:
⅓ cup brown sugar
¼ cup granulated sugar
2 teaspoons cinnamon
1 cup chopped nuts
1 6-ounce package chocolate chips

Cream butter and sugar together. Add eggs one at a time; beat well after each addition. Combine dry ingredients and add to egg mixture alternately with the sour cream. Add vanilla. Combine topping ingredients. Spread half the dough in a greased and floured 9 × 13-inch pan. Cover with half of the topping mixture. *Carefully* spread remaining dough on top. Sprinkle remaining topping over top of the dough. Bake in a 350°F oven for 30-35 minutes.

SERVES 15-20

Springtime Rhubarb Coffeecake

1½ cups granulated sugar
½ cup shortening
1 egg
1 cup buttermilk
1 teaspoon salt
1 teaspoon baking soda
1 teaspoon vanilla
2 cups flour
2 cups finely chopped rhubarb

TOPPING:
1 Tablespoon butter
1 Tablespoon cinnamon
½ cup granulated sugar

Mix cake ingredients, except the rhubarb, in a large bowl. Stir in the rhubarb. Pour into a 9 × 13-inch pan. Combine the topping ingredients and sprinkle over the cake batter. Bake at 350°F for 30-35 minutes. Serve warm.

SERVES 8-10

Kristina Kringle

BUTTER PASTRY:
½ cup butter
1 cup flour
2 Tablespoons cold water

CREME PUFF PASTRY:
1 cup water
½ cup butter
1 cup flour
4 eggs
1 teaspoon vanilla

ALMOND ICING:
1 Tablespoon melted butter
1¼ cups powdered sugar
½ teaspoon almond extract
3 Tablespoons cream or milk
¼ cup toasted almonds

BUTTER PASTRY: Cut butter into flour. Sprinkle with cold water to moisten. Toss with a fork until dough clings together. Gather into a ball and pat into a 10-inch circle. Set aside.
CREME PUFF PASTRY: Bring water and butter to a boil. Dump in flour all at once and beat until it pulls away from the pan. Beat in the eggs one at a time; add the vanilla with the last egg. Spread mixture on butter pastry, all the way to the edge. Bake at 375°F for 40 minutes or until golden.
ALMOND ICING: Stir together the melted butter, powdered sugar, almond extract, and cream. When pastry is cool, spread icing on top and sprinkle with toasted almonds. Cut into wedges to serve.

SERVES 6-8

Yummy Coffee Cake

1 18½-ounce box butter-flavored, white or yellow cake mix
¾ cup oil
½ cup granulated sugar
1 teaspoon vanilla
4 eggs
1 cup sour cream
1 cup pecans, chopped
1 teaspoon cinnamon
4 teaspoons brown sugar
White icing (optional)

Mix thoroughly the cake mix, oil, sugar, and vanilla. Add eggs one at a time; mix well after each addition. Mix in the sour cream and pecans. Pour half of the batter in a tube or bundt pan and sprinkle with a mixture of the cinnamon and brown sugar. Top with the remainder of the batter. Bake at 350°F for 1 hour. When cool, top of cake may be drizzled with white icing.

SERVES 16-20

Strawberry Spice Loaf

BATTER:
3 cups sliced fresh strawberries or 2 10-ounce packages frozen strawberries
3 cups all purpose flour
2 cups granulated sugar
1 teaspoon salt
3 teaspoons cinnamon
1 teaspoon nutmeg
1 teaspoon soda
1¼ cup cooking oil
4 eggs, beaten

SPREAD:
12 ounces cream cheese
½ cup strawberry juice (reserved)

Let fresh strawberries stand at room temperature while preparing the batter so juice can settle. If using frozen berries, thaw in container. Combine dry ingredients in a large bowl; mix thoroughly. In a separate bowl combine oil and eggs. Drain strawberries, reserving the juice, and mash. Add oil and egg mixture to strawberries; mix well. Make a well in the center of the dry ingredients and pour in the strawberry mixture. Mix until thoroughly combined. Grease and flour 2 9-inch loaf pans. Divide the batter equally into the pans. Bake at 350°F for 1 hour or until cake tester inserted into loaf comes our dry. Cool slightly before removing from pans. To make spread, soften cream cheese and beat in ½ cup reserved juice from berries. Use as spread on strawberry bread for sandwiches.

YIELD: 2 loaves

NOTE: Good finger sandwiches for a brunch.

Cranberry Nut Bread

2 cups flour
½ teaspoon salt
1½ teaspoons baking powder
½ teaspoon baking soda
1 cup granulated sugar
Juice and grated rind of 1 orange
2 Tablespoons salad oil
Boiling water
1 egg, beaten
1 cup chopped raw cranberries
1 cup chopped nuts

Sift together the flour, salt, baking powder, baking soda, and sugar two times. Add the orange juice and grated rind. To the salad oil add enough boiling water to make ¾ cup liquid and add to the dry ingredients. Add the egg; mix well. Stir in the cranberries and nuts. Pour batter into a greased loaf pan. Bake at 325°F for 1 hour. Store 24 hours before serving.

YIELD: 1 loaf

SUGGESTION: This bread makes delicious tea sandwiches when sliced and spread with butter and cream cheese. It is also good toasted for breakfast.

Zucchini Pineapple Bread

3 eggs
1 cup oil
2 cups granulated sugar
2 teaspoons vanilla
2 cups coarsely shredded zucchini
1 8½-ounce can crushed pineapple, well drained
3 cups flour
2 teaspoons baking soda
1 teaspoon salt
½ teaspoon baking powder
1½ teaspoons cinnamon
¾ teaspoon nutmeg
1 cup chopped nuts or currants

Cream together the eggs, oil, sugar, and vanilla. Stir in the zucchini and pineapple. In a separate bowl combine the remaining ingredients. Stir the dry ingredients gently into the zucchini mixture until just blended. Divide the batter into 2 greased and sugared 5 × 9-inch loaf pans. Bake at 350°F for 1 hour. Cool in pans for 10 minutes and then turn onto a rack.

YIELD: 2 loaves

Danish Orange Bread

1 cup Wesson oil
2 cups granulated sugar
4 eggs
2 teaspoons baking soda
1⅓ cups buttermilk
4 cups flour
1 teaspoon salt

Grated peel of one orange
1 cup nuts, chopped

GLAZE:
Juice of 2 oranges
⅔ cup granulated sugar

Mix oil and sugar. Add eggs. Dissolve baking soda in buttermilk and blend into oil and sugar mixture. Then add flour, salt, orange peel, and nuts. Pour batter into 2 greased loaf pans and bake at 350°F for 1 hour. To make glaze, mix orange juice and sugar; boil for 1 minute. Remove bread for pans and brush with glaze while bread is hot.

YIELD: 2 loaves

Doughnut Rhyme

In 1851 Lucretia Allyn Gurney came to Oregon and settled near what is now Oswego. She passed this donut recipe down to her children and grandchildren.

"1 cup of sugar, 1 cup of milk,
2 eggs beaten as fine as silk;
Salt and nutmeg, lemon will do,
Baking powder teaspoons two;
Lightly stir the flour in,
Roll on pie-board, not too thin.
Drop with care the doughy things
Into the fat that briskly swells
Evenly the spongy cells.
Watch with care the time for turning,
Fry them brown just short of burning.
Rollin sugar, serve them cool.
Price a quarter for this rule."

Josephine County Historical Society

Moistest Date Bread Ever

2 teaspoons baking soda
2 cups boiling water
1 pound dates, chopped
2 cups granulated sugar
2 Tablespoons butter
2 eggs
1 teaspoon vanilla
1 teaspoon salt
3 cups flour
1 cup chopped nuts

Dissolve soda in boiling water. Pour soda water over chopped dates. Set mixture aside for 1 hour. Cream sugar, butter, eggs, vanilla, and salt together. Combine creamed mixture with date mixture which has been sitting for 1 hour. Add flour and nuts. Grease and flour 2 loaf pans. Divide mixture between the 2 pans. Bake loaves at 325°F for 1 hour. Cool 10-15 minutes then remove from pans. Cool completely before slicing.

YIELD: 2 loaves

"Substitute 1 tablespoonful of cornstarch for each egg required in baking cookies and doughnuts."

Twentieth Century Cookbook, 1906

3-C Bread

2½ cups flour
1 cup granulated sugar
1 teaspoon baking powder
1 teaspoon baking soda
1 teaspoon cinnamon
¾ teaspoon salt
3 eggs
½ cup oil
½ cup milk
2 cups grated carrots
1⅓ cups flaked coconut
½ cup maraschino cherries, chopped or sliced
½ cup raisins
½ cup nuts

Combine flour, sugar, baking powder, baking soda, cinnamon, and salt. Beat together eggs, oil, and milk; stir into dry ingredients. Stir in remaining ingredients and pour into 2 greased and floured 5 × 9-inch loaf pans. Bake at 350°F for 55-60 minutes.

YIELD: 2 loaves

Lemon Bread

1½ cups granulated sugar, divided
⅓ cup butter
3 Tablespoons lemon extract
2 eggs
1½ cups sifted flour
1 teaspoon baking powder
1 teaspoon salt
½ cup milk
Juice of 1 large lemon

Line bottom and sides of greased 8 or 9-inch loaf pan with wax paper. Mix 1 cup of the sugar with the butter and lemon extract. Beat in eggs. Sift together dry ingredients and alternately add to sugar mixture along with milk. Beat just enough to blend. Pour into pan and bake at 350°F for 1 hour. Remove from pan while still warm. Combine lemon juice with remaining ½ cup of sugar and mix well. Drizzle over top of loaf. Wait 24 hours before cutting. Wrapped in foil, this will keep 3 months in refrigerator or 1 year frozen.

YIELD: 1 loaf

"One pound Soda, 1½ pounds Cream Tartar, ¼ pound cornstarch makes the best (and double the strength of any on the market) Baking Powder known. Try it. A.E. Crosby, chemist."

Twentieth Century Cookbook, 1906

Ellen's Apricot Bread

¾ cup chopped dried apricots
½ cup warm water
1 egg
1 cup granulated sugar
2 Tablespoons melted butter
2 cups flour
3 teaspoons baking powder
¼ teaspoon baking soda
Pinch salt
½ cup fresh orange juice
1 cup chopped nuts

Soak apricots in ½ cup warm water ½ hour. Beat the egg; add sugar and melted butter. To this mixture add dry ingredients alternated with orange juice. Add the apricots and chopped nuts. Pour into greased and floured 5 × 9- inch bread pan or 2 4 × 8-inch pans. Bake at 325°F 1 hour for large pan or 50 minutes for the small pans.

YIELD: 1 large loaf or 2 small loaves

Pumpkin Bread

3 eggs
3½ cups granulated sugar
1 30-ounce can pumpkin
1 cup oil
5 cups flour
1 teaspoon cinnamon
1 teaspoon allspice
1 teaspoon cloves
½ teaspoon nutmeg
1½ teaspoons salt
4 teaspoons soda
2 cups chopped nuts
2 cups chopped dates

Cream together eggs, sugar, pumpkin, and oil. Add dry ingredients and mix well. Stir in nuts and dates. Bake at 350°F for 1 hour in 3 greased and floured loaf pans.

YIELD: 3 loaves

Blueberry-Orange Nut Bread

3 cups sifted flour
¾ cup granulated sugar
3 teaspoons baking powder
¼ teaspoon baking soda
1 teaspoon salt
3 eggs
½ cup milk
½ cup butter, melted
1 Tablespoon grated orange peel
⅔ cup orange juice
1 cup fresh or frozen blueberries
½ cup chopped walnuts

Sift together flour, sugar, baking powder, baking soda and salt. Beat together eggs, milk, melted butter, orange peel, and juice. Stir liquid ingredients into dry ingredients just until dry ingredients are moistened. Fold in blueberries and nuts. Pour into greased 5 × 9 × 3-inch loaf pan and bake at 350°F for 60-70 minutes. Remove from pan and cool. Wrap in foil to store.

YIELD: 1 loaf

Whole Wheat Muffins

½ cup butter or margarine
1 cup packed brown sugar
1 egg
2 cups whole wheat flour
1 teaspoon baking soda
1 cup milk or water
½ teaspoon vanilla
½ cup chopped nuts

Cream butter and sugar together and then add the egg. Add flour and soda alternately with milk to creamed mixture. Mix in vanilla and nuts. Fill greased muffin cups or paper baking cups two-thirds full. Bake in 425°F oven for 12-15 minutes.

YIELD: 12-14

6-Weeks Bran Muffins

5 teaspoons baking soda
2 cups boiling water
1 cup shortening
2 cups granulated sugar
4 eggs
1 quart buttermilk
4 cups flour
1 teaspoon salt
4 cups All-Bran Cereal
2 cups 40% Bran Flakes cereal
2 cups chopped dates

Add baking soda to boiling water and cool. Cream shortening and sugar; then add eggs and baking soda mixture. Add remaining ingredients and mix well. Spoon batter into greased muffin tins and bake at 375°F for 25 minutes. Remaining batter may be kept for 6 weeks in refrigerator. Keep batter in a tight container in the refrigerator, but do not stir batter again after refrigerating.

YIELD: 5 dozen muffins

Blueberry Muffin Cakes

½ cup butter
¾ cup granulated sugar
2 eggs
2⅓ cups flour
2½ teaspoons baking powder
½ teaspoon salt
½ teapsoon nutmeg
¾ cup milk
1½ cups fresh blueberries

TOPPING:
½ cup melted butter
¾ cup granulated sugar
¼ teaspoon cinnamon

Cream butter and sugar until light and fluffy. Beat in eggs until well blended. Mix in the flour, baking powder, salt, and nutmeg; then add milk. Fold in blueberries. Fill greased muffin tins three-quarters full. Bake at 350°F for 25-30 minutes or until light brown. Remove muffins from pans and cool slightly. For topping, roll muffins in melted butter and then in combined cinnamon and sugar mixture.

SERVES 12-16

NOTE: To freeze, place muffins on a cookie sheet and put in freezer until frozen solid. Then wrap and return to freezer.

Fresh Peach or Apple Muffins

1 cup peeled and chopped fresh apples or peaches
1 teaspoon lemon juice
1 cup milk
1 egg
¼ cup melted Crisco
⅔ cup granulated sugar
½ teaspoon salt
¼ teaspoon cinnamon
3 teaspoons baking powder
2 cups unsifted flour

Sprinkle the fruit with lemon juice and set aside. Mix remaining ingredients, adding flour last. Fold in fruit just before baking. Fill greased muffin tins two-thirds full and bake at 450°F for 20 minutes.

YIELD: 20-24 muffins

Corn Bread

1 cup butter or margarine
1 cup granulated sugar
4 eggs
1 4-ounce can California green chiles, seeded and chopped (optional)
1 16-ounce can cream-style corn
½ cup shredded mild Cheddar cheese
1 cup sifted flour
1 cup sifted yellow corn meal
4 teaspoons baking powder
½ teaspoon salt

Cream butter and sugar. Mixing well, add eggs, one at a time. Add chiles, corn and cheese; mix well. Sift flour and corn meal together with baking powde and salt; add to corn mixture. Blend well. Pour into greased and floured 9 × 13-inch pan. Place pan in preheated 350°F oven and immediately reduce hea to 300°F. Bake for 1 hour. Serve warm.

SERVES 1

Beer Bread

3 cups self-rising flour
3 Tablespoons granulated sugar
1 12-ounce can beer

Mix all ingredients together. Pour into greased loaf pan and let rise 30 minutes Bake at 350°F for 70 minutes or until golden brown.

YIELD: 1 loa

In 1846 more than 160,000 bushels of wheat were produced in the Oregon country. An act of the provisional government made it legal tender valued at $1.00 a bushel. By 1880 the five "wheat counties" of Eastern Oregon, Umatilla, Wasco, Sherman, Guilliam, and Morrow, produced a million bushels. By 1890, that figure was doubled.

Coffee Bread

1 package dry yeast
¼ cup warm water
¼ cup granulated sugar
3 Tablespoons butter
1½ teaspoons salt
¾ cup milk, scalded
1 egg
2½-3 cups flour
2 Tablespoons softened butter

FILLING:
1 cup chopped nuts
½ cup granulated sugar
1 teaspoon cinnamon

GLAZE:
1 cup powdered sugar
1 Tablespoon softened butter
2 Tablespoons milk

Soften the yeast in the warm water. Combine the sugar, butter, salt, and milk in a mixing bowl and cool to lukewarm. Stir in the egg and yeast. Gradually add 2 cups of flour and beat until smooth. Mix in enough of the remaining flour to make the dough easy to handle. Knead the dough on a lightly floured surface until smooth and satiny, about 5-8 minutes. Place in a greased bowl, turning dough to grease all sides. Cover and let rise in a warm place until doubled in bulk, about 1-1½ hours. Punch down and turn out on a floured surface. Roll out dough into a 15 × 20-inch rectangle and spread with the soft butter. Mix the filling ingredients together and sprinkle over the dough rectangle. Roll up the dough like a jelly roll, starting with a long side of the rectangle. Place rolled dough on a greased cookie sheet with the seam down. Bring the ends together to form a circle and seal by pinching them together. Slice through the top layer of dough at 1-inch intervals. Cover and let rise in a warm place until doubled, approximately 45-60 minutes. Bake the ring at 350°F for 25-30 minutes until golden brown. Make a glaze by beating together and heating over low heat the powdered sugar, butter, and milk. Spread over the warm ring.

SERVES 8

Yulekaka

2 packages dry yeast
¼ cup warm water
2 cups milk, scalded
½ cup shortening
⅔ cup granulated sugar
2 teaspoons salt
¼ teaspoon crushed cardamom seed
2 eggs, beaten
8 cups sifted flour, divided
½ cup raisins
½ cup currants
1 cup candied fruit
½ cup chopped maraschino cherries
White powdered sugar frosting
Maraschino cherries

Soften the yeast in the warm water. Combine the scalded milk, shortening, sugar, salt, and cardamom; cool to lukewarm. Add the yeast and eggs; mix together. Add 4 cups of flour and beat in well. Add the raisins, currants, candied fruit, and maraschino cherries. Add the remaining 4 cups of flour; beat in well. Knead the dough until smooth and elastic. Let rise in a warm place until doubled in bulk. Punch down and let rise again until doubled. Form 2 round loaves in greased 9-inch round cake pans, or use all of dough to form a wreath in a greased tube pan. Let rise again until doubled. Bake at 350°F for 45-60 minutes. When cool, frost bread with white powdered sugar frosting and decorate with additional maraschino cherries.

YIELD: 2 round loaves or 1 large wreath

NOTE: Yulekaka is a Norwegian Christmas bread.

Caramel Breakfast Rolls

2 1-pound loaves frozen bread dough, thawed
1 cup packed brown sugar
1 5½-ounce package regular vanilla pudding and pie filling mix
½ cup butter, melted
¼ cup half and half
½ cup chopped pecans

Cut 1 loaf of dough into small pieces and place in a greased 9 × 13-inch baking dish. Combine and mix well the brown sugar, pudding mix, melted butter, and half and half. Drizzle half of this mixture over the dough pieces and sprinkle with ¼ cup nuts. Cut the second loaf of dough into small pieces and place on top of the first layer. Drizzle remaining brown sugar mixture over the dough and sprinkle with the rest of the nuts. Cover and refrigerate several hours or overnight. Bake uncovered at 325°F for 50 minutes. While still warm turn baking dish upside down onto a platter or cookie sheet to remove rolls.

SERVES 10-12

Potato Rolls

1 package yeast
½ cup lukewarm water
⅓ cup shortening
½ cup granulated sugar
1 teaspoon salt
1 cup mashed potatoes
1 cup scalded milk
2 eggs, well beaten
6-7 cups flour

Dissolve yeast in lukewarm water. Add shortening, sugar, salt, and mashed potatoes to scalded milk. When cool, add yeast. Mix thoroughly and add eggs. Stir in enough flour to make a stiff dough. Put in refrigerator several hours or overnight. When ready to make rolls, punch dough down and form into rolls. Let rolls rise about 2½ hours. Bake at 400°F for 10-12 minutes or until golden brown.

YIELD: 4-5 dozen rolls

NOTE: This dough makes wonderful cinnamon rolls.

Leila's Feather Rolls

1 package dry yeast
2 teaspoons granulated sugar
¼ cup warm water
1 cup milk
½ cup shortening
⅓ cup granulated sugar
1 teaspoon salt
3 eggs
4½ cups sifted flour
Melted butter

Combine yeast, 2 teaspoons sugar, and warm water. Stir until dissolved. Scald milk and add shortening, ⅓ cup sugar, and salt. Stir until shortening is melted. Beat eggs and stir into milk mixture. Stir in yeast and 3 cups flour. Beat well with a mixer. Stir in remaining 1½ cups flour. It will be a sticky dough. Cover and refrigerate overnight. Turn out on a floured board and shape into crescent, cloverleaf or Parker House rolls. Let stand 4 hours covered with a cloth. Brush with melted butter and bake at 400°F for 10 minutes or until golden brown!

YIELD: 36-48 rolls

Sourdough Biscuits

"Mix 1 pint of flour and 1 teaspoon of salt with 1 pint of warm water or canned milk. Beat into a smooth batter. Keep in a warm place until well soured or fermented. Add another teaspoon of salt and 1½ teaspoons of soda dissolved in ½ cup of tepid water and enough flour to make the dough easy to handle. Knead until dough is no longer sticky, cup up into biscuits and cook in a pan containing plenty of grease."

Oregon: End of the Trail, 1951

Rich White Batter Bread

1 package dry yeast
½ cup warm water
⅛ teaspoon ground ginger
3 Tablespoons granulated sugar
1 13-ounce can evaporated milk
1 teaspoon salt
2 Tablespoons salad oil
4-4½ cups unsifted all purpose flour
Melted butter or margarine

Dissolve yeast in water in a large mixer bowl. Blend in ginger and 1 Tablespoon of sugar. Let stand in warm place until mixture is bubbly, about 15 minutes. Stir in remaining 2 Tablespoons sugar and the milk, salt, and salad oil. With mixer at low speed, add flour, 1 cup at a time, beating very well after each addition. Beat in last cup of flour with a wooden spoon; add flour just until dough is very heavy and stiff, but too sticky to knead. Place dough in a well-greased 2-pound coffee can or divide into 2 1-pound coffee cans. Cover with well-greased plastic can lids. Dough can be frozen at this point if you wish. To bake, let covered cans stand in a warm place until dough rises and pops off the lids. For dough at room temperature this will take 1-1½ hours for a 2-pound can or 45-60 minutes for a 1-pound can. For frozen dough it will take 6-8 hours for a 2-pound can or 4-5 hours for a 1-pound can. Discard the lids and bake at 350°F for 60 minutes for a 2-pound can or 45 minutes for 1-pound cans. The crust will be very brown when removed from the oven. Brush the tops of the loaves with butter. Cool 5-10 minutes and loosen the crust around the edges with a long, thin knife. Slide bread from cans. Let cool in an upright position on a rack.

YIELD: 1 large or 2 small loaves

VARIATION: Use 1½ cups whole wheat flour plus 3 cups all purpose flour. Replace the sugar with honey.

Rolled French Bread

1 Tablespoon yeast
1½ cups warm water
2 Tablespoons oil
1 Tablespoon granulated sugar
1½ teaspoons salt
4 cups flour (approximately)

Dissolve yeast in ½ cup warm water. Add remaining 1 cup water, oil, sugar, salt, and 2 cups flour; mix well. Then add remaining flour. No kneading is necessary. Punch dough down every 10 minutes for a total of 5 times. Divide dough in half. Roll each half into a 9 × 13-inch rectangle, then tightly roll each piece into a loaf. Let each loaf rise until doubled in size, about 1 hour. Bake at 350°F for 35 minutes. Serve warm.

YIELD: 2 loaves

Challah

2 packages dry yeast
½ cup very warm water
2 Tablespoons granulated sugar
6 Tablespoons oil
1½ cups warm water
3 eggs
2 teaspoons salt
7 cups all purpose flour (approximately)
1 Tablespoon cold water
Poppy seeds (optional)

Dissolve yeast in ½ cup very warm water, stirring in the sugar to speed the yeast reaction. Let stand until bubbly. Pour oil and 1½ cups water into a large bowl. Add eggs, reserving 1 yolk for top of bread, and salt to the water and oil. Mix well. Add yeast mixture. Stir in 4 cups flour, then 3 more cups. Turn out on a floured board and knead until smooth and elastic, about 5 minutes. Place in a greased bowl, turning over to grease top. Cover with a cloth and let rise in a warm place until doubled in bulk, about 1 hour. Punch down. Divide dough into 9 pieces. Roll pieces into 8-10 inch ropes. Braid together 3 ropes to form 1 loaf. Repeat to form 2 more loaves. Place loaves on cookie sheets, allowing room to double. Mix the reserved egg yolk with 1 Tablespoon cold water and brush over loaves. Sprinkle with poppy seeds, if desired, and set in warm place, covered lightly, to rise again, about 1 hour. Bake at 375°F for 45 minutes, or until loaves sound hollow when tapped and are lightly browned. Turn out onto racks to cool.

YIELD: 3 loaves

Granary Bread

3½-4 cups all purpose flour, divided
2 packages dry yeast
1 Tablespoon salt
⅓ cup honey
3 Tablespoons butter
2½ cups hot water (120-130°F)
2½ cups whole wheat flour
1 teaspoon oil to brush loaves
Milk or butter (optional)

Mix 2½ cups white flour, yeast, salt, honey, and butter in large bowl. Pour in the water. Beat until smooth. Add 1 cup whole wheat flour and beat again. Add 1 cup white flour and remaining whole wheat flour as needed. Cover dough with a towel and let it rest for 20 minutes. Punch down and knead for 30 seconds. Divide into 2 sections and shape into round loaves. Flatten slightly. Place in 2 greased 9-inch round cake pans and brush with oil. Cover with plastic and put in refrigerator for 2-24 hours. (It is best if refrigerated for about 6 hours.) Remove from refrigerator 10 minutes before placing in oven. Bake at 400°F for 30-40 minutes. Brush with milk or butter for a soft crust.

YIELD: 2 loaves

Cheese Bread

7-8 cups all purpose flour
⅓ cup granulated sugar
1 Tablespoon salt
2 Tablespoons dry yeast
2 cups water
⅔ cup milk
3 cups grated sharp Cheddar cheese (about ¾ pound)
1 egg, beaten
1 teaspoon cold water
1 teaspoon sesame seeds

Combine 2½ cups flour, sugar, salt, and yeast in a bowl. Combine water and milk in a saucepan and heat over low heat to 120-130°F. Pour into a large mixing bowl. Gradually add dry mixture and beat for 2 minutes. Add cheese and additional ½ cup of flour. Beat again until smooth. Gradually stir in enough remaining flour to make a stiff dough, about 4 cups. Turn onto a floured board and knead until smooth, 8-10 minutes. Place in a greased bowl and turn dough to grease top. Cover and let rise until doubled in bulk, about 1-1½ hours. Punch dough down and turn out onto floured board. Divide dough in half. Set 1 piece aside, and divide other half into 3 pieces. Roll each piece into a 10-inch rope. Braid these 3 ropes and place in a greased pan. Repeat with other half of dough. Cover and let rise about 1 hour or until dough rises slightly above the top of pans. Brush tops with a mixture of beaten egg and cold water. Sprinkle with sesame seeds. Bake on lowest shelf of oven at 350°F for about 30-35 minutes. Remove from pans and cool on racks. If tops get dark during baking, cover with tin foil.

YIELD: 2 loaves

Gourmet Cheese Bread

1 package dry yeast
¼ cup warm water
1 Tablespoon instant minced onion
2¼ teaspoons dill seed
2 Tablespoons granulated sugar
1 teaspoon salt
¼ teaspoon baking soda
4 slices bacon, cooked drained and crumbled
1 Tablespoon lukewarm bacon drippings
1 egg, unbeaten
1 cup cottage cheese
2¼ cups flour
Butter
Salt

Soften yeast in water. Combine yeast, onion, dill seed, sugar, salt, soda, bacon bacon drippings, egg, and cottage cheese. Heat all of this to lukewarm. Ad flour to form a stiff dough, beating after each addition. Cover. Let rise for hour until light and doubled in size. Stir down. Turn into greased 1½ to 2-quar casserole. Let rise for 30-40 minutes. Bake at 350°F for 40-45 minutes. Brus with butter and sprinkle with additional salt.

YIELD: 1 loa

Dilly Bread

1 package dry yeast
¼ cup warm water
1 cup small curd cottage cheese
1 Tablespoon butter
2 plus Tablespoons granulated sugar
2 Tablespoons dried minced onion
2 plus teaspoons dill seed
1 teaspoon salt
¼ teaspoon baking soda
1 egg
2½ cups flour (approximately)

Dissolve yeast in warm water. Heat cottage cheese and butter in a saucepan until warm. In a separate bowl mix together the sugar, onion, dill seed, salt, baking soda, and egg. Add the dissolved yeast and warm cottage cheese mixture; mix thoroughly. Add flour to make a stiff dough; stir with a large spoon. Cover bowl and let dough rise in a warm place until doubled in bulk, about 1 hour. Stir down dough, but do not knead. Put in a well-greased bread pan and let rise until doubled in bulk, about 40 minutes. Bake at 350°F for 35 minutes or until done.

YIELD: 1 loaf

Whole Wheat Sesame Bread

3 packages dry yeast
¾ cup very warm water
½ teaspoon granulated sugar
3 cups lukewarm milk
⅓ cup oil
⅓ cup packaged brown sugar
¼ cup molasses
⅓ cup sesame seeds
2 eggs
1 Tablespoon salt
3 cups whole wheat flour
7-8 cups all purpose flour
1 egg, beaten
Sesame seeds

Dissolve yeast in ¾ cup warm water; stir in granulated sugar. In a large bowl combine milk, oil, brown sugar, molasses, and sesame seeds; mix well. To the large bowl add the yeast mixture, 2 eggs, salt, and whole wheat flour. Mix well. Add all purpose flour 1 cup at a time and mix until well blended. This is a soft, sticky dough. Turn out to knead, using additional flour as necessary to prevent sticking. Knead about 7 minutes or until smooth and elastic, or use a heavy mixer with dough hook and follow manufacturer's directions. (However, it is too large an amount of dough for most mixers.) Put dough in a greased bowl, turn once to grease top, and cover. Put in a warm place and let rise about 1 hour or until doubled. Punch down. Shape into 3 loaves and put in greased loaf pans. Cover and let rise about ½ hour or until dough is above top of pans. Brush tops with beaten egg and sprinkle with additional sesame seeds. Bake at 350°F for 35-45 minutes until bread sounds hollow when tapped. Turn out on racks to cool.

YIELD: 3 loaves

Sunflower Whole Wheat Bread

3 cups warm water (110°F)
¾ cup honey, at room temperature
2 packages dry yeast
¼ cup butter, softened
4 cups whole wheat flour (preferably stone ground)
3-6 cups unbleached flour
2 teaspoons salt
1 cup unsalted sunflower seeds

In a very large mixing bowl, combine and mix the water, honey, and yeast until yeast is softened, about 5 minutes. Blend the butter, whole wheat flour, 1 cup unbleached flour, salt, and sunflower seeds into the yeast mixture by hand or with an electric mixer for 7 minutes on low speed. Slowly add 2-3 cups unbleached flour; beat with a wooden spoon until a stiff dough forms. Sprinkle 1 cup of the remaining flour on a bread board, turn the dough out on the board and knead; add flour if dough is sticky. Knead 8-10 minutes or until dough is smooth and elastic. Place it, smooth-side down, in a greased bowl and turn the dough to grease its top. Cover the bowl with a damp towel and place in a warm (80-85°F) draft-free place until dough has doubled in bulk, about 1 hour. Knead the dough for 1 minute, cover, and let rise in a warm place again until doubled. Punch down a second time. Divide the dough in half, shape in 2 loaves, and place in 2 greased 5 × 9-inch loaf pans. Place loaves in a warm place and allow to rise to the top of the pans, about 45 minutes. Bake the loaves in a preheated 350°F oven for about 1 hour or until they are well browned and hollow sounding when tops are tapped. Turn loaves out onto a rack to cool.

YIELD: 2 loaves

VARIATION: A slightly denser and even more nutritious bread may be made by using all whole wheat flour.

Salt-Rising Bread

A young pioneer bride who crossed the plains from Illinois in 1852 brought this recipe with her.

"Scald ½ pint new milk. Stir into it enough corn meal to make a stiff mush. Set in a warm place to rise overnight. The next morning add to this one pint of tepid water, a pinch of salt, one tablespoon sugar and enough flour to drop from a spoon. Pour this into a pitcher and cover it. Set in a pot of hot water, keeping the water the same temperature, as on this depends the rising. Let stand until it rises to the top of the pitcher. Then take 6 cupfuls flour, a dessert spoon of salt and one tablespoon lard. Add the batter and mix to a stiff dough, adding tepid water as needed. Make into loaves. Let rise nearly to the top of the pan and bake."

Josephine County Historical Society

Beer-Wheat Bread

2 cups flat beer
½ cup corn meal
½ cup molasses
2 Tablespoons butter
2 teaspoons salt
2 packages dry yeast
1 Tablespoon granulated sugar
½ cup wheat germ
½ cup whole bran cereal
2 cups whole wheat flour
3 cups all purpose flour (approximately)
Margarine

Heat together the beer, corn meal, molasses, butter, and salt. Cool to lukewarm; add yeast, sugar, and mix thoroughly. Add wheat germ, bran cereal, and whole wheat flour; beat well. Stir in all purpose flour; add more as needed to knead. Knead 10 minutes. Cover and let rise 1 hour or until doubled. Punch down and let rise again until doubled. Form into 2 round loaves and place in 2 greased 8-inch round cake pans which have been dusted with corn meal. Let rise again until doubled. Bake at 375°F for 30-40 minutes. After loaves are removed from oven, brush tops with margarine.

YIELD: 2 loaves

Swedish Limpa Bread

4 cups water
1 cup packed brown sugar
4 teaspoons caraway seed
2 Tablespoons shortening
2 teaspoons grated orange peel
2 packages dry yeast
2 teaspoons salt
6 cups all purpose flour (approximately)
4 cups rye flour (approximately)
Butter

Boil together water, sugar, caraway seed, shortening, and orange peel for 3 minutes. Let the mixture cool to lukewarm and add the yeast. Stir thoroughly; gradually add the salt and 3 cups of all purpose flour. Add the rye flour and mix well. Add the remainder of the white flour to make a stiff dough. Turn out on a floured surface and knead dough until smooth and elastic. Then place in an oiled bowl, turning the dough over to oil the top. Cover and let rise in a warm place until doubled in bulk, about 1-1½ hours. Punch down dough, knead lightly and shape into 2 round loaves. Place on a greased cookie sheet, cover and let rise again, about 1 hour. Bake in a 350°F oven for 1 hour. To glaze and soften tops, butter tops of loaves when hot from the oven. Cool on a rack.

YIELD: 2 loaves

Chili-Cheese Bread

3 cups grated Monterey Jack cheese
1 4-ounce can chiles or jalapeno peppers, chopped
1 cup mayonnaise
1 loaf French bread

Mix cheese, peppers, and mayonnaise well. Spread on cut surfaces of a loaf of French bread that has been sliced in half horizontally. Bake at 350°F for 20-30 minutes. Cut in slices to serve.

SERVES 6-8

Cheese-Olive Bread

3 cups grated Cheddar cheese
1 3-ounce jar pimiento-stuffed green olives, sliced
1 cup mayonnaise
1 loaf French bread

Mix cheese, olives, and mayonnaise. Spread on cut surfaces of a loaf of French bread which has been sliced in half horizontally. Bake at 350°F for 20-30 minutes. Cut in slices to serve.

SERVES 6-8

Cheese Spread

1 pound margarine, at room temperature
½ pound grated sharp Ceddar cheese
1 teaspoon Worcestershire sauce
¼ pound grated Romano cheese
¼ teaspoon garlic powder
½ teaspoon paprika
Sour dough bread

Slowly whip together all ingredients with mixer until light and fluffy. Spread on sour dough bread slices and toast under broiler.

YIELD: 3-4 cups

Rosemary Bread

¼ pound butter
1 Tablespoon finely chopped scallions
1 Tablespoon finely chopped parsley
¼-½ teaspoon rosemary
French bread

Mix butter with scallion, parsley, and rosemary. Spread on sliced French bread and heat. Bread may be wrapped in foil for a softer texture.

YIELD: 1 loaf

Crackling Bread

"2 cups corn meal
½ teaspoon soda
¼ teaspoon salt
1 cup buttermilk
1 cup cracklings, diced

Sift corn meal, salt and soda together. Add milk and stir in cracklings. Form into oblong cakes and place on greased baking sheets. Bake, hot, for 30 minutes.
CRACKLINGS: Cut fat back into thin 1½ inch squares. Fry in deep fat until they are curled and golden brown. Drain cracklings on absorbent paper. Serve warm or cold or use for crackling bread."

Tillamook County Pioneer Museum

EGGS, CHEESE, AND GRAINS

Kenneth R. O'Connell

Cream Cheese

"A very easy way of making cream cheese is to lay a piece of muslin in a large basin, but do not let it quite touch the bottom; this may be prevented by putting weights in the edge of the muslin lying outside the basin. Pour in your cream (sour) and let it stand a day and a night, by which time all the thin part of the cream will have run through the muslin into the basin, and the cream will be quite thick. Draw the muslin together over the cream, and give it a squeeze, the press out any milk that may remain. Tie it round with a string pretty tight and hang it in a rough towel doubled four times. Dig a hole in the garden and bury it in the cloth, and let it remain four or five days when it will be ripe. Press it into shape."

Peterson's Magazine, 1877; Tillamook County Pioneer Museum

Easy Cheese Fondue

1 10½-ounce can Cheddar cheese soup, undiluted
1 garlic clove, minced
2 egg yolks, beaten
½ cup beer, apple juice or cider
Zucchini, cauliflower, broccoli or French bread cubes

Heat soup and garlic to just below boiling. Remove from heat. Stir half of the hot soup into egg yolks and then blend this mixture back into the remaining soup. Stir in beer and heat thoroughly, stirring constantly. Keep warm over low heat. Use zucchini, cauliflower, broccoli, or cubes of French bread to dip in fondue.

SERVES 4

Zippy Fondue

2 pounds Velveeta cheese, cubed
1 4-ounce can Ortega chili strips
½ 15-ounce can stewed tomatoes, diced
1 teaspoon garlic powder
1 teaspoon onion powder
1 teaspoon Worcestershire sauce
1 Tablespoon vegetable oil
1 Tablespoon prepared mustard
⅛ teaspoon monosodium glutamate
1 10½-ounce can Cheddar cheese soup

Mix together all ingredients and heat in double boiler or fondue dish.

YIELD: Approximately 1 quart

Brunch Casserole

1½ pounds Brown 'n' Serve link sausage
5 eggs
2 cups milk
⅛ teaspoon salt
1 teaspoon prepared mustard
7 slices bread
1 cup grated Cheddar cheese

Cut sausages in quarters and brown in a frying pan. Drain on paper towels. Beat eggs well; add milk, salt, and mustard. Remove crusts from bread and slice into 1-inch squares. Add sausage, bread, and cheese to egg mixture; stir well. Pour into a 2-quart casserole and refrigerate overnight. To bake allow casserole to reach room temperature, then place casserole dish in a shallow pan of water to prevent crust from forming while cooking. Bake for 1 hour at 350°F.

SERVES 6

"Tinware can be polished by rubbing it with a raw onion."

Klamath County Museum

Company Strata

12 slices white bread
12 ounces sharp processed cheese, sliced
1 10-ounce package frozen chopped broccoli, cooked and drained
2 cups diced cooked ham
6 eggs, slightly beaten
3½ cups milk
2 Tablespoons instant minced onion
½ teaspoon salt
¼ teaspoon dry mustard

From the slices of white bread cut 12 "doughnuts and holes." Remove the top crusts from the remaining scraps of bread and fit the scraps in the bottom of a 9 × 13 × 2-inch baking dish. Layer the sliced cheese, broccoli, and ham over the bread. Arrange the "doughnuts and holes" on top. Combine the eggs, milk, onion, salt, and mustard; pour over the bread. Cover and refrigerate 6 hours or overnight. Bake uncovered at 350°F for 55 minutes. Let stand 10 minutes before cutting.

SERVES 12

VARIATION: Bacon, shrimp, crab or other meats may be substituted for the ham.

Strudel Jacob

8 ounces Farmer's cheese, grated
6 ounces sharp Cheddar cheese, grated
4 ounces Mozzarella cheese, shredded
⅔ cup grated Parmesan cheese
4 sprigs fresh parsley, chopped
1 cup sliced fresh mushrooms
2 cups Italian-flavored or plain bread crumbs, divided
Garlic powder, oregano, and cayenne pepper to taste
1 egg, beaten
4 strudel pastry sheets (phyllo)
1 cup melted butter

Mix cheeses together. Add parsley, mushrooms, 1 cup bread crumbs, seasonings and egg. Mix well. Set aside. Wet and wring out a dish towel or tea towel and lay on a flat surface. Unroll strudel pastry leaves. Carefully place one leaf on the damp towel. With a soft paint brush paint the leaf with melted butter. Sprinklw with ¼ cup bread crumbs. Lay a second pastry leaf over the first and repeat with melted butter and crumbs. Take half the cheese mixture, compress in hands to form a roll and lay it along the shorter edge of the pastry sheet. Using the towel to lift the pastry sheets, roll it jelly-roll style, starting at the end with the cheeses. Lift onto a cookie sheet. Tuck the ends under the bottom of tне roll. Make another roll like the first. Make slight indentations 1 inch apart in the rolls. Bake at 375°F for 15-33 minutes until lightly browned. Cut and serve.

SERVES 6

Hearty Breakfast Casserole

3 medium baking potatoes
Boiling water
6-8 slices bacon, diced
¼ cup minced onion
1 cup grated Swiss cheese
½ cup cottage cheese
5 eggs, beaten
½ teaspoon salt

Cook potatoes in boiling water until tender. Peel and dice. Fry bacon; remove and drain, reserving bacon drippings. Lightly brown potatoes and onion in bacon drippings. Remove and combine with bacon, cheeses, eggs, and salt. Turn into shallow buttered baking dish. Bake at 350°F for 30-40 minutes or until set in center.

SERVES 6-8

Cheese Blintzes

1 cup water
1 cup milk
2 cups flour
4 eggs
2 Tablespoons oil
2-3 teaspoons granulated sugar
½ teaspoon salt
1 teaspoon vanilla
Oil
Butter or margarine
Sour Cream
Jam

FILLING:
1 8-ounce package cream cheese, softened
1 16-ounce package Ricotta cheese
1 egg
¼ cup granulated sugar
1 teaspoon vanilla

Blend the first 8 ingredients in a blender, making sure thay are thoroughly blended. The crepes will cook more easily if the batter sits at least 30 minutes after it is blended then is stirred by hand just before using. Lightly oil a 6-inch skillet and heat on medium heat until a drop of water bounces when dropped on the surface. Lift the skillet and add about 2 Tablespoons batter, tipping the pan to spread the batter; then return pan to the heat. Cook the crepe only on one side. When the surface looks dry, covered with tiny bubbles, and is very slightly browned around the edges, it is done. Loosen the edges all around with a spatula or fork and turn the crepe out onto a tea towel. When cool, crepes may be stacked.
FILLING: Use a mixer to whip together the cheeses. Add the egg, sugar, and vanilla; mix well. Spoon a well-rounded Tablespoon of filling onto the cooked side of the crepe. Fold up the bottom edge, then each side and then the top edge, making a rectangular envelope shape. Repeat with the remaining crepes and filling. These may be cooked immediately or frozen individually on a baking sheet then stored in a plastic bag in the freezer. To cook, fry seam-side down in butter over medium heat until brown, then turn over carefully and brown. Use lower heat to cook frozen blintzes; do not thaw first. Serve with sour cream and jam.

SERVES 6-8

Mixed Cheese Pancakes

3 cups flour
2 teaspoons salt
4 teaspoons baking powder
1 teaspoon baking soda
2 Tablespoon granulated sugar
8 eggs
2⅔ cups milk
2 cups grated Cheddar cheese
2 cups cottage cheese
1 cup sliced fresh mushrooms
½ cup chopped green onion

Mix the flour, salt, baking powder, baking soda, and sugar in a bowl. Beat the eggs, stir in the milk, and add to the dry ingredients. Mix until smooth. Fold in the cheeses, mushrooms, and onion. Bake on a hot well-greased griddle until browned on both sides.

SERVES 8-10

Stuffed Eggs Au Gratin

6 hard-cooked eggs
¼ cup butter or margarine, melted
½ teaspoon Worcestershire sauce
¼ teaspoon prepared mustard
2-3 green onions, minced with tops
1 teaspoon minced parsley
3 slices boiled ham, minced
Salt and pepper to taste
1 cup grated American or mild Cheddar cheese

WHITE SAUCE:
½ cup butter or margarine
¼ cup flour, unsifted
2 cups milk
Salt and pepper to taste
Chopped parsley or chives

Cut the eggs in half lengthwise and slip out the yolks. In a bowl, mash the yolks with the melted butter, Worcestershire sauce, and mustard. Then mix in the onions, parsley, and ham. Season to taste with salt and pepper. Fill the egg whites with this mixture and arrange them in the bottom of a buttered casserole or pie pan. Make a white sauce by melting the butter and stirring in the flour. Add the milk gradually, stirring continually, while heating the sauce over medium low heat. Heat until sauce comes to a boil and thickens, then season with salt and pepper and add parsley for color. Pour the white sauce over the eggs, and sprinkle the grated cheese on top. Bake at 325°F for 25-30 minutes.

SERVES 3-4

Creamy Cheese Enchiladas

6 flour tortillas
3 cups shredded Monterey Jack cheese
6 Tablespoons chopped green onion
¼ cup butter
¼ cup flour
2 cups chicken broth
1 cup sour cream
1 4-ounce can green chiles, seeded and chopped

Fill each tortilla with ½ cup cheese and 1 Tablespoon green onion. Roll each individually and place in an 8-inch square shallow baking dish. Melt butter in saucepan over medium heat. Add flour, stirring constantly. Add chicken broth to make a thick sauce. Remove from heat and add sour cream and chiles; stir until smooth. Pour over tortillas. Bake at 350°F for 20 minutes.

SERVES 6

To make cottage cheese, milk was set in a container on the back of the wood stove to warm. The milk would separate and the whey was poured off. This was used to feed the hogs. The milk solids were scopped into a flour sack and hung up to drip. When the remaining whey had dripped through, the result was cottage cheese. Some farmers made the cheese richer by adding heavy cream.

Mary's Easy Quiche

CRUST:
3 cups flour
1½ cups Crisco
½ teaspoon salt
1 egg, beaten
1 Tablespoon vinegar
3 Tablespoons cold water

FILLING:
1 pound bacon, fried and crumbled
3 cups minced ham
10 eggs, partially beaten
3 cups milk
1½ pounds Swiss cheese, shredded
2 4-ounce cans mushrooms, drained

CRUST: Place flour, Crisco, and salt in a bowl and cut the Crisco into the flour. Combine the egg, vinegar, and cold water; add to the above mixture, stirring to combine thoroughly. Divide dough in two and roll out between sheets of wax paper. Pat into 2 9 × 13-inch casserole dishes.
FILLING: Mix together all the filling ingredients and pour half into each pie crust. Bake at 375°F for 30 minutes.

SERVES 16

Quiche Michele

1 cup sliced fresh mushrooms
½ cup diced ham
2 Tablespoons butter
2 eggs, beaten
1 cup whipping cream
½ cup shredded Cheddar cheese
¼ teaspoon ground nutmeg
½ teaspoon salt
Dash of pepper
1 9-inch pie shell, baked

In saucepan cook mushrooms and ham in butter for about 5 minutes. Set aside. In mixng bowl combine eggs, cream, cheese, nutmeg, salt, and pepper. Place ham and mushroom mixture in bottom of pie shell; pour egg mixture over the top. Bake in 350°F oven for 25 minutes. Let stand 10 minutes before serving.

SERVES 6-8

Vegetable Quiche

½ cup chopped green onion
¼ pound mushrooms, sliced
1 garlic clove, minced
2 Tablespoons margarine
1 10-ounce package frozen chopped spinach
3 eggs, lightly beaten
¼ cup half and half
1 teaspoon salt
1 teaspoon basil
½ teaspoon celery salt
6 ounces Swiss cheese, shredded (1½ cups)
1 9-inch pie shell, unbaked
2 medium tomatoes, sliced
1 Tablespoon Parmesan cheese
1 Tablespoon dried bread crumbs

Using a medium-size skillet, sauté onion, mushrooms, and garlic in margarine; set aside. Cook spinach according to package directions; squeeze all moisture out by pressing with a spoon against a sieve, and set aside. Combine eggs, half and half, and seasonings; set aside. Put the sautéd mixture, spinach, and cheese in the bottom of the pie shell. Pour the egg mixture over the top. Arrange tomatoes around the outer edge of the pie shell. Combine Parmesan and bread crumbs; set aside. Bake quiche at 425°F for 15 minutes, and then at 350°F for 20 minutes. Sprinkle cheese mixture on top of tomatoes. Bake 10 minutes longer at lowered temperature. Let stand 5 minutes.

SERVES 8

Huevos Rancheros

Oil, divided
2 cups minced onion (not dehydrated)
2 garlic cloves, crushed
2 1-pound cans tomatoes, broken up
2 8-ounce cans green chiles
1 teaspoon granulated sugar
1 teaspoon salt
¼ teaspoon fresh ground pepper
¼ teaspoon ground coriander
6 corn tortillas
6 eggs
1 ripe avocado, peeled, and thinly sliced
Grated Monterey Jack cheese
Chopped ripe olives or scallions

Heat enough oil to cover bottom of skillet. Cook onion and garlic over low temperature until transparent. Add tomatoes, chiles, sugar, salt, pepper, and coriander. Bring to boil. Reduce to low heat and simmer uncovered 30-45 minutes, stirring frequently. In a small skillet place oil to depth of ⅛ inch. Over medium-high heat fry tortillas, one at a time, until firm. Drain well. With a large spoon, make 6 hollows in the tomato sauce. Drop 1 egg in each hollow and poach until cooked to doneness. Remove eggs and place 1 egg on each tortilla. Spoon sauce around each egg and garnish with avocado slices, cheese, and olives.

SERVES 6

VARIATION: Rather than poaching the eggs, they may be fried in a separate skillet, continuing as above.

Eggs Continental

¾ cup fine bread crumbs
4 hard-cooked eggs, sliced
3 slices bacon, diced
¼ pound fresh mushrooms, sliced
1 cup sour cream
2 Tablespoons chopped parsley
¼ teaspoon salt
¼ teaspoon paprika
½ cup grated Cheddar cheese

Line casserole dish with bread crumbs. Arrange sliced eggs on top. Fry bacon until crisp, then add mushrooms and sauté. Drain off the fat. Mix bacon and mushrooms with sour cream, parsley, salt, and paprika. Spread this mixture over the eggs. Top with grated cheese. Bake at 375°F for 20 minutes.

SERVES 4

Mexican Soufflé

Butter
3 4-ounce cans whole green chiles
2 cups grated Monterey Jack cheese
2 cups grated medium sharp Cheddar cheese
6 large eggs
1 cup flour
4 cups whole or 2% milk
Salt and pepper to taste

Butter the bottom of a 3-quart soufflé dish. Cut chiles into 1-inch pieces. Layer the chiles and cheeses in bottom of soufflé dish. Beat together the eggs, flour, milk, salt, and pepper; pour over chiles and cheeses. Bake in preheated 350°F oven for 1 hour. Let stand 5 minutes before serving.

SERVES 8

For over 100 years Tillamook County in Oregon has been famous for its cheese. A Canadian named Peter McIntosh moved to that area and brought with him the fine art of making real Cheddar. His cheeses were famous throughout the Pacific Northwest, and in the gold-mining camps of Alaska, his golden cheese was often traded ounce-for-ounce with the metal the miners worked so hard to mine.

Eggs Fantastic

1 12-ounce package regular Jimmy Dean sausage
¼ pound fresh mushrooms, sliced
1 medium onion, chopped
Salt and pepper to taste
6 eggs
3 Tablespoons sour cream
¼-⅓ cup Mexican tomato and yellow chili hot sauce (La Victoria Salsa Supreme)
8 ounces Velveeta cheese, sliced
8 ounces medium Cheddar cheese, sliced
8 ounces Mozzarella cheese, sliced

Sauté crumbled sausage, mushrooms, and onion with salt and pepper. Drain very well on paper towels. Combine eggs and sour cream in blender and blend for 1 minute. Pour eggs in greased 7½ × 11½-inch baking dish. Bake at 400°F for 8-10 minutes until set in the middle. Spoon hot sauce over eggs and add sausage mix. Then layer the 3 cheeses beginning with the Velveeta. Casserole may be refrigerated or frozen at this point and baked later. Bake uncovered at 300°F for 45 minutes. Remove from oven and let set 5-10 minutes before cutting and serving.

SERVES 6-8

Poached Eggs Mushroom

1 10½-ounce can cream of mushroom soup
⅓ cup milk
¼ cup sherry
1 Tablespoon butter or margarine
4 eggs
Toast or English muffins

Mix and heat soup, milk, sherry, and butter in a large skillet; break eggs into the sauce. Cover and cook over very low heat for a few minutes, or until eggs are cooked to desired firmness. Serve on toast or English muffins.

SERVES 4

Rice-Broccoli Bake

1 medium onion, diced
½ cube margarine
1 10½-ounce can cream of mushroom soup
½ pound Cheddar cheese, shredded
½ cup sour cream, thinned
2 10-ounce packages frozen, chopped broccoli, thawed and drained
2½ cups cooked rice
Buttered bread crumbs

Wilt onion in margarine. Mix all ingredients together except crumbs and place in an 8 × 8-inch casserole. Top casserole with buttered crumbs. Bake at 350°F for 30 minutes covered, and then another 15 minutes uncovered.

SERVES 6-8

Cheese-Rice Casserole

1 large onion, diced
¼ pound butter or margarine melted
1¾ cups uncooked rice
2 10½-ounce cans consommé
1 4-ounce can mushrooms, undrained
1½ cups grated yellow cheese
½ cup sliced almonds

Mix all ingredients and bake in covered casserole for 1½ hours at 325°F.

SERVES 6-

Rice Elena

3-4 cups cooked rice
2 cups sour cream
2 4-ounce cans chopped green chiles
1 pound Monterey Jack cheese, grated
Salt to taste
¼ cup grated Cheddar cheese

Butter a 2-quart casserole. Mix all ingredients together except Cheddar cheese. Pour in casserole. Sprinkle Cheddar cheese on top. Bake at 350°F for 30 minutes.

SERVES 12

French Rice

1 cup butter, melted
2 medium onions, chopped
2 cups uncooked white rice
1 cup water
2 garlic cloves, minced
2 teaspoons chopped fresh parsley
2 10½-ounce cans consommé
1 4-ounce can mushrooms, drained

Mix all ingredients and place in a greased casserole. Bake at 350°F for 1 hour; stir every 15 minutes.

SERVES 4

Green Rice

6 cups cooked rice
¾ cup melted butter
1 bell pepper, seeded and minced
2 small onions, minced
1¼ cups milk
1 cup minced fresh parsley
2-3 cups grated Cheddar cheese
3 eggs, beaten

Combine all of the above ingredients and place in greased casserole dish. Bake covered in 350°F oven for 30 minutes; uncover and bake an additional 20 minutes.

SERVES 8-10

NOTE: Great with a fish dinner.

Spicy Fried Rice

2 Tablespoons butter
5 scallions, chopped including green ends
6 ounces *fresh* bay shrimp, cooked
2 cups cooked rice
1 teaspoon ginger
½ teaspoon garlic powder
¼ teaspoon ground cloves
1 teaspoon salt
½ teaspoon pepper
2 Tablespoons soy sauce
2 eggs
Chopped scallion greens or shrimp (optional)

Melt butter in large frying pan and sauté scallions for 2 minutes. Add shrimp and cook 2 more minutes; stir constantly. Add rice and cook until warmed, turning often. Add spices and soy sauce. Stir well. Beat eggs and pour over the top. Stir mixture until eggs are set, about 1 minute. Turn onto serving platter. May be garnished with scallion greens or extra shrimp.

SERVES 4-6

"When in haste to do up a shirt, sprinkle it lightly, wrap it in paper and pop it in a hot oven for 4 minutes. Then remove and iron."

Klamath County Museum

Rice - Zucchini Casserole

1½ pounds small zucchini
¾ cup shredded sharp Cheddar cheese
½ cup uncooked regular long grain rice
1 10½-ounce can mushroom soup
1 cup water
1 3-4 ounce can sliced mushrooms, undrained
1 teaspoon salt
¼ teaspoon pepper
1-2 slices bacon

Wash zucchini well and slice ¼-inch thick. Arrange one third of the zucchini in bottom of well-buttered 2-quart casserole. Top with one third of the cheese and half of the rice. Make another layer of one third of the zucchini and one-third of the cheese, then a layer using all the remaining rice. Arrange remainder of zucchini on top. In a small pan combine soup, water, mushrooms with their liquid, salt, and pepper; heat and pour into the casserole. Sprinkle remaining cheese over casserole. Cut bacon in 1-inch pieces and arrange on top. Cover and bake in 350°F oven for about 25 minutes; uncover and bake about 20 minutes longer, or until rice is tender and zucchini is tender-crisp.

SERVES 4-6

Fettuccine Alfredo

1 12-ounce package fettuccine
¼-½ cup butter to taste
1 pint cream
1 cup grated Parmesan cheese
Salt and pepper to taste

Cook fettuccine according to directions on package. Drain and return to pan. Add butter, cream, cheese, and salt and pepper. Stir, mixing all ingredients thoroughly until cream and butter are absorbed by noodles. Heat through and serve immediately.

SERVES 10

Pasta Primavera

1 cup sliced zucchini
1½ cups broccoli flowerets or green beans
1½ cups snow peas
1 cup baby peas
6 stalks asparagus, sliced
Boiling, salted water
16-ounces spaghetti
3 Tablespoons olive oil, divided
12 cherry tomatoes, cut in half
2 teaspoons minced garlic, divided
Salt
Freshly ground black pepper
¼ cup chopped Italian parsley
⅓ cup pine nuts
10 large mushrooms, sliced
⅓ cup butter
½ cup freshly grated Parmesan cheese
1 cup heavy cream
⅓ cup chopped fresh basil
⅓ cup chicken consommé (optional)
Cherry tomatoes
Grated Parmesan Cheese (optional)

Blanch zucchini, broccoli, snow peas, baby peas and, asparagus one at a time in boiling salted water for 1-2 minutes each until just crisp-tender. Drain and refresh under cold water. Set aside. This can be done ahead of time. Cook pasta in lots of boiling salted water until al dente, about 8-11 minutes. Drain. While pasta is cooking heat 1 Tablespoon oil and sauté tomatoes, 1 teaspoon of garlic, and all the salt, pepper, and parsley. Set aside. In another large pan with remaining 2 Tablespoons oil sauté pine nuts until brown. Add remaining teaspoon garlic; all the blanched vegetables, and raw mushrooms. Simmer a few minutes until hot. In a pan large enough for pasta and vegetables, melt butter. Add ½ cup cheese, cream, and basil. Stir to blend and melt cheese. Add pasta and toss to coat with sauce. If sauce gets too thick, thin with a little chicken consommé. Add about one- third of the vegetables; toss again. Divide pasta among broad soup plates and top with remaining vegetables. Garnish with a few cherry tomatoes. Top with more grated Parmesan, if desired.

SERVES 6

Layered Noodle Spinach Dish

4 ounces medium noodles
2 10-ounce packages frozen chopped or leaf spinach
3 Tablespoons butter
2 Tablespoons flour
½ teaspoon salt
¼ teaspoon paprika
⅛ teaspoon white pepper
1 cup milk
½ pound Gruyere cheese, grated

Cook and drain noodles, then cook and drain spinach. Make white sauce with butter, flour, salt, paprika, pepper, and milk. Remove sauce from heat and stir in spinach. Grease a 8 × 12 × 2-inch pan. Layer half of the noodles, half of the cheese, all of the spinach/white sauce, the remaining half of noodles, and the remaining half of cheese. Bake at 400°F for 15 minutes, or until bubbly.

SERVES 8

Grits Casserole

1½ cups grits
6 cups water
3 eggs, slightly beaten
1 pound Cheddar cheese, grated
2 teaspoons seasoned salt
Dash Tabasco sauce
1 cup butter
½ teaspoon cayenne pepper

Cook grits in water for 2-5 minutes. Add remaining ingredients and pour into a well-greased 2-quart casserole. Bake uncovered at 350°F for 1 hour.

SERVES 12-15

Barley Pine Nut Casserole

1 cup pearl barley
6 Tablespoons butter
¼-½ cup pine nuts or almonds
1 medium onion, finely chopped
¼ cup chopped green onion or chives
¼ teaspoon salt
¼ teaspoon pepper
2 14-ounce cans chicken broth, undiluted
Parsley

Rinse barley and drain. In fry pan, heat 2 Tablespoons butter. Add nuts and stir until lightly toasted. Remove from heat and set nuts aside. Add remaining 4 Tablespoons of butter to pan, along with barley and onion. Cook until lightly browned. Stir in nuts, green onion, salt and pepper. Spoon into 1½-quart casserole. Freeze or chill at this point if desired. Heat broth to boiling and pour over barley mixture. Stir to mix. Bake at 375°F for 70 minutes, or until liquid is absorbed. Garnish with parsley and serve immediately.

SERVES 6

'he cost of moving a family to the Oregon Territory included a covered wagon osting approximately $100.00 and a three oxen team for about $225.00. The ɔagon could be completely outfited for about $215.00

Food Staples

12 sacks flour	36.00
400 pounds bacon	40.00
100 pounds coffee	30.00
Yeast powder	5.00
50 pounds salt	1.00
3 pounds pepper	.50
2 bushels beans	3.00
15 gallons vinegar	4.00
50 pounds lard	5.00
200 pounds sugar	25.00
4 bushels dried apples	6.00
1 bushel dried peaches	2.00
50 pounds rice	5.00

Sundries

40 pounds candles	10.00
1 gross matches	1.00
1 coffee mill	.75
2 coffee pots	1.50
8 tin cups and plates	1.00
2 frying pans	2.50
4 butcher knives	2.00
6 knives, forks and spoons	2.00
2 kettles	1.25
2 bread pans	1.00

Camp Needs

Tent	15.00
10 gallon water tub	1.25
2 water buckets	.50
1 small tin pail	1.00
75 feet rope	2.50
2 axes	2.50
10 pounds nails	.75
Hand tools	2.50
Whet stone	.10

'otal cost including wagon and oxen $539.60

MEATS

Gwyneth P. O'Connell

Filet of Beef Wellington

Valley River Inn

4 6-ounce beef fillets, trimmed
Salt and pepper
16 ounces Duxelle
12 ounces puff pastry (any recipe)
2 ounces egg yolk
1 ounce cold water
Red wine sauce

DUXELLE:
18 ounces fresh mushrooms, finely chopped
2 ounces cooked ham finely chopped
Salt and pepper to taste
Cayenne pepper
Parsley, finely chopped to taste
3 ounces goose liver paté (optional)

FILET: Lightly season the entire filet with salt and pepper. Place in a frying pan which has been preheated to 400°F and brown on all sides for 30 seconds. Remove the filets and let them cool, but do not refrigerate.

DUXELLE: Put a frying pan on the fire and let it get red hot. Add the mushrooms. Stir gently to insure evaporation of the water content of the mushrooms. Add the ham. Season with salt and pepper and a tiny pinch of cayenne pepper. Remove from the fire; add the parsley and goose liver paté, if desired. Mix thoroughly.

PUFF PASTRY: Using your favorite recipe, make according to directions. Then roll dough into a 16 × 16-inch square which is $\frac{1}{16}$-inch thick. Let it settle for 10 minutes and then cut into 4 squares which are 8 × 8 inches each.

EGG YOLK: Beat, and add cold water.

ASSEMBLY: Spread one-fourth of the Duxelle evenly on all sides of each browned filet. Place each filet in the middle of a pastry square. Fold the dough around it. With a butter brush, paint a little egg yolk on the overlapping edges of the dough. (It will stay together this way during the cooking process without separating.) Lay seam-side down on a cookie sheet. Brush the remainder of the egg yolk mixture on the top of the Filet Wellington; this will give it a beautiful color during cooking. Bake for 15-25 minutes in preheated 400°F oven. Cooking time depends on degree of doneness desired. Serve with a red wine sauce.

SERVES 4

Tournedos-a-la-Thwing

¼ cup wine vinegar
1 teaspoon minced onion
½ teaspoon minced parsley
⅛ teaspoon ground pepper
3 egg yolks
1 Tablespoon butter, melted
Pinch salt
3 Tablespoons butter, melted
1 Tablespoon chopped chives
1 Tablespoon tarragon
1 Tablespoon chopped parsley
6 tournedos (fillets bound with beef fat)
¾ cup butter
Salt and pepper to taste
6 rounds of bread, toasted

Prepare Béarnaise by boiling vinegar, onion, ½ teaspoon parsley, and pepper until it is reduced to 2 Tablespoons. Strain. In a double boiler over simmering water, place egg yolks, 1 Tablespoon butter, and pinch salt. Add seasoned vinegar mixture and cook, beating constantly until thickened. Remove from heat and while beating, add the 3 Tablespoons butter, chives, tarragon, and 1 Tablespoon parsley. Set aside. Sauté tournedos in ¾ cup butter, 4 minutes on each side, and season with salt and pepper. Serve tournedos on toast; cover with sauce.

SERVES 6

Classic French Pepper Steak

Coarse pepper
2-inch thick New York strip steak
Salt
Butter
½ cup red wine
1 beef bouillon cube
¼ cup water

With the heel of your hand, press the pepper firmly into the steak. Salt both sides. Sauté over high heat in small amount of butter, quickly searing both sides. Reduce heat to medium and cook 5 minutes on each side. Test for desired degree of doneness. Remove from skillet and keep warm on heated platter. Add wine, bouillon cube, and water to skillet. Heat quickly until slightly reduced. Pour over steak and serve.

YIELD: Determined by amount of steak used

London Broil

2 pounds flank steak or ¾-inch round steak
1 garlic clove
½-1 teaspoon salt
2-3 Tablespoons soy sauce
1 Tablespoon tomato paste
1 Tablespoon oil
½ teaspoon pepper
½ teaspoon oregano

Score flank steak or trim all fat from round steak. Mash garlic with salt, and add remaining ingredients. Mix well and rub into steak. Wrap in wax paper and let stand in refrigerator 5-6 hours or overnight. Broil 5-8 minutes on each side or until done. Slice across grain and serve with any remaining sauce.

SERVES 4-6

Stir-Fried Beef and Broccoli

1 pound beef sirloin, trimmed of fat and gristle
1 Tablespoon cornstarch
2 Tablespoons dry sherry
2 Tablespoons soy sauce
1 pound broccoli
2-3 Tablespoons peanut oil
1 teaspoon salt
2-3 Tablespoons water
2-3 Tablespoons peanut oil
2 slices fresh ginger
2 green onions, sliced thin
1 teaspoon granulated sugar
2 Tablespoons oyster sauce (optional)
Cooked rice

Slice meat across grain into pieces ⅛ × 1 × 2-inches. Combine cornstarch, sherry, and soy sauce. Marinate meat in this mixture. (May marinate several hours if desired.) Cut the flowers off the broccoli and reserve them. Remove the stringy skin from broccoli stalks and cut diagonally into ⅛-¼ inch pieces. Add to broccoli flowerets. Heat wok or large fry pan and pour in 2-3 Tablespoons peanut oil. When the oil begins to smoke, add the broccoli and stir-fry until coated with oil. Add the 1 teaspoon salt and mix well. Pour in the water, and cover the wok for 2-3 minutes. When broccoli is done, transfer it to a plate. (It should still be crunchy and bright green.) Remove any liquid from wok. Pour 2-3 Tablespoons oil into reheated wok. When it begins to swirl and smoke around the edges, add ginger and green onion. Stir briefly and add the beef. Stir-fry until most of the beef has lost its pink color. Add sugar and optional oyster sauce. Stir and return broccoli to wok. Stir just long enough to heat through. Serve with rice.

SERVES 6

Oriental Stuffed Flank Steak

RICE STUFFING:
½ cup chopped onion
1 garlic clove, minced
¼ cup margarine
1½ cups cooked rice
½ cup chopped parsley
½ cup grated Parmesan cheese
½ teaspoon salt
¼ teaspoon pepper

STEAK:
1¾-2-pound flank steak
¼ teaspoon garlic powder
2 Tablespoons soy sauce
½ teaspoon pepper
2 Tablespoons margarine
1 beef bouillon cube
1 cup water
¾ teaspoon powdered ginger

STUFFING: Sauté onion and garlic in margarine until onion is golden. Remove pan from heat. Stir in rice, parsley, cheese, salt, and pepper. Set aside.
STEAK: Wipe flank steak with damp paper towel. With sharp knife, lightly score diamonds on both sides of steak. Rub ⅛ teaspoon garlic powder on each side. Then brush each side with 1 Tablespoon soy sauce and ¼ teaspoon pepper. Lay steak flat and spread with 1 Tablespoon margarine; then spread rice stuffing over steak, keeping about 1½ inches from edges. Roll up from end to end, around stuffing. Tie roll in 3 places with twine. Spread remaining Tablespoon of margarine over rolled steak surface. Place in roasting pan. Mix bouillon cube and water and pour over roll. Sprinkle with powdered ginger. Roast at 350°F for 45-60 minutes, basting occasionally. Slice steak before removing twine; it is easier to get even slices. Pour pan juices into bowl to serve with meat.

SERVES 4

Marinated Flank Steak

2 small or 1 large flank steak
3 garlic cloves
2 Tablespoons brown sugar
½ teaspoon fresh ginger
¼ cup soy sauce
¼ cup red wine
Freshly ground pepper
1 beef bouillon cube, dissolved in 1 cup water

Score steak on both sides. Place steak in a bowl containing mixture of all remaining ingredients so that it is completely submerged. Leave tightly covered in refrigerator for 2 days, turning every half day. Remove from refrigerator 1 hour before cooking. Barbecue or grill, searing each side 3-4 minutes only!

SERVES

Flank Steak in Honey Marinade

1 flank steak
Instant meat tenderizer
¼ cup soy sauce
2 Tablespoons vinegar
½ teaspoon ginger
¾ cup salad oil
3 Tablespoons honey
1½ Tablespoons garlic powder

Sprinkle steak with meat tenderizer and pierce with fork. Blend together the soy sauce, vinegar, ginger, oil, honey, and garlic powder. Marinate the meat in sauce at least 10 hours, or overnight. Broil or barbecue 7 minutes on each side. Slice on diagonal.

SERVES 6

Pepper Steak

1½ pounds round steak, cut in ½-inch strips
½ cup flour
1 teaspoon salt
¼ teaspoon pepper
⅓ cup salad oil
1 8-ounce can tomato sauce
1 cup water
½ cup chopped onion
1 small garlic clove, minced
1 beef bouillon cube
1½ teaspoons Worcestershire
1 medium green pepper, cut in strips
Cooked rice

Coat steak in mixture of flour, salt, and pepper. Using a large skillet, brown the steak strips in the oil. When brown, add tomato sauce, water, onion, garlic, and bouillon cube. Cover and simmer 1½ hours, or until meat is tender. Uncover and stir in Worcestershire sauce and green pepper. Simmer 5-10 minutes longer. Serve on rice.

SERVES 6

In 1837 two men, Jason Lee and Erving Young, headed a group of prominent men determined to break the monopoly on cattle in Oregon. The only herd prior to that date was owned by the Hudson Bay Company. They sold milk to the new settlers, but refused to part with any of their livestock. Lee and Young organized an expedition to California to drive a large herd of beef and dairy cattle to Oregon for the settlers. By 1870 cattle ranching was firmly established in the vast range lands of central and south-eastern Oregon.

Italian Swiss Steak

1½ pounds round steak, cut into serving pieces and tenderized
Flour, salt, and pepper
Shortening
2 large onions, peeled and sliced
1½ cups canned tomatoes
2 green peppers, sliced
1 cup water (optional)
8 ounces Mozzarella cheese, shredded

Dredge round steak in flour, salt, and pepper mixture and brown in shortening in heavy fry pan or Dutch oven. Add onions, tomatoes, and peppers. Cover and cook over low heat for 1½-2 hours or until meat is tender. If more juice is desired, add 1 cup hot water. Just before serving, cover each piece of meat with Mozzarella cheese. Cover pan again for a few minutes to melt the cheese, and serve immediately. Do not allow the cheese to melt too much.

SERVES 4

Special Beef Parmesan

1½ pounds round steak or chuck
1 egg
⅓ cup Parmesan cheese
⅓ cup bread crumbs
⅓ cup oil
½ cup chopped onion
1 teaspoon each salt and pepper
¼-⅓ cup granulated sugar (or less)
1 6-ounce can tomato paste
2 cups hot water
½ pound Mozzarella cheese, grated

Prepare and flatten meat by trimming fat, cutting meat into 6-8 pieces. Lay between wax paper and strike with bottom of large pan (no edges, please). Flatten to ½-inch thick. Beat egg with fork. Mix Parmesan cheese and bread crumbs together. Dip meat in egg and then the bread mixture. Brown in skillet with oil and place in 9 × 13-inch baking dish. In remaining oil sauté onion then add salt, pepper, sugar, tomato paste, and water. Boil 5 minutes. Pour two thirds of this sauce over meat. Cover with Mozzarella cheese and add remaining sauce. Bake at 300°F for 1½ hours.

SERVES 6

Beef Stroganoff

1½ cups sliced onion (2 medium onions)
¼ cup vegetable oil
½ pound mushrooms, sliced (canned or fresh)
2 pounds round or boneless chuck steak, cut in thin strips
2 Tablespoons flour
¾ pound tomatoes (1 12-ounce can or 3 medium tomatoes, peeled)
1½ teaspoons salt
⅛ teaspoon pepper
¼ teaspoon Worcestershire sauce
½ cup sour cream
½ cup red wine
Cooked rice

Sauté onion in oil for 10 minutes, mushrooms also, if you use fresh. Canned mushrooms are added after the onion has cooked for 10 minutes. Cover and continue cooking for 5 minutes. Scrape onion and mushrooms into a bowl and set aside. Save remaining oil in pan to brown meat slowly and thoroughly. Sprinkle meat with flour and stir until well-blended. Cut tomatoes into chunks and add them to the meat. Add salt, pepper and Worcestershire sauce. Cover and simmer slowly for 1 hour, stirring occasionally. Add reserved sautéd mushrooms and onion, sour cream, and wine. Simmer another ½ hour. Serve over rice.

SERVES 8

Tangy Beef Stroganoff

1 pound round steak, cubed
Flour
2-3 Tablespoons oil
½ cup chopped onion
1 6-ounce can mushrooms and juice
1 garlic clove, chopped or pressed
Salt and pepper to taste
½ pint sour cream
1 Tablespoon Worcestershire sauce
3 teaspoons chili sauce
3 teaspoons prepared yellow mustard
1 Tablespoon lemon juice
1 beef bouillon cube
Water as needed
Cooked brown rice

Dip cubed steak in flour and sauté in oil. Drain oil. Add next 10 ingredients. Simmer 1 hour, adding the water if necessary. Stir and serve over brown rice.

SERVES 4

Round Steak Supreme

3-4 pounds round steak, cut into large cubes
2 beef bouillon cubes
2 cups boiling water
¾ cup ketchup
3 Tablespoons prepared mustard
3 Tablespoons Worcestershire sauce
1 large onion, quartered
2 green peppers
1 4¼-ounce can sliced mushrooms
Cornstarch
Cooked rice

Place steak in heavy skillet. Dissolve bouillon in boiling water, reduce heat and add ketchup, mustard, and Worcestershire sauce. Pour over meat, cover, and simmer 1 hour. Add onion and cook 10 minutes. Add green pepper, sliced ½-inch wide the long way, and the mushrooms; cover and simmer 20 minutes. Thicken with cornstarch if needed. Serve over rice.

SERVES 6

NOTE: This is a good company dish, especially for a large crowd.

Beef Burgundy

6 slices bacon, cut in ¼-inch pieces
3 pounds lean beef stew or round steak, cut in 1-inch pieces
3 cups Burgundy wine
2 cups beef bouillon soup or 2 cups water and 2 beef bouillon cubes
1 Tablespoon tomato paste
1 garlic clove, minced
½ teaspoon dried thyme leaves, crushed
1 bay leaf
¼ cup chopped parsley
1 teaspoon salt
½-1 pound fresh mushrooms, sliced
¼ cup margarine
1 3½-ounce jar cocktail onions
½ cup flour
Cooked Rice
Parsley

Cook bacon and set aside. Brown beef in bacon fat. Drain off fat, if necessary. Add bacon, wine, bouillon, tomato paste, garlic, thyme, bay leaf, parsley, and salt. Bring to a boil. Place in 2½-quart casserole and bake covered for 3 hours at 325°F. Fifteen minutes before serving, sauté mushrooms in margarine. Drain onions, saving liquid. Add mushrooms and onions to casserole. Blend flour in onion liquid and 1 cup of liquid from casserole. Mix well. Pour into casserole and mix. Continue baking until mushrooms and onions are heated. Let casserole stand at least 10 minutes before serving. Serve with rice and garnish with parsley.

SERVES 6

Marinated Chuck Steak

3-4 pounds chuck steak, 1½ inches thick
Unseasoned tenderizer
¼ cup vinegar
½ cup red wine
¼ cup oil
1 medium onion, cut up
1 large garlic clove
½ teaspoon salt
½ teaspoon pepper
1 teaspoon rosemary
1 teaspoon Worcestershire sauce
¼ teaspoon ground bay leaves
1 Tablespoon Dijon prepared mustard

Treat chuck with tenderizer. Combine all remaining ingredients in blender, then pour over meat and refrigerate 2-6 hours. Grill over medium-hot fire about 6 inches from coals. Baste with marinade every 5 minutes. Cook a total of 30-35 minutes, or until done as desired, turning once. Let rest 10 minutes. Slice across grain.

SERVES 6

Old-Fashioned Beef Stew

2 Tablespoons cooking oil
2 pounds beef, cubed
2 medium onions, sliced
2 medium celery stalks with tops, sliced
2 teaspoons salt
1 teaspoon pepper
1 medium bay leaf
1 teaspoon dried marjoram
1 teaspoon garlic powder
1 teaspoon sweet basil
2 large carrots, sliced
2 pounds tomatoes (canned or fresh)
1 10-ounce package frozen corn
1 10-ounce package frozen cut green beans
3 medium potatoes, washed and cubed
1 10½-ounce can beef bouillon
2 cups red wine
Roux of 2 Tablespoons butter and 2 Tablespoons flour mashed together (optional)

In heavy 6-quart Dutch oven, heat oil just to smoking. Add meat all at once and brown rapidly, stirring constantly until all of the cubes are browned. Reduce heat and add onions, celery, and spices. Cook until onion is just tender. Add remaining ingredients except roux. Stir well to combine. Cook over medium-low heat until meat is tender and all vegetables are very tender, approximately 1 hour. Add more wine or beef stock during cooking to keep meat from drying out. Stew should be very moist but not runny. If gravy is thin, add roux; cook and stir until thickened and flour taste is gone.

YIELD: 5 quarts

Carbonade

3 pounds boneless beef, cut in ½-inch slices
Oil
4 cups slivered onion
2 Tablespoons flour
1 10½-ounce can beef broth, undiluted
1½ cups beer
1½ teaspoons salt
½ teaspoon thyme
1 Tablespoon vinegar
2 garlic cloves, pressed or chopped finely
1 stalk celery
Sprig of parsley
Bay leaf

In fry pan, brown meat in oil. Remove. Sauté onion in oil, using same fry pan. Layer meat and onion in casserole dish. Set aside. Blend flour into same fry pan being used. Add beef broth, beer, salt, and thyme. Boil, stirring in vinegar and garlic. Pour into casserole dish with meat and onions. Place celery, parsley, and bay leaf on top. Cover and bake at 300°F for 2½ hours. Remove celery, parsley, and bay leaf before serving.

SERVES 6

Easy Stew

1-2 pounds stew meat
2 Tablespoons Crisco
1 package dry onion soup mix
1 10½-ounce can mushroom soup, undiluted
2 cups water
4 potatoes, peeled and quartered
6-8 carrots, cut up
1 10-ounce package frozen peas, cooked and drained
1 10½-ounce can consommé, undiluted
2-3 stalks celery, cut up
½ green pepper, cut up
Cornstarch (optional)

Brown stew meat in Crisco. Drain oil. Add onion soup mix, mushroom soup, and water. Simmer 20 minutes. Add potatoes and carrots, and simmer 3 hours. Add peas, consommé, celery, and green pepper. Simmer 40 minutes. Thicken with cornstarch, if necessary.

SERVES 6

Bar-B-Q Beef

5-pound boned roast
1 cup ketchup
1 cup barbecue sauce
1 cup water
1 onion, chopped
2½ teaspoons vinegar
2 teaspoons Worcestershire sauce
Garlic powder, salt, and pepper to taste

Place meat in roasting pan or dutch oven. Mix all ingredients and pour over roast. Cover and cook for at least 5 hours at 300°F or until meat flakes off into pieces and becomes part of the sauce.

YIELD: 10 servings

Marinated Chuck Roast

3-5 pound chuck roast, cut 1½-inches thick
½ cup strong coffee
½ cup soy sauce
1 large onion, finely chopped
1 garlic clove, minced
1 Tablespoon Worcestershire sauce
1 Tablespoon vinegar

Marinate meat in a mixture of all the remaining ingredients for 12 hours at room temperature, turning several times. Remove from marinade and broil meat in oven, or cook on charcoal grill, basting frequently with marinade. Cook to desired doneness, but it is best served medium-rare.

SERVES 6-8

Dill Pot Roast

3-5 pound chuck roast
1 teaspoon garlic salt
½ teaspoon dill weed
1 teaspoon paprika
¾ cup beef bouillon soup
2 small onions, sliced
6-8 large carrots, peeled and cut
2 Tablespoons cornstarch
2 Tablespoons water

Place meat in roasting pan; sprinkle with herbs and bouillon. Put sliced onions on top. Put peeled and cut carrots around meat. Roast at 350°F covered for 3 hours. Make gravy by adding cornstarch and water mixture to drippings after roast is cooked.

SERVES 6-8

Spanish Short Ribs

1 Tablespoon peppercorns
½ cup pimiento-stuffed green olives
1 garlic clove, minced
½ teaspoon grated lemon peel
¼ cup olive oil
4 pounds short ribs
Meat tenderizer

Process peppercorns in blender or food processor until cracked. Add olives, garlic, lemon peel, and oil. Blend until thick and smooth. Sprinkle meat with tenderizer over all sides and pierce with a fork. Spread olive oil mixture on all sides of short ribs and marinate for 3-4 hours. Barbecue over medium coals until done, 30-45 minutes.

SERVES 6

NOTE: A good, economical recipe for a difficult-to-use meat!

Camping Stew

1 pound ground beef
1 medium onion, chopped
1 16-ounce can tomatoes, undrained
1 16-ounce can green beans, drained
1 12-ounce can Niblets corn, drained
1 16-ounce can sliced carrots, undrained
1 8-ounce can tomato sauce
2 cups cooked macaroni
Salt and pepper to taste
1 bay leaf
½ teaspoon garlic powder

AT HOME: Brown beef in skillet. Drain off fat, if necessary. Add onion and cook until onion is just tender. Add remaining ingredients. Cook until carrots are tender, about 10 minutes. Cool.
TO TAKE CAMPING: Place in covered container. Freeze or chill, depending on how long you want it to keep. If frozen solid in a 6-cup container, it will take 24 hours to defrost and will keep unrefrigerated (but not exposed to direct heat or sun) 6-8 hours longer. If chilled thoroughly and placed in camping cooler with ice packs, it will keep 2-3 days.
TO EAT: Heat through over camp stove or fire and serve in bowls for a 1-dish meal.

SERVES 4

NOTE: Serve with crusty buttered rolls.

Scrumptious Stroganoff

1½ pounds lean ground beef
4 Tablespoons butter
1 cup chopped onion
1 garlic clove, chopped
½ pound fresh mushrooms, sliced
3 Tablespoons flour
2 teaspoons instant beef bouillon
1 Tablespoon ketchup
1 Tablespoon A-1 Sauce
½ teaspoon salt
⅛ teaspoon pepper
1 10½-ounce can beef consommé or bouillon
½ cup white wine
¼ teaspoon dried dill
1½ cups sour cream

Brown meat in 1 Tablespoon butter, then add remaining butter and sauté onion, garlic, and mushrooms until onion is clear, 3-4 minutes. Remove pan from heat and remove meat and onions from pan, set aside. Mix flour, instant bouillon, ketchup, A-1 Sauce, salt, and pepper in fry pan. Gradually add beef consommé, return to heat, and bring to boil. Put meat back in pan, reduce heat, and simmer 5 minutes. Stir in wine, dill, and sour cream. Heat thoroughly.

SERVES 4

Taco Casserole

1 pound ground beef
½ teaspoon garlic salt
1 9½-ounce package corn chips
1 cup grated Cheddar cheese
2 cups shredded lettuce
SAUCE:
1 16-ounce can stewed tomatoes
1 teaspoon granulated sugar
¾ teaspoon dried oregano
½ teaspoon Worcestershire sauce
¼ teaspoon salt
⅛ teaspoon pepper
¼ teaspoon hot sauce
¼ cup chopped green pepper
¼ cup chopped onion

Cook ground beef until browned; drain off excess fat. Stir in garlic salt. Coarsely crush corn chips and place in bottom of ungreased 8-inch square baking dish. Spoon hot meat over chips. Top with cheese. Bake at 350°F 10-12 minutes or until heated through. While casserole is baking, prepare taco sauce by stirring together all sauce ingredients. Break up large tomato pieces. Sprinkle casserole with shredded lettuce; pour on taco sauce and serve immediately.

SERVES 4

Tamale Pie Goes Festive

CORN MEAL CRUST:
1 cup corn meal
2 teaspoons salt
2½ cups boiling water
2 Tablespoons butter

FILLING:
2 medium onions, chopped
1 garlic clove, minced
2 Tablespoons lard or drippings
1½ pounds lean ground beef
1 15-ounce can pitted ripe olives
2 cups cubed leftover roast
½ cup diced celery
½ cup diced green pepper
1 8-ounce can whole kernel corn
1½ cups cooked tomatoes
1 Tablespoon chili powder
2 teaspoons salt
½ teaspoon allspice
¼ teaspoon pepper
½ cup grated American cheese

Stir corn meal and salt into boiling water and cook until thickened, stirring constantly. Stir in butter and cook over water (double-boiler style) for 20 minutes. Line bottom and sides of a 2-quart casserole with mixture. Cook onions and garlic in hot fat for 5 minutes. Add ground beef and brown. Add remaining ingredients, except cheese and simmer 10 minutes. Pour filling into corn meal lining. Bake at 350°F for 45 minutes. Sprinkle with cheese. Bake an additional 15 minutes.

SERVES 8

Chili-Ghetti

2 Tablespoons butter
1 garlic clove, minced
¾ cup chopped onion
1 pound ground beef
2½ cups tomatoes (1-pound 3-ounce can)
3 15-ounce cans chilli with meat
1 8-ounce package spaghetti
3 cups shredded Cheddar cheese
1 cup sour cream
½ cup grated Parmesan cheese

In large skillet melt butter; brown garlic, onion, and ground beef. Drain off excess fat, and add tomatoes and chili; simmer 45 minutes. Meanwhile cook spaghetti and drain. Remove skillet with chili mixture from heat and stir in Cheddar cheese until melted. Fold in sour cream. Combine chili mixture and spaghetti, mixing well. Place in buttered baking dish, top with Parmesan cheese and bake 45 minutes in 350°F oven.

SERVES 8

Chili

3 pounds ground chuck or sirloin
2-3 medium onions, chopped
2 garlic cloves, minced
1 green pepper, chopped
½ teaspoon dried oregano
½ teaspoon ground cumin
2-3 Tablespoons chili powder, depending on taste
Salt and pepper to taste
2 6-ounce cans tomato paste
1 quart water
2 15-ounce cans kidney beans, drained

Brown meat and onion. Drain off all fat. Add garlic and green pepper; sauté until soft. Add seasonings, tomato paste and water. Simmer 2 hours. Then add kidney beans. Simmer ½ hour more.

SERVES 6

Spanish Rolls

20 hard rolls (approximately)
1 pound ground beef
6 hard-boiled eggs, finely chopped
1 large onion, chopped
1 pound sharp Cheddar cheese, grated
½ teaspoon garlic
1 8-ounce can tomato sauce
1 5-ounce can chopped ripe olives, drained
3 Tablespoons melted butter
1 teaspoon salt
1 teaspoon Tabasco

Take hard rolls, cut a little off one end and scoop out center. (Cut around inside with knife and pull out with fork.) Brown ground beef in skillet and add rest of ingredients. Fill rolls and replace ends. Wrap in foil. Bake 1 hour at 275°-300°F, or if you have a microwave, don't wrap in foil, but rather, heat in a paper napkin for 30-45 seconds each.

SERVES 4

NOTE: Can be frozen and popped in microwave for quick meal.

Leaburg Lasagna

1 28-ounce can Italian-style tomatoes or 1 16-ounce can peeled tomatoes plus 2 8-ounce cans stewed tomatoes
1 teaspoon salt
1½ teaspoons oregano
2 6-ounce cans tomato paste
½ teaspoon pepper
1 teaspoon onion salt
1 teaspoon salt, divided
2 pounds ground chuck or ground round
¼ cup olive oil (to be used in cooking meat if ground round is used)
1 cup finely minced onion
2 garlic cloves, finely minced
1 12-ounce package lasagna noodles
¾ pound Ricotta cheese or 1 pint small curd creamed cottage cheese
½ pound Mozzarella cheese, grated
¾ cup Parmesan cheese.

Simmer first 6 ingredients in uncovered pan. Salt cold fry pan with the ½ teaspoon salt. Put crumbled meat in pan and add olive oil, if necessary, then add onion and garlic. Add remaining ½ teaspoon salt. Cook until meat is browned. Add meat mixture to tomato mixture. Simmer 2½-3 hours. Preheat oven to 350°F. Cook lasagna noodles according to package directions. Cover the bottom of a baking dish with one third of the sauce. Place one half of the lasagna noodles crisscross over the bottom layer of sauce. Cover the layer of noodles with half of the Ricotta cheese, half of the Mozzarella, and one third of the Parmesan cheese. Repeat, ending up with a layer of sauce on top. Sprinkle the remaining one third Parmesan cheese on top. Bake until bubbly, approximately 30-40 minutes. Let stand about 15 minutes before serving.

SERVES 6

A winter staple for the Oregon Indians was made by pounding the cambium (a thin layer between the outer and inner bark) of the cedar, pine and hemlock trees with roots and berries. This was formed into large cakes, about a foot square and one inch thick. These were dried in the sun and stored for the winter months.

Company Casserole

4 cups uncooked medium-size egg noodles
2 pounds ground beef
1 Tablespoon butter
4 8-ounce cans tomato sauce
1 cup cottage cheese
1 8-ounce package cream cheese
¼ cup sour cream
⅓ cup chopped scallion or onion
1 Tablespoon chopped green pepper
2 Tablespoons butter, melted

Cook and drain noodles. Sauté beef in large skillet, using 1 Tablespoon butter, until brown. Stir in tomato sauce and remove from heat. Set aside. Combine in a bowl the cottage cheese, cream cheese, sour cream, scallion, and green pepper. Using a 3-quart casserole, spread half of the noodles, then cover with the cheese mixture. Add rest of noodles. Pour 2 Tablespoons melted butter over top of noodles. Cover with meat mixture. Bake uncovered for 30 minutes at 375°F.

SERVES 6

Zucchini Beef Casserole

1 pound ground beef
1 onion, chopped
1 Tablespoon oil
1 cup uncooked instant rice
½ teaspoon oregano
½ teaspoon salt
⅛ teaspoon pepper
4 cups sliced zucchini, sliced (peeling optional)
2 cups cottage cheese
1 10½-ounce can mushroom soup, undiluted
1 cup shredded sharp Cheddar cheese

Brown meat and onion in oil. Add rice and seasonings, and stir a few minutes. Drain off excessive grease. Layer in a 9 × 13-inch casserole, half of sliced zucchini, all of the meat mixture, the cottage cheese, remainder of zucchini, the soup and grated cheese. Bake at 350°F for 40 minutes.

SERVES 6

Pizza-"R"-Way

1 large loaf Rhodes white bread dough
1 cup good homemade tomato sauce or 1 8-ounce can good commercial tomato sauce flavored with 1½ teaspoons Italian Seasonings
1½-2 cups shredded Mozzarella cheese
Any or all of the following: sliced fresh mushrooms, sliced fresh tomatoes, sliced fresh green pepper, sliced olives
Thinly sliced pepperoni or salami, browned sausage or ground round, to taste
½ cup shredded Mozzarella cheese

Place frozen dough lengthwise in middle of 11 × 16-inch baking pan with sides. When dough thaws (3-5 hours) evenly spread it along bottom of pan and up sides of dish. Spread tomato sauce evenly on top of dough. Sprinkle with most of the cheese, reserving about ½ cup for top of pizza. Cover with your choice of pizza ingredients. Top with remaining cheese. Bake at 375°F for 20-30 minutes or until crust is nicely browned and cheese is bubbly and brown.

SERVES 6

Sweet and Sour Meatballs

2 pounds ground beef
1 large onion, grated
⅓ cup water
½ cup bread crumbs and crushed corn flakes, mixed
½ cup ketchup
1 garlic clove, minced
Salt and pepper to taste
1 large onion, diced
1 small head cabbage, diced

SAUCE:
½ cup ketchup
Juice of 4 lemons
2 8-ounce cans tomato sauce
1 cup brown sugar

Mix first 7 ingredients together. Form medium-size balls and broil. Sauté diced onion in oil until golden, using heavy skillet. Add cabbage and sauté lightly. Place onion- cabbage mixture in bottom of Dutch oven. Place broiled meatballs on top. Then add sauce.
SAUCE: Combine and heat ingredients, then pour over meatballs. Cover and cook in 350°F oven for 1 hour.

SERVES 8

Bernie's Spaghetti and Meatballs

SPAGHETTI SAUCE:
1 46-ounce can tomato juice, divided
2 Tablespoons granulated sugar
1 6-ounce can tomato paste
1 cup canned mushrooms, drained
4 Tablespoons olive oil
1 large onion, cut up
1 green pepper, cut up
2 Tablespoons barbecue sauce
Dash garlic salt
Pinch rosemary
¼ teaspoon oregano
2 bay leaves

MEATBALLS:
1½ pounds ground round
½ pound ground pork
2 egg yolks
2 Tablespoons bread crumbs
2 Tablespoons soft butter
2 teaspoons lemon juice
2 teaspoons salt
½ teaspoon pepper
½ cup finely chopped onions
Shortening
Cooked pasta

SAUCE: Pour 1-2 cups of tomato juice into a blender jar, reserve the remainder. Add the other sauce ingredients except the bay leaves. Mix sauce in blender until well blended. Pour into a 4-quart kettle with another 2 cups tomato juice and bay leaves. Cover and cook slowly for 2 hours on medium-low heat. Make meatballs while sauce is cooking.
MEATBALLS: Thoroughly mix meatball ingredients, except shortening, together. Shape into 25-30 meatballs. Brown meatballs in shortening, add to sauce along with remaining tomato juice. Cook 2 more hours. Remove bay leaves before serving over pasta.

SERVES 6-8

Special Meatloaf and Stuffing

1½ cups lean ground beef
½ cup soft bread crumbs
2 eggs
1 9-ounce packet Italian salad dressing mix
½ cup boiling water
1 6-ounce box stuffing mix (chicken or rice)
½ cup chopped celery
½ cup mayonnaise
1 teaspoon curry powder
½ cup marmalade or apricot jam, melted.

Mix the first 4 ingredients. Press and shape into an 8 ×10-inch layer on a baking sheet. Mix other ingredients except jam and put on meat in a strip down the middle. Roll meat over stuffing and seal the edges. Place seam-side down on sheet. Chill for 1 hour. Bake 40 minutes at 350°F, basting with jam.

SERVES 8

Glazed Burgundy Burgers

1 pound ground round or ground sirloin, shaped into 4 beef patties
¼ pound fresh mushrooms, sliced
2 Tablespoons chopped shallots
1 garlic clove, minced
2 Tablespoons butter
1 teaspoon Spice Island Beef Stock Base (dry)
1 teaspoon Dijon prepared mustard
¾ cup Burgundy or other dry red wine

Brown hamburgers on both sides, transferring cooked burgers to warm platter. Sauté mushrooms, shallots, and garlic in butter until tender. Set aside. Combine beef stock base, mustard, and wine. Return burgers to fry pan and pour sauce over meat. Cook over high heat until sauce reduces to glaze. To serve, spoon glaze over burgers, top with mushrooms and shallots.

SERVES 4

Patti's Beans

1 pound ground beef
¼ pound bacon, chopped
½ cup chopped onion
½ cup brown sugar
½ cup ketchup
2 Tablespoons vinegar
1 teaspoon salt
1 15-ounce can lima beans
1 15-ounce can kidney beans
1 31-ounce can pork and beans
1 teaspoon dry mustard

Brown ground beef, bacon, and onion. Add the sugar, ketchup, vinegar and salt. Partially drain the lima, kidney and pork and beans; add to the meat mixture. Stir in mustard. Bake 1 hour at 350°F, or cook very slowly in oven as it seems to enhance the flavor.

SERVES 20

Picnic Salami

4 pounds ground beef
¼ cup curing salt
2 Tablespoons Liquid Smoke
1½ teaspoons garlic powder
1½ teaspoons ground pepper

In a large bowl thoroughly mix the above ingredients. Cover and chill for 24 hours. Divide mixture into fourths. Shape each into an 8-inch log and place each on a 12 × 18-inch piece of nylon net. Roll up tightly and tie ends with string. Place logs on broiler pan with rack, and bake in a 225°F oven for 4 hours. Keeps in refrigerator for up to three weeks and freezer up to two months.

YIELD: 4 logs

Frosted Meatloaf

2 pounds ground beef
½ cup Kraft French Dressing
½ cup dry bread crumbs
½ cup chopped onion
2 eggs, beaten
1 teaspoon salt
½ teaspoon pepper
1 teaspoon garlic flakes
2 cups hot mashed potatoes
1 egg, beaten
½ cup mayonnaise
1 teaspoon salt
¼ teaspoon pepper
¼ cup Parmesan cheese
Sliced tomato, olives, mushrooms, pimiento, or parsley as desired

Combine meat, French dressing, bread crumbs, onion, eggs, salt, pepper, and garlic flakes. Mix well and shape into an oval loaf in a shallow baking dish. Bake at 350°F for 1 hour. Remove from oven and place on baking sheet or heat-proof serving platter. Combine potatoes, egg, mayonnaise, salt, pepper, and cheese, and frost the meatloaf. Broil until potato topping is golden brown and puffy! Garnish with tomato, olives, mushrooms, pimiento, or parsley.

SERVES 6

Veal Parmigiana

1-1½ pounds veal, ½-inch thick
2 eggs, beaten
3 Tablespoons fine dry bread crumbs
2 Tablespoons butter
2 Tablespoons oil
6 ounces spaghetti noodles
8 ounces Mozzarella cheese, shredded
6 Tablespoons grated Parmesan cheese

SAUCE:
2 Tablespoons margarine
1 cup chopped onion
2 15-ounce cans tomato purée
2 teaspoons dry basil
2 teaspoons granulated sugar
1 teaspoon oregano
1 teaspoon salt
½ teaspoon pepper
½ teaspoon garlic powder
6-8 mushrooms, sliced
½ cup dry red wine

Pound veal slices, dip them into egg, then bread crumbs. Heat butter and oil in fry pan and lightly brown veal. Cook spaghetti noodles, drain and turn into shallow casserole dish. To make sauce, heat margarine and sauté onion, then add remaining sauce ingredients and simmer 10-12 minutes. Top spaghetti noodles with half of the tomato sauce, then all the veal slices, half the cheeses, the remaining tomato sauce, and the remaining cheeses. Bake covered at 375°F for 30 minutes (1 hour if casserole is cold).

SERVES 4-6

Rollini Di Vitella with Rice Piedmont

1 medium garlic clove, chopped finely
1 teaspoon chopped fresh rosemary
3 Tablespoons finely chopped parsley
½ teaspoon salt
¼ teaspoon pepper
1 pound veal, cut into 8 very thin slices
8 paper-thin slices Prosciutto or Italian salami
5 Tablespoons olive oil or butter
½ cup Marsala or sweet sherry wine
1 4-ounce can mushrooms undrained

Mix garlic, rosemary, parsley, salt and pepper. Spread mixture lightly on each veal slice. Top each veal slice with 1 slice Prosciutto. Roll up the veal slices and fasten with toothpicks. Heat skillet and add oil; brown veal rolls quickly on both sides. Drain any remaining oil, then add wine. Simmer 2-3 minutes until wine is absorbed. Add mushrooms with liquid; simmer for 15-20 minutes. Serve with **Rice Piedmont.**

SERVES 4

Rice Piedmont

1 cup Uncle Ben's white rice
Salted water
1 10-ounce package frozen peas
½ cup shredded Romano Parmesan cheese
⅓ cup melted butter
Dash nutmeg

Boil rice in salted water as directed on package; do not overcook; if anything, undercook. Cook frozen peas 5 minutes only. Mix rice and peas together; stir in cheese and butter; season with nutmeg. Serve with **Rollini Di Vitella.**

An early settler of Cottage Grove, Oregon remembers the special taste of the foods that were home canned in the early days of the town. "You cooked your food from start to finish, where now you buy it half cooked in a can from the store and you've lost all the goodness."

Seasons of Harvest: Recollections of Lane County, 1975

Veal Scallopini a la Genovise

1 pound veal steak, ¼-inch thick
2 Tablespoons oil
1 garlic clove, crushed
2 Tablespoons flour
1 teaspoon capers
1 onion, chopped
1 teaspoon salt
1 teaspoon pepper
Pinch sage
Pinch nutmeg
¼ cup sauterne or dry white wine
¼ cup tomato paste
½ cup water or more
¼ pound fresh mushrooms
1 Tablespoon butter
1 4-ounce jar stuffed green olives
Pasta
Few green onion tops, finely chopped

Cut meat in 1 to 2-inch squares. Heat oil and sauté garlic. Add meat and sauté lightly until golden brown. Turn down heat. Sprinkle flour over meat and add capers, onion, salt, pepper, sage, and nutmeg. Then add wine, tomato paste and water. Cover and cook about 20 minutes or until tender. Slice mushrooms and sauté in melted butter. Add to veal along with olives. Cover and simmer until slightly thickened, about ½ hour. Serve over spaghetti, shell pasta, or homemade noodles. Garnish with green onion tops.

SERVES 4-6

Veal with White Wine

1½ pounds boneless veal or beef
6 slices bacon, cut in half
Flour
2 Tablespoons bacon fat or oil
1 16-ounce can of onions
1 Tablespoon flour
1½ cups beef broth
½ cup dry white wine
Salt and pepper to taste

Cut meat into 12 chunks. Wrap each piece of meat with a half slice of bacon and dredge lightly with flour. Heat fat in a heavy skillet. Add meat and onions, browning on all sides. Remove from pan and pour off all but 1 Tablespoon fat. Stir in 1 Tablespoon flour and blend until smooth. Add broth and wine; return meat and onions to skillet. Cover and simmer 1½-2 hours, until meat is very tender. Season to taste.

SERVES 4

Veal in Mushroom Cream Sauce

2 pounds veal, cut into 8 thin slices
3 Tablespoons butter
2 Tablespoons chopped green onion, with some tops
¾ pound fresh mushrooms, sliced (3 cups)
Salt and pepper to taste
¼ cup dry white wine
1 cup heavy cream or evaporated milk
2 Tablespoons butter
8 thin slices prosciutto, wafer-thin boiled ham, or Smithfield ham
8 thin slices Fontina, Gruyere, Swiss, or Mozzarella cheese
4 cups cooked hot buttered noodles (spinach noodles are delicious)

Pound veal lightly with a flat meat mallet to make it thinner. Melt 3 Tablespoons butter in saucepan. Sauté onion and mushrooms lightly. Season with salt and pepper. Sprinkle with wine; shake pan and cook about 10 seconds. Add cream and cook over medium-high heat about 3 minutes or until cream cooks to a sauce-like consistency. Remove from heat and set aside. Melt 2 Tablespoons butter in a heavy skillet. Lightly brown the veal about 2 minutes on each side over medium-high heat. Place veal in center of an ovenproof warmed serving platter. Trim ham slices to fit neatly over each piece of veal and arrange in serving dish. Spoon creamed mushrooms over each piece of veal with ham. Place one slice of cheese (trimmed to fit veal) over each piece. Run briefly under the broiler just until the cheese melts and begins to lightly brown. Spoon hot buttered noodles in a ring around the veal slices. Serve piping hot.

SERVES 4

Scrapple

No part of the meat from slaughtered farm animals was wasted. Scrapple was a favorite use for the leftovers of hog. This recipe came from the diary of a pioneer woman who traveled to Oregon in 1866. It was served with eggs as a diversion from bacon or ham.

"Boil the head, heart and lean scraps of a hog until flesh slips off easily. Remove bone, gristle and fat, then chop fine. Set liquor in which meat was boiled aside until cold. Remove the fat and return to stove. When it boils, add meat, salt and pepper. Season with sage. When boiling, add corn meal as for any corn meal mush. Cook an hour, stirring constantly at first and then gently. Pour into pan, not too deep, and mold. Chill. Cut into slices when set and fry brown as you do mush."

Josephine County Historical Society

Sweet and Sour Pork

⅓ cup packed brown sugar
1 Tablespoon cornstarch
½ teaspoon grated fresh ginger or ¼ teaspoon ground ginger
1 Tablespoon soy sauce
1 Tablespoon sherry
¼ cup wine vinegar
¼ cup chicken broth
2 pounds boneless lean pork, cut in 1-inch cubes
1 egg, beaten
½ cup cornstarch
5 Tablespoons salad oil, divided
1 medium onion, cut in 1-inch squares
2 medium carrots, diagonally sliced, ¼-inch thick
1 garlic clove, mashed
1 green pepper, seeded, cut in 1-inch squares
1 8¼-ounce can pineapple chunks, drained
2 medium tomatoes, cut in 1-inch cubes
Cooked rice

Make sauce by mixing first seven ingredients in bowl. Set aside to use later. Dip pork in beaten egg, drain briefly, roll in cornstarch until lightly coated all over, and shake off excess. In a large frying pan over medium heat, pour in 3 Tablespoons of oil. Add pork; cook, turning constantly until browned, about 7 minutes. Lift pork from pan and set aside. Scrape off and discard any brown particles, but leave oil in pan. Add 2 Tablespoons of oil to pan and turn to high heat. Add onion, carrots, and garlic, cooking and stirring for about 3 minutes or until vegetables are tender but crisp. Add green pepper, pineapple, tomatoes, and reserved sauce. Stir and cook until mixture boils. Add pork and stir 1 minute longer to heat thoroughly and coat pork with the sauce. Serve with rice.

SERVES 6

Golden Pork Chops

6 pork chops
1 10½-ounce can Golden Mushroom soup
2 Tablespoons minced onion
½ soup can white wine

Place pork chops in baking dish. Combine soup, onion, and wine, and pour over chops. Bake for 1 hour at 350°F. If desired, brown under broiler before serving.

SERVES 4-6

Pork Chops Supreme

8 thick pork chops
Salt
8 thin onion slices
8 thin lemon slices
½ cup packed brown sugar
½ cup ketchup

Heat oven to 350°F. Season chops with salt, and place in large baking dish. Top each pork chop with an onion slice and a lemon slice. Mix together the brown sugar and ketchup; spoon 2 Tablespoons of mixture on top of each chop. Cover and bake 1 hour. Uncover and bake 30 minutes longer, basting occasionally.

SERVES 6-8

Florentine Chops

6 pork loin chops, ½-¾-inch thick
Shortening or oil
1½ pounds fresh spinach, washed, chopped, and lightly steamed
2 Tablespoons grated onion
6 Tablespoons butter
6 Tablespoons flour
1¼ cups strong chicken stock
1¾ cups milk
Salt and white pepper to taste
Nutmeg to taste
2 egg yolks, slightly beaten
1½ cups grated Swiss cheese
6 Tablespoons freshly grated Parmesan cheese
Cooked rice

Brown chops in a lightly greased pan. Lower heat, cover, and cook 30 minutes or until tender. Keep warm. Combine cooked spinach with grated onion and set aside. In saucepan, melt butter. Stir in the flour and cook over low heat for 3 minutes. Slowly stir in chicken stock and milk and continue to stir until thickened. Add salt, pepper, and nutmeg. Stir a little of this sauce into egg yolks and then return the yolk mixture to the sauce, stirring until smooth and thick. Mix 1 cup of sauce with spinach mixture and spread it over bottom of a large, greased, shallow casserole. Arrange chops on top of spinach. Meanwhile, stir the Swiss cheese into the remaining sauce and stir over low heat until cheese is melted. Pour sauce over chops, sprinkle with Parmesan cheese and bake uncovered at 400°F for 15 minutes or until bubbling and cheese is slightly browned. Serve with rice.

SERVES 6

Pork Chop Delight

- thick pork chops or chicken breasts
- ½ cup flour
- ½ cup shortening
- ¼ pounds fresh whole button mushrooms
- 16-ounce can whole boiled onions, drained
- ⅓ cups canned milk, undiluted
- 2 10½-ounce cans mushroom soup, undiluted
- ¼ cup white wine or vermouth (optional)
- 2½ cups grated processed cheese
- 2 Tablespoons grated fresh onion
- ½ teaspoon garlic powder
- Few pinches of rubbed basil
- Salt and pepper to taste
- Paprika

Coat chops with flour and brown in melted shortening. Remove chops and place in large casserole dish. Arrange mushrooms and onions attractively over chops. Combine milk, soup, wine, cheese, grated onion, garlic powder, basil, and salt and pepper in saucepan. Heat until barely blended. Pour mixture over meat, mushrooms, and onions. Dust heavily with paprika, cover with foil, and refrigerate at this point, if desired. Bake at 325°F for 1 hour.

SERVES 8

Sweet Lemon Spareribs

- 3 pounds country-style spareribs
- Water
- 1 6-ounce can lemonade concentrate
- 2 lemonade cans water
- 3 Tablespoons soy sauce
- 3 Tablespoons ketchup
- 3 Tablespoons packed brown sugar
- ½ teaspoon salt
- 1-2 teaspoons vinegar
- Cornstarch dissolved in water

Place ribs in pan, cover with water and bring to a boil. Simmer for 1 hour. Pour off water. Combine lemonade, 2 cans water, soy sauce, ketchup, brown sugar, salt, and vinegar and pour two-thirds over ribs. Cover and cook over medium-low heat, on top of stove, 1 hour or until tender. Add more mix as necessary. Remove ribs from pan. Pour remainder of sauce in pan, add cornstarch mixture, and cook until sauce is thickened and done. Serve sauce separately to pour over ribs.

SERVES 4-6

Simple Simon Spareribs

4 pounds country-style spareribs
⅔ cup white sauterne wine
3 Tablespoons red wine vinegar
⅔ cup packed brown sugar
¼ cup soy sauce

Trim excess fat from ribs and arrange them in a single layer in a large, shallow pan. Combine wine, vinegar, brown sugar, and soy sauce. Pour over ribs. Bake uncovered at 350°F for 2-2½ hours, basting occasionally.

SERVES 4-5

Summer Baked Ham

10-12-pound fully cooked bone-in ham
1 medium onion, sliced
2 bay leaves
¼ cup packed brown sugar
4 sprigs parsley
Ground cloves to taste (about 5-6 whole)
Pepper to taste
2½ cups beer
Whole cloves

GLAZE:
½ cup packed brown sugar
¼ cup honey

Place ham fat-side up in a shallow pan. Place onion and bay leaves on top and sprinkle with sugar, parsley, ground cloves, and pepper. Insert meat thermometer in thickest part of meat, away from the bone. Pour beer around ham. Cover pan tightly with foil. Bake at 350°F, basting every 30 minutes with beer in pan, until thermometer registers 130°F, about 3 hours. Pour off all drippings from pan, reserving 2 Tablespoons. Mix the reserved drippings with the brown sugar and honey to make a glaze. Remove bay leaves. With a sharp knife, remove any skin from ham and score by making diagonal cuts in fat ¼-inch deep and 1¼-inches apart to form a diamond pattern. Stud the center of each diamond with a clove. Brush the surface of the ham with half the glaze. Return the ham to a 400°F oven and bake 30 minutes longer, basting every 10 minutes with the remainder of the glaze.

SERVES 20

Ham and Mushroom Crepes

12 crepes
3 Tablespoons butter
1½ pounds mushrooms, sliced
1 Tablespoon flour
½ cup whipping cream
12 thin slices cooked ham (about ¾ pound)
1 Tablespoon butter
1 Tablespoon flour
1 cup light cream or milk
1 cup grated Swiss, Gruyere or Danish Samsoe cheese
Fresh parsley, chopped

Prepare crepes. Melt 3 Tablespoons butter over medium heat until bubbly. Add mushrooms and sauté until just lightly browned. Sprinkle with 1 Tablespoon flour and stir. Add whipping cream and cook over medium heat until mixture is thickened and liquid is reduced to about ⅓ cup (approximately 8 minutes). Set aside. Place a piece of ham on each crepe and spoon on about ¼ cup of the mushroom filling. Roll and arrange seam-side down in a buttered 9 × 13-inch dish. Make a sauce by heating 1 Tablespoon butter in a small saucepan. Stir in 1 Tablespoon flour and cook until bubbly. Gradually stir in light cream and cook, stirring over medium heat until thickened. Pour sauce over crepes and sprinkle with cheese. Bake uncovered at 400°F for 15 minutes. Sprinkle top with chopped parsley before serving. May also be covered and refrigerated for up to 3 days.

YIELD: 12 crepes

Hawn's Ham Loaf

⅝ cup packed dark brown sugar
1 teaspoon ground cloves
2 pounds ground ham
1 pound ground sirloin
13 slices stale bread crumbs
2½ cups whole milk
3 eggs
⅝ teaspoon dry mustard
Salt and pepper to taste

Spread brown sugar over bottom of loaf pan, then sprinkle cloves over brown sugar. Combine meat, bread crumbs, milk, eggs, mustard, and salt and pepper with hands. Pack into loaf pan and bake 1 hour at 375°F. Invert to serve.

SERVES 12-16

SUGGESTION: Excellent served with a mustard sauce.

Ham with Asparagus

3 pounds asparagus
5 Tablespoons butter
4 Tablespoons flour
2-2¼ cups milk and asparagus juices combined
Nutmeg, salt, and pepper to taste
12 thin slices of ham, halved
6 hard-boiled eggs, sliced
1½ cups grated Swiss or Cheddar cheese
Paprika
Butter

Cook asparagus. Drain juice and reserve to later combine with milk. Melt 5 Tablespoons butter in pan. Add flour and stir constantly for 3-4 minutes without browning. Boil milk and asparagus juice and add hot liquid to the flour mixture. Cook and stir until sauce is thickened. Remove from heat and add the nutmeg, salt, and pepper. In a 9 × 13-inch casserole, layer half of the asparagus, ham, eggs, and sauce. Repeat, ending with layer of sauce. Spread the grated cheese over all; sprinkle with paprika and dot with butter. Bake at 350°F for 30 minutes, or until bubbly.

SERVES 4-6

Ham and Cheese Puff

2 cups ground cooked ham (about ¾ pound)
2 cups grated Swiss cheese
1 stalk celery, finely minced or ground
½-⅔ cup mayonnaise
1 teaspoon prepared mustard
12 slices of white bread, toasted
6 eggs
2¼ cups milk
Parsley

Combine ham, cheese, and celery with mayonnaise and mustard to make a spread. Put on 6 of the toast slices. Put the other 6 slices together to make 6 whole sandwiches. Cut each diagonally into quarters and stand crust edge down in a buttered 9 × 13-inch pan. Beat the eggs and add the milk, then pour over the sandwiches. Chill in the refrigerator overnight. Bake at 325°F for 35 minutes. Garnish with parsley. To serve, cut between sandwiches.

SERVES 8

After-Game Ham Sandwich

½ pound ham, cubed
½ pound sharp cheese, cubed
⅓ cup diced green onion
2 hard-boiled eggs, diced
½ cup sliced green olives
3 Tablespoons mayonnaise
½ cup chili sauce
8-10 rolls (sourdough, hamburger buns, etc.)

Combine ham, cheese, onion, eggs, and olives. Add mayonnaise and chili sauce. Mix well and spread on rolls. Wrap in foil. Bake at 400°F for 10 minutes or until filling is hot and cheese melting. Can make ahead and refrigerate. Allow more time to bake.

YIELD: 8-10 sandwiches

Baked Ham and Cheese Sandwiches

16 slices bread (remove crusts)
8 slices ham
8 slices Swiss cheese
4 eggs
3 cups milk
Dash dry mustard
Dash salt

SAUCE:
4 Tablespoons butter
4 Tablespoons flour
½ teaspoon salt
¼ teaspoon pepper
½ teaspoon dry mustard
2 cups milk
1 cup nippy Cheddar cheese

Put bread out to dry. Put 8 slices in buttered baking dish. Top each with ham, cheese, and another slice of bread. Beat eggs with milk, mustard, and salt. Pour over sandwiches and refrigerate overnight. Bake at 325°F for 1 hour or until brown. Serve topped with sauce.

SAUCE: Melt butter over low heat in a heavy saucepan. Blend in flour, salt, pepper, and dry mustard. Cook over low heat, stirring until mixture is smooth and bubbly. Remove from heat. Stir in milk. Bring to a boil, stirring constantly. Boil 1 minute. Add Cheddar cheese. Stir until cheese is melted.

SERVES 6-8

Roast Leg of Lamb with Herb Stuffing

7-pound boned and rolled leg of lamb (the butcher will do this for you with a few days' notice)
2 Tablespoons oil
1 small green pepper, halved, seeded
2 medium carrots, peeled
2 medium onions
2 stalks celery
2 garlic cloves, peeled
2 10½-ounce cans condensed beef bouillon
¼ cup flour
½ cup cold water or white wine

STUFFING:
1 cube butter
¼ teaspoon each marjoram, mint leaves, basil, oregano, sage, thyme
1 small bay leaf
3 slices bread
1 Tablespoon lemon juice

Carefully unroll butcher's tie on roast. Prepare herb stuffing by placing all stuff ing ingredients in a blender and blending to a smooth paste. Spread herb stuff ing over inside surface of meat. Retie following butcher's original ties. Heat oi in heavy roasting pan or skillet. Brown lamb on all sides, about 15 minutes Transfer meat, if necessary, to roasting pan. Roast at 350°F for 30 minutes Place pepper, carrots, onions, celery, and garlic in blender and blend until fine ly chopped. Stir into pan drippings with meat. Roast 35 minutes longer or unti meat thermometer registers 140°F for rare or 150°F for medium. Transfer mea to heated platter and keep warm. Place roasting pan over heat and adc bouillon. Boil; lower heat and simmer 5 minutes. Strain liquid into mediun saucepan and discard vegetables. Skim excess fat from surface. Heat slowly tc boiling. Combine flour and water to a smooth paste. Whisk flour mixture intc gravy by pouring in slowly while beating constantly. Continue stirring unti mixture thickens. Carefully remove strings from meat. Slice several servings o meat and pour one fourth of the gravy the length of the roast. Pass remainin gravy. Roast may be frozen before or after cooking. For uncooked, defros stuffed roast and cook as above. To reheat cooked roast, defrost, cover wit foil and roast at 350°F for 30 minutes or until heated through. Meat may b surrounded with **Fresh Spring Vegetables** (see index).

SERVES 6-

Many Basque immigrants came to Oregon in the 1870s. The southeaster region of the state was similar to the fine sheep pasture of their native lands the Pyrenees provinces of Spain. Many of the Spanish cultural traditions are stil practiced in the Basque settlements of the Harney County area in southeaster Oregon.

Mustard Lamb Roll

4½-5-pound boned and rolled leg of lamb
⅓ cup Dijon-style prepared mustard
1 Tablespoon soy sauce
¼ teaspoon garlic salt
¼ teaspoon ground ginger
1 teaspoon rosemary, rubbed
1 Tablespoon salad oil

Place meat on rack in roasting pan. Mix together mustard, soy sauce, garlic salt, ground ginger, rosemary, and salad oil. Spread mixture over roast, coating completely, and roast in a 350°F oven until meat thermometer reaches 150°F for rare meat or 160°F for well done, about 1½-2 hours.

SERVES 6-8

Roast Leg of Lamb with Rosemary Stuffing

1-1¼ cups fresh bread crumbs
2 Tablespoons milk
3 Tablespoons shallots, minced
2 Tablespoons butter
1½ cups ground lamb
2 garlic cloves, mashed
⅓ teaspoon crushed or ground rosemary
¼ plus teaspoon salt
½ teaspoon pepper
8-9 pound butterflied leg of lamb

MUSTARD AND HERB SAUCE:
3-4 garlic cloves, mashed
½ teaspoon ground rosemary
1½ teaspoon soy sauce
½ cup strong Dijon prepared mustard
4-5 Tablespoons olive oil

Make paste from bread crumbs and milk. Sauté shallots in butter. Combine paste, shallots, ground lamb, garlic, rosemary, salt, and pepper. Open out butterflied leg of lamb and spread mixture over, then roll and tie roast securely. Make mustard sauce by combining garlic, rosemary, soy sauce, and mustard with a wire whisk. Beat in oil by droplets to make a very thick viscous sauce. Place roast on rack in roasting pan and coat with herb and mustard sauce. Insert meat thermometer in thickest part of roast and bake at 325°-350°F for 2½-4 hours or until thermometer reads 140°F, for rare.

SERVES 8-12

Crown Roast of Lamb, Stuffed

½ cup spicy brown prepared mustard
1 Tablespoon soy sauce
1 teaspoon ground thyme
½ teaspoon garlic powder
½ teaspoon ground ginger
18-rib crown roast of lamb (about 5 pounds)

Combine mustard, soy sauce, thyme, garlic, and ginger. Rub meat (not bones) all over with mustard mixture and place in roasting pan. Refrigerate covered 1½-2 hours or overnight. Remove meat from refrigerator and let come to room temperature, approximately 1 hour. Preheat oven to 450°F.

FOR APPLE AND ONION DRESSING: Stuff center of roast with prepared dressing (see below). Insert meat thermometer between two ribs, without touching bones. Reduce oven setting to 350°F and bake for 35 minutes per pound or until thermometer registers 165°F (medium). Transfer to meat platter.

FOR SUMMER VEGETABLE FILLING: Cover "crown" bones with foil to prevent discoloration. Crumple a ball of aluminum foil and place in the center of the lamb to help keep the shape during baking. Reduce oven setting to 350°F and bake for 35 minutes per pound. When the roast has one more hour to bake, remove from oven and discard foil ball (not the foil on the bones). Stuff the center with prepared filling (see below) and return to 350°F oven for final hour of baking. When done, transfer the roast to meat platter and remove foil from bones. Garnish roast by piercing a hole halfway through each tomato (use a small knife) then pushing a tomato onto each rib bone. (Olives may be used in place of the tomatoes.)

SERVES 6-8

Apple and Onion Dressing

¼ cup butter
½ cup chopped onion
½ cup chopped celery
¼ teaspoon garlic powder
2 cups diced tart apples with skins
½ cup raisins
1 cup dry bread cubes, ½-inch
¼ cup chopped fresh parsley or 1 Tablespoon dried
Salt and pepper to taste

Melt butter in pan. Sauté onion, celery, and garlic until just tender. Combine with remaining ingredients. Stuff into cavity of crown roast.

Summer Vegetable Filling

4 medium carrots, julienned in 3-inch strips
4 medium zucchini, julienned in 3-inch strips
1 small head broccoli, broken into small florets
1 small head cauliflower, broken into small florets
Salt and pepper to taste
¼ cup butter, melted
¼ cup chopped fresh parsley or 1 Tablespoon dried
2 Tablespoons dried basil
18 cherry tomatoes or large pitted green or ripe olives

Toss all the vegetables. Season with salt and pepper. Pack into crown roast. Melt butter and herbs. Pour over vegetables.

Ghivetch

1½ pounds lean meat, cubed (lamb preferable)
Several Tablespoons olive oil
¾ cup beef broth
1 garlic clove
¼ teaspoon tarragon
1¼ teaspoons salt
1 bay leaf, crushed
½ cup sliced carrots
1 cup fresh beans
1 large potato, cubed
1 onion, sliced
1 zucchini, sliced
½ small head cauliflower, separated
½ green pepper, sliced
½ cup fresh peas (optional)
½ cup sauterne or dry sherry
1 large tomato, peeled and chopped
1½ cups sliced fresh mushrooms

In a heavy pan, brown meat in olive oil. Place meat in a 1½ to 2-quart baking dish. Combine broth, garlic, tarragon, salt, and bay leaf in the browning pan and bring to a boil. Take off stove and cool if dish is to be refrigerated. To the cubed meat add the carrots, beans, potato, onion, zucchini, cauliflower, green pepper, and peas. To the broth mixture, add the sauterne, then pour over vegetables and meat. Refrigerate overnight, if desired. Cover tightly and bake the meat and vegetables in a 350°F oven for 1-1¼ hours. Vegetables should be firm at the end of baking time. Add tomato and mushrooms 15-20 minutes before done.

SERVES 6

Lamb Curry with Coconut and Kashmiri Pulao Rice

1½ Tablespoons shortening
2 medium potatoes, cubed
2 medium onions, chopped
1½-2 pounds lamb, cubed
2 teaspoons garam masala (available at specialty stores)
1 Tablespoon coriander powder
1 Tablespoon cumin powder
1 teaspoon garlic powder
½ teaspoon turmeric
1 Tablespoon paprika
1 teaspoon cayenne pepper
1 Tablespoon salt
2 Tablespoons water
2 tomatoes, quartered
1 cup water
1 12-ounce can coconut milk
Green coriander
Grated ginger

Melt shortening in pan over medium-high heat. Add potatoes and brown. Remove and set aside. Add chopped onions to pan and fry until brown. Add lamb and brown. Mix garam masala, corinader, cumin, garlic powder, turmeric, paprika, cayenne, and salt together in bowl. Add 2 Tablespoons water and blend thoroughly to make a paste. Add paste to lamb when lamb is thoroughly browned. Mix well and fry for additional 2 minutes. Add tomatoes to lamb and stir. Add 1 cup water together with browned potatoes. Cover and simmer 15-20 minutes or until lamb is tender. Add coconut milk, stir and keep on low heat to simmer for additional 5 minutes. Garnish with green coriander and grated ginger. Serve with Kashmiri Pulao Rice, below.

Kashmiri Pulao Rice

2 cups water
1 cup uncooked long grain white rice
1 teaspoon granulated sugar
¾ Tablespoon salt
1 teaspoon garlic powder
1 Tablespoon dried mint flakes, crushed
2 Tablespoons shortening
4 whole cloves
½-inch cinnamon stick
2 small onions, chopped
1 4-ounce package slivered almonds
½ cup golden raisins
2 garlic cloves, minced
½ green hot pepper, chopped

Bring water to a boil and immediately add rice. Stir. Cover pan, lower heat and simmer for 20 minutes. Remove lid and stir rice well. Remove to platter and allow to cool. Mix cooled rice with sugar, salt, garlic powder, and mint. Set aside. Melt shortening in a wok. Add whole cloves and cinnamon stick. Add onions and brown. Add almonds, raisins, garlic, and green hot pepper; stir and fry for 1 minute, then add to rice mixture. Mix well and stir fry for 2-3 minutes until thoroughly warm.

SERVES 6-8

Sweet and Sour Lamb Shanks

2 Tablespoons shortening
6 lamb shanks
2 teaspoons salt
Dash pepper
1 chicken bouillon cube
2 cups water
1 garlic clove
1 bay leaf
4 whole cloves
1 teaspoon Worcestershire sauce
¼ cup vinegar
2 Tablespoons brown sugar
½ teaspoon dry mustard
1 small onion, chopped
Cooked noodles or rice
Fresh or canned green grapes

Melt shortening and brown shanks. Season with salt and pepper. Dissolve bouillon cube in water. Add to shanks along with garlic, bay leaf, cloves, Worcestershire, vinegar, brown sugar, mustard, and onion. Cover and simmer about 1½ hours or until tender. Serve with noodles or rice and garnish with heated grapes.

SERVES 3-4

Lamb in Grape Leaves

3 Tablespoons olive oil
3 medium onions, finely minced
1 cup uncooked rice
1 teaspoon finely minced mint
½ pound ground lamb
Pinch of Cinnamon
½ teaspoon salt
Grape leaves (your own or from a specialty store, approximately 18-ounce jar)
Water
Fresh lemon juice and wedges

Heat oil and sauté onions, rice, and mint for 10 minutes. Add lamb, cinnamon, and salt. Place heaping Tablespoon of mixture on each grape leaf and roll, folding in the ends. Pack bundles snugly in casserole dish or pan and add slight amount of water to prevent scorching. Cover and steam for 1 hour until tender. Squeeze fresh lemon juice over all and serve with additional lemon wedges.

SERVES 6-8

POULTRY

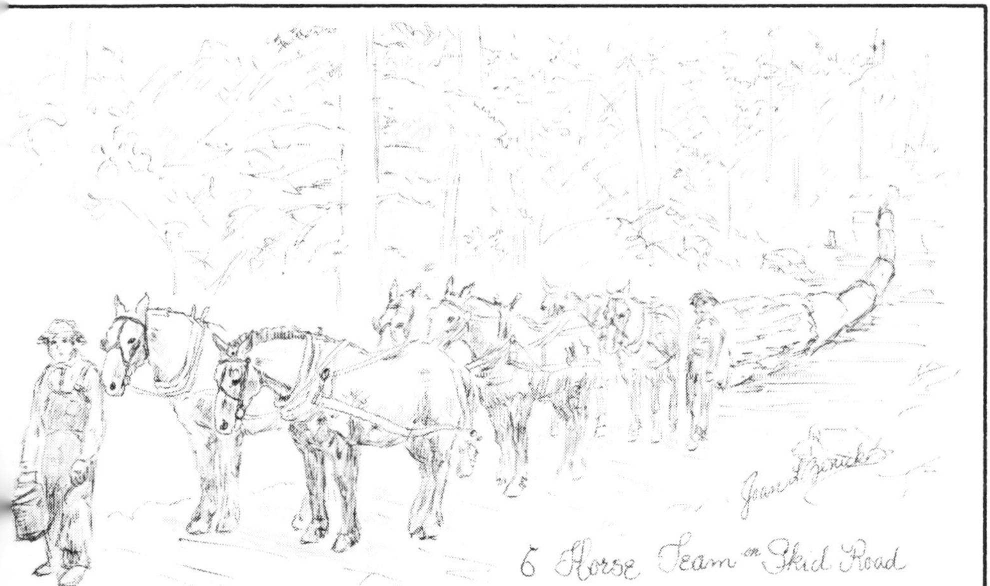

6 Horse Team on Skid Road

Joan L. Zenick

Turkey Tetrazzini

Tablespoons butter
teaspoon salt
teaspoon pepper
cup flour
cups chicken stock or
canned chicken broth
dashes Tabasco sauce, divided
pound fresh mushrooms, sliced
Tablespoons butter
2 egg yolks
2 Tablespoons dry sherry
6 Tablespoons heavy cream
6 cups cubed cooked turkey
(1 large turkey breast)
8 ounces spaghetti, cooked
Parmesan cheese
Butter

lelt 8 Tablespoons butter and add salt, pepper, and flour to saucepan. Stir with wire whisk until blended. Add boiling chicken stock and stir vigorously until mooth. Season with a touch of Tabasco sauce. Sauté mushrooms in 4 Table-poons butter until lightly browned. Do not drain. Set mushrooms aside. To the hicken sauce, add egg yolks, slightly beaten with a little hot sauce, and stir in herry and cream. Cook, stirring until heated. Do not let boil. Add reserved ıushrooms and turkey. Place alternate layers of spaghetti, sauce, and generous prinkling of Parmesan cheese in a 9 × 13-inch buttered casserole. Sprinkle top ıyer with additional Parmesan cheese and dot with butter. Bake at 350°F for 5-50 minutes, covered. When heated, pop under broiler for a few minutes un-l brown.

SERVES 12-14

Green Noodle Turkey Casserole

10½-ounce can cream of
mushroom soup
soup can milk
pound sharp cheese, grated
alt and pepper to taste
5 ounces green spinach noodles,
cooked
2 cups chopped cooked turkey
or 2 6½-ounce cans tuna, drained
Grated cheese
¼ cup slivered almonds

lix soup, milk, and ¼ pound cheese together in saucepan. Heat until cheese ıelts. Stir in salt and pepper. Pour small amount of sauce into large baking ish. Layer with noodles, turkey, and more sauce. Repeat layers. Top with addi-onal grated cheese and slivered almonds. Bake at 375°F for about 1 hour.

SERVES 6

Turkey-Broccoli Bake

2 10-ounce packages frozen chopped broccoli
1 Tablespoon lemon juice
2 Tablespoons butter or margarine
2 Tablespoons flour
½ teaspoon salt
2 cups milk
½ cup shredded Swiss cheese
2 cups julienne turkey
½ cup soft bread crumbs
¼ cup grated Parmesan cheese
1 Tablespoon butter, melted

Prepare broccoli according to package directions. Drain well and mix with lemon juice. Spread mixture into 9-inch round baking dish. In a saucepan, melt 2 Tablespoons butter. Blend in flour and salt. Add milk all at once. Cook, stirring constantly, until mixture thickens and bubbles, then remove from heat and stir in the Swiss cheese until melted. Add turkey and spoon mixture over broccoli. Combine bread crumbs, Parmesan cheese, and 1 Tablespoon butter; sprinkle over casserole. Bake at 350°F for 20-25 minutes or until heated through.

SERVES 6

Ground Beef Dressing for Turkey

½ pound raw chestnuts
1 pound lean ground beef
¼ cup butter
½ cup minced onion
1 garlic clove, minced
¾ cup chopped celery
1 cup bread cubes (about 2 slices of toast)
3 Tablespoons pine nuts
½ cup currants or raisins
2 Tablespoons tomato sauce
2 peeled, shredded apples
Chopped parsley to taste

To prepare chestnuts boil them for 10 minutes and peel them while hot. Roast them under the broiler until brown and chop before adding to mixture. Sauté ground beef in fry pan. Remove meat and add butter to fry pan. Sauté onion, garlic, and celery in the butter. Add bread cubes and sauté until they get the flavor of the butter. Turn into large bowl and combine with all of the ingredients.

YIELD: Dressing for a 10-12-pound turkey

In 1864, the first Leghorn chickens wre introduced to Oregon. Poultry became an indispensable segment of farm life. By the early 1900s, eggs and poultry were being produced on a large scale, especially in the temperate Willamette Valley.

Stir-Fried Chicken

1-1½ pounds boneless chicken breasts
1 Tablespoon cornstarch
1½ Tablespoons dry sherry
2½ Tablespoons soy sauce, divided
10 fresh mushrooms
1 small green pepper
3-4 Tablespoons peanut oil
2 green onions, cut in 1-inch lengths
1 stalk celery, sliced
2 slices fresh ginger
1 teaspoon salt
½ cup cashews
1 6-ounce package frozen pea pods (optional)
Cooked rice

Cut chicken into ½ to ¾-inch cubes and place in dish. Combine cornstarch, dry sherry, and 1½ Tablespoons soy sauce; mix well. Pour over chicken; may be marinated several hours. Wash mushrooms and cut each vertically into 4 pieces. Wash and remove seeds from green pepper and cut into 1-inch square pieces. Heat wok or large pan and pour in 3 Tablespoons oil. Add chicken to wok when the oil is hot, but has not yet begun to smoke. Stir fry 2 minutes and remove with slotted spoon. (Chicken may not be completely done at this point.) If necessary, add another Tablespoon of oil to wok. When it starts to smoke, stir fry mushrooms and green pepper 1 minute. Add green onions, celery, ginger, salt, and remaining 1 Tablespoon soy sauce, stirring well. Then put chicken back in the wok and stir fry with the vegetables until the chicken is entirely cooked. Stir in cashews and pea pods. Remove ginger slices before serving with rice.

SERVES 6

NOTE: If you like a lot of sauce, add ¾ cup chicken broth mixed with 1 teaspoon cornstarch after the chicken and vegetables have been combined. Stir until sauce is clear and thickened. This step is recommended if pea pods are added.

Chicken Tetrazzini with Asparagus

The Pine Tavern

4-pound chicken
2 cups chicken broth
¼ cup chopped carrots
¼ cup chopped celery
4 Tablespoons butter
4 Tablespoons flour
1 cup light cream
Lemon juice to taste
2 Tablespoons sherry or sauterne
Salt and pepper to taste
2 cups cooked spaghetti
½ pound uncooked asparagus
4 Tablespoons Parmesan cheese
1 cup crumb topping

Cook chicken in broth with chopped carrots and celery. Remove chicken and pick from bones. Melt butter in saucepan over low heat. Add flour and stir until smooth; add chicken broth, from which you have removed chicken, and cream; stir until smooth. Add lemon juice and wine. If necessary, add salt and pepper. Spread spaghetti on bottom of greased casserole; next place a layer of asparagus and arrange chicken pieces on top. Cover with sauce; add cheese and topping. Bake in 325°F oven for 25 minutes.

SERVES 8

VARIATION: Broccoli may be substituted for asparagus.

Chicken Divan

8 chicken breasts
2 10-ounce packages frozen broccoli spears or 1½ pounds fresh broccoli
2 10½-ounce cans cream of chicken soup
1 cup mayonnaise
1 teaspoon lemon juice
½ teaspoon curry powder or ½ teaspoon oregano
2 6-ounce jars marinated artichoke hearts, drained (optional)
Slivered almonds

Cook, debone, and dice the chicken breasts. Cook broccoli until tender and spread it in a 9 × 13-inch baking dish. Distribute chicken over the broccoli. Combine soup, mayonnaise, lemon juice, curry powder, and artichoke hearts. Spread mixture over the chicken and sprinkle slivered almonds on top. Bake at 350°F for 30-45 minutes.

SERVES 6-8

VARIATION: Before baking, sprinkle the following over the chicken and broccoli: ¾ cup shredded sharp Cheddar cheese, ½ cup bread crumbs or garlic cheese croutons, 2 Tablespoons butter, melted.

Guava Chicken

10-12 chicken breasts or thighs
Juice of 1 lemon
1 10-ounce jar Guava jelly (available at specialty stores)
2 Tablespoons cornstarch
4-5 drops red food coloring
¼-½ cup sesame seeds

Wash chicken pieces and pat dry. Place chicken in a large baking dish. Squeeze juice of lemon over the chicken. Stir Guava jelly with fork until loose and liquid. Pour jelly over chicken. Bake uncovered for 1½ hours at 325°F. Baste 3-4 times with jelly and juices from pan. Remove chicken from the oven. Pour the juices into a saucepan and thoroughly stir in the cornstarch with a whisk. Add food coloring. The sauce should be a rosy color. Cook sauce over low heat until thickened and clear. Pour the Guava sauce over the chicken and sprinkle with sesame seeds. Return the chicken and sauce to the oven at once for at least 15 minutes or until ready to serve.

SERVES 6-8

Paella a la Valenciana

3½-pound frying chicken, cut up, or pieces that you desire
2 garlic cloves, minced
4 green onions, chopped
¼ cup olive oil
¼ pound ground pork
2 medium tomatoes, peeled and chopped
1 10-ounce package frozen green peas
1 8½-ounce can artichoke hearts, cut up
2 teaspoons paprika
1½ cups raw rice
2 teaspoons salt
4 cups chicken broth, or bottled clam juice
Pinch saffron
10-12 cooked medium shrimp
10-12 clams or mussels, uncooked
Stuffed green olives (optional)

In a paella pan or deep skillet, brown chicken, garlic, and onions in olive oil. Add pork and brown quickly. Add tomatoes, peas, artichoke hearts, paprika, and rice. Cook until rice is well coated with oil. Add salt, broth, and saffron. Cook uncovered until rice is almost tender, about 15 minutes. Add shrimp and clams and continue cooking until rice is tender and clams have just opened. Just before serving garnish with stuffed olives.

SERVES 6

Stuffed Chicken Legs Flambé

PER SERVING:
2 chicken legs (including thigh)
¼ cup minced ham
2 Tablespoons minced onion
2 Tablespoons parsley
2 Tablespoons raisins
Salt, pepper, garlic to taste
1 cup dry white wine
2 Tablespoons butter
Cooked white rice ring
1 cup sautéed mushrooms (optional)
6 Tablespoons brandy, heated

Bone each chicken leg by carefully skinning meat down bone with sharp knife Carefully cut around joint to avoid cutting skin. Cut bone off to leave small foot joint at end of drumstick. Combine ham, onion, parsley, raisins, and seasonings Stuff each drumstick with half this mixture. Marinate in white wine overnight or 8 hours. Remove legs, reserving wine. Melt butter in skillet and brown legs Place legs in baking dish. Pour reserved wine marinade into butter and heat Pour over the legs. Bake at 375°F for 45 minutes. Add more wine if juices begin to dry up. To serve, arrange legs in center of hot rice ring, not on rice Garnish rice ring with mushrooms, if desired. Heat pan juices and pour into small pitcher. Just before serving, pour heated brandy over legs and ignite Quench flames at the table with pan juices.

SERVES 1 person

NOTE: Reheats well. To freeze use fresh chicken only. Prepare through the stuffing of legs. Wrap each leg separately in freezer wrap. Thaw before marinating and complete recipe. Delicious with curried fruit and watercress salad.

Chicken Parisienne

4-6 medium-size chicken breasts
1 10½-ounce can condensed cream of mushroom soup
1 3-ounce can mushrooms and liquid
1 cup sour cream
½ cup cooking sherry
Paprika
Cooked rice

Place chicken breasts skin-side up in 7 × 11 × 1½-inch dish. Combine soup mushrooms and liquid, sour cream, and sherry. Pour mixture over the chicken Sprinkle with paprika. Bake at 350°F for 1-1¼ hours. Serve with hot, fluffy rice.

SERVES 4-

Chicken Cacciatore
from the Jacksonville Inn

- -4-pound frying chicken
- Tablespoons peanut oil or butter
- large onion, diced
- inch salt and pepper
- ½ teaspoon thyme
- Dash monosodium glutamate
- ½ cup white wine
- ½ cup canned tomatoes

ut chicken into serving pieces. Heat oil in skillet and brown chicken on all ides, about 10 minutes. Add onion, season with salt, pepper, thyme, and MSG. Vhen slightly brown, drain oil, add wine, and simmer until wine is abosrbed. dd tomatoes. Cover and simmer 20-30 minutes or until done.

SERVES 6

)regon lies in the Western fly-way for the migratory water fowl. Ducks and eese pass through the state twice a year. Several Canadian varieties winter on he rivers and lakes in Oregon. The pioneers relied on this plentiful source of neat.

Chicken Véronique

- cup flour
- teaspoon salt
- teaspoon black pepper or ¾ teaspoon white pepper, divided
- -6 chicken breasts (halves)
- cup peanut oil
- cup white wine
- 2 cups orange juice
- 2-3 Tablespoons honey
- 2-3 Tablespoons chopped fresh parsley
- 2-3 Tablespoons grated or slivered orange peel
- 1¼ cups halved seedless white grapes
- Grapes, orange slices, and fresh parsley

ombine flour, salt, and half the pepper; dust chicken breasts. In a heavy skillet rown chicken in peanut oil. Add wine, orange juice, honey, and parsley; simier over low heat for 35 minutes. Add remaining half of pepper and the range peel, cooking 10 minutes longer. Remove chicken to serving dish. Add rapes to gravy and cook 2-3 minutes, stirring constantly. Pour mixture over ie chicken. Garnish with additional grapes, orange slices, and parsley.

SERVES 4-6

Curried Chicken

Salt
Paprika
2½-3-pound fryer or favorite pieces, such as breasts and thighs
2 Tablespoons butter
1 apple, chopped fine
1 onion, chopped fine
3 teaspoons curry powder
1 10½-ounce can cream of mushroom soup
1 cup cream

Salt and paprika the chicken and spread it out in a layer in a shallow buttered baking dish. Melt butter in a saucepan and sauté the onion and apple. Add curry powder, soup, and cream. Pour the sauce over the chicken and bake at 350°F for 1½ hours, or until the chicken is tender.

SERVES 6

Viva La Chicken

4 whole chicken breasts or 1 chicken, cut up
1 dozen corn tortillas
1 10½-ounce can cream of chicken soup
1 10½-ounce can cream of mushroom soup
1 cup canned milk
1 cup chicken broth
1 large onion, chopped
1 8-ounce can chili salsa
1 4-ounce can diced green chiles
1 6-ounce can ripe olives
1 pound Monterey Jack cheese, grated

Bake or boil the chicken until done; skin, debone, and dice. Cut tortillas into 1 inch strips. Mix together soups, milk, broth, onion, salsa, chiles, olives, and cheese, reserving about ¾ cup of cheese for topping. In a large oiled casserole dish, layer half of the ingredients starting with tortillas, then chicken, and finally sauce. Repeat, ending with sauce. Bake 1½ hours at 300°F. During last 15 minutes of baking, top the dish with remaining ¾ cup of cheese.

SERVES 6-8

NOTE: This dish may be prepared and refrigerated the day before. Good with green salad and guacamole dressing.

Chicken Breasts Mandalay

4 chicken breasts, skinned and halved
3 Tablespoons flour
1 Tablespoon curry powder
2 teaspoons salt
4 Tablespoons vegetable oil
2 Tablespoons brown sugar
2 chicken bouillon cubes
1 small onion, cut up
1 cup water
1 7¾-ounce jar junior apricots (baby food), or 2 4½-ounce jars
2 Tablespoons lemon juice
2 teaspoons soy sauce
Cornstarch
1 8¾-ounce can apricot halves

Shake breasts in mixture of flour, curry powder, and salt. Brown very lightly in oil in fry pan. Remove chicken and place in large baking dish. Stir sugar, bouillon, onion, water, junior apricots, lemon juice, and soy sauce into fry pan drippings. Heat to boiling. Pour over chicken. Bake covered for 1 hour at 350°F or until chicken is tender. Remove chicken to serving dish. Add cornstarch to sauce until desired thickness is reached. Pour over chicken and top with canned apricot halves.

SERVES 6

Coq Au Vin Blanc

1 frying chicken, cut up
Salt and pepper to taste
Flour
½ cube butter
Juice of 1 lemon
1 garlic clove, crushed
½ cup white wine
½ cup chicken broth
2 Tablespoons flour
1 4-ounce can mushrooms, undrained
1 5-ounce jar tiny onions
1 medium zucchini or 2 small, sliced

Skin chicken pieces and discard the skin. Season chicken with salt and pepper, and dust with flour. Brown slowly in butter. Add lemon juice, garlic, and wine. Cover and simmer about 30 minutes until almost tender, adding a bit more wine if necessary. Stir broth into 2 Tablespoons flour and pour over chicken. Add mushrooms with juice, onions, and sliced zucchini. Simmer 5-10 minutes longer until tender. Remove chicken and vegetables to serving platter. Blend sauce and pour over chicken.

SERVES 6

Mary's Chicken

8 chicken breasts
8 thinly sliced ham pieces
8 slices Swiss cheese
½ cup cream of chicken soup
½ cup sour cream
½ cup dry white wine

Debone and skin the chicken breasts; pound into an oblong shape. In the center of each breast place one slice each of ham and cheese, cut to fit breasts. Roll the breasts and secure them with a toothpick. Place breasts in a casserole. Mix together the soup, sour cream, and wine; pour over the chicken breasts. Cover the dish and bake for 1-1½ hours at 325°F.

SERVES 8

Sweet and Sour Chicken

2-3 pounds chicken, cut up
1 8-ounce jar apricot preserves
1 package onion soup
1 8-ounce jar Thousand Island Dressing

In a baking dish place washed chicken pieces—do not layer. First spoon apricot preserves on each piece of chicken, then sprinkle with onion soup, and finally pour dressing over each piece. Cover and bake at 350°F for 1½ hours.

SERVES 4

Oriental V-Chicken

2 pounds chicken wings
3 Tablespoons brown sugar
½ cup cooking oil
3 Tablespoons soy sauce
¼ cup sherry
Dash monosodium glutamate
1 small garlic clove, minced
1 4-ounce can mushrooms, drained, or ½ pound fresh
Cooked rice

Disjoint wing tip and discard or save them for soup. Wash and dry the wings, the fry in skillet (no oil) until brown. Add remaining ingredients and stir until mixed. Cover and simmer for 25 minutes. Remove the cover and increase heat until liquid is almost gone. Serve over hot rice.

SERVES 4-5

Chicken and Artichoke Casserole

3-3½-pound chicken, cut up
1 teaspoon salt
¼ teaspoon pepper
½ teaspoon paprika
4 Tablespoons butter or margarine
1 14-ounce can artichoke hearts, drained and halved
¼ pound mushrooms, sliced
2 Tablespoons flour
⅔ cup chicken broth
3 Tablespoons dry sherry
¼ teaspoon rosemary

Rinse chicken and pat dry. Sprinkle with salt, pepper, and paprika. In fry pan, brown chicken pieces in melted butter. Transfer chicken to a shallow 3-quart casserole and arrange artichokes in between. Set aside. Drain all but 3 Tablespoons drippings from frying pan; add mushrooms and cook until golden. Stir flour into mushrooms and cook 1 minute. Then add broth, sherry, and rosemary. Cook, stirring until thickened. Pour sauce evenly over chicken and artichokes. Cover and bake in 375°F oven for 40 minutes.

SERVES 4-6

Yellow Rice and Chicken

1 Tablespoon salt
1 frying chicken, cut up
½ cup olive oil
2 garlic cloves, sliced
1 onion, chopped
1 green pepper, chopped
3 cups water
1 15-ounce can whole tomatoes
1 teaspoon saffron
1½ cups uncooked rice
Salt and pepper to taste
1 8½-ounce can petite green peas, heated
1 2-ounce jar sliced pimiento

Salt the chicken. Heat olive oil in large pot or Dutch oven. Brown garlic in oil. Fry chicken in oil, turning frequently to prevent burning. When chicken is light brown, add onion and green pepper. When these become glazed, drain off most of oil. Add water, tomatoes, and saffron. Boil 5 minutes. Add rice and boil additional 5-10 minutes. Stir with a fork. Place covered pan in 325°F oven and cook until rice is dry (about 25 minutes). Stir with a fork and add salt and pepper to taste. Garnish with peas and pimiento.

SERVES 6

Bob's Mom's Chicken

Flour
10 chicken breasts or parts
½ cup butter or Wesson oil
1 10½-ounce can chicken broth, undiluted

GLAZE:
1 10-ounce jar marmalade
⅓ cup prepared mustard
¼ cup packed brown sugar
½ teaspoon salt
½ teaspoon pepper

Sauté floured chicken parts in ½ cup butter until browned. Add broth and cover, cooking until chicken is tender (30-40 minutes). Meanwhile in a small saucepan make the glaze by stirring together the marmalade, mustard, brown sugar, salt, and pepper; heat until bubbly. Place chicken in baking dish and brush liberally with the glaze. Bake for 20-30 minutes at 350°F or broil until bubbly, turning and brushing with glaze.

SERVES 5-6

Tahitian Chicken

¾ cup vegetable oil
¾ cup flour
2 frying chickens, cut up
3 Tablespoons cornstarch
1 cup granulated sugar
1 cup water
1 cup vinegar
3 Tablespoons soy sauce
Cooked white rice

Heat oil in a large frying pan. Flour the washed chicken and brown it in the hot oil. Meanwhile mix the remaining ingredients, except rice, together in a small mixing bowl. Place chicken in a 9 × 13-inch baking dish, single layer. Pour soy mixture over chicken. Bake 1 hour at 350°F. Serve with white rice.

SERVES 8

Oregon has had a long history as a logging center in America. In the early days, the camp cook was a very important person in a logging camp. The hard-working lumberjacks each consumed approximately 8,000 calories every day, and it was up to the cook to keep the men well fed and content. A 1,000- man crew would eat 1,000 pounds of fresh meat, 200 pounds of smoked meat, a ton of fresh fruits and vegetables, 900 pounds of flour, 600 pounds of sugar, 140 pounds of butter, 240 dozen eggs, and gallons upon gallons of coffee, tea, and milk each day.

Sour Cream Chicken Enchiladas

2 whole chicken breasts
2 $10\frac{1}{2}$-ounce cans cream of chicken soup
1 pint sour cream
1 4-ounce can chopped green chiles (save some for garnish)
Vegetable oil
1 dozen corn tortillas
$\frac{3}{4}$ cup chopped onion
3 cups grated Cheddar or Monterey Jack cheese, or combination of both
Ripe olives

Boil chicken breasts 20-25 minutes. Remove meat from bone and chop. Mix chicken meat, soup, sour cream, and chiles together. Heat oil in small fry pan; dip each tortilla into the hot oil until softened, and drain on paper towels. Spread a thin layer of creamed mixture over the bottom of a 9 × 12-inch pan. Spread equal amounts of creamed mixture down the middle of each tortilla (reserve some creamed mixture for top) and sprinkle with chopped onion and cheese (reserve some cheese for top). Roll up tortilla and place seam-side down in prepared pan. Pour remaining mixture over the top of rolled tortillas and sprinkle with remaining cheese. Bake 25-30 minutes at 350°F. Garnish with black olives and additional chiles.

SERVES 6-8

NOTE: Can be prepared ahead of time and refrigerated before baking.

Spicy Barbecued Chicken

3-pound frying chicken or 3 pounds favorite pieces
4 Tablespoons ketchup
2 Tablespoons vinegar
1 Tablespoon lemon juice
2 Tablespoons Worcestershire sauce
$\frac{1}{4}$ cup water
3 Tablespoons melted butter
2 teaspoons hickory salt
1 teaspoon dry mustard
2 teaspoons chili powder
$\frac{1}{4}$ teaspoon cayenne pepper
1 teaspoon paprika

Put chicken on individual pieces of foil. In a small mixing bowl combine the remaining ingredients and spoon over each piece of chicken. Seal tightly and put on a cookie sheet. Bake for 15 minutes at 500°F. Reduce heat to 350°F and continue baking for 1 hour.

SERVES 4-6

Easy Company Chicken

4 chicken breasts (½ pound each) skinned and boned
Salt, pepper, and flour
3 Tablespoons butter
2 Tablespoons oil
8 thin 2 × 4-inch slices prosciutto ham
8 thin 2 × 4-inch slices Fontina cheese
4 teaspoons grated Parmesan cheese
2 Tablespoons chicken stock

Lay chicken on wax paper and cover with another strip of wax paper. Pound the chicken pieces lightly to flatten them. Season the pieces with salt and pepper and dip them in flour. Shake off excess flour. In heavy skillet melt butter and oil over moderate heat. Brown the chicken lightly on both sides—do not overcook. Transfer chicken to shallow buttered baking dish. Place a piece of prosciutto and then a piece of Fontina cheese on each piece of chicken. Sprinkle with Parmesan cheese and dribble chicken stock over them. Bake uncovered in the middle of the oven for about 10 minutes at 350°F or until the cheese is melted and lightly browned. Serve at once.

SERVES 4

Orange Chutney Chicken

3 pounds frozen chicken breasts, thawed
1 teaspoon salt
¼ teaspoon pepper
2 Tablespoons salad oil
½ cup orange juice
½ cup chutney, chopped
¼ cup granulated sugar
2 Tablespoons lemon juice
2 oranges, peeled and cut in ½-inch slices
1 Tablespoon cornstarch
2 Tablespoons water

Preheat oven to 350°F. Sprinkle chicken with salt and pepper. Heat oil and brown chicken. Place chicken in 9 × 13 × 2-inch baking pan; add orange juice. Cover and bake for 45 minutes. Combine chutney, sugar, and lemon juice. Place orange slices over chicken; pour on chutney mixture. Continue baking uncovered for 15 minutes or until chicken is tender. Remove chicken to serving platter. Combine cornstarch and water. Place baking pan on surface unit, bringing liquid to a boil. Lower heat and stir in cornstarch mixture, stirring constantly, until mixture thickens. Pour over chicken and serve.

SERVES 6

Chicken in White Wine

1 large chicken, cut up, or favorite parts for 4 people
2 Tablespoons olive oil
8 small onions or shallots, peeled
4 slices bacon, lightly cooked and chopped
2 bay leaves
Pinch dried thyme
Salt and pepper to taste
¼ pound small fresh mushrooms
2 Tablespoons chopped parsley
½ cup dry white wine
½ cup chicken stock
Pat butter
Fresh parsley (optional)

Rinse chicken and dry thoroughly. Heat oil and place chicken skin-side down in pan; sauté the chicken on both sides until golden brown. Remove chicken from pan and keep warm while browning onions. Return chicken to pan with remaining ingredients except butter and fresh parsley. When liquid comes to boil, lower heat, partially cover pan and simmer 30 minutes or until chicken is tender and liquid from chicken runs clear when pierced. Place chicken on heated serving dish. Adjust seasoning in sauce and add butter. When butter is melted, pour sauce over chicken and sprinkle with fresh parsley, if desired.

SERVES 4

VARIATION: Reconstituted dry black mushrooms may be used instead of fresh mushrooms.

Cheese-Crisp Baked Chicken

2 cups bread crumbs, older the better
1 cup shredded Cheddar cheese
2 Tablespoons chopped parsley
1 teaspoon salt
¼ teaspoon pepper
½ teaspoon garlic salt
1 frying chicken, cut into serving pieces (if small, then 1½ chickens)
¾ cup melted margarine

Combine crumbs, cheese, parsley, and seasonings. Dip chicken into margarine, then crumb mix. Arrange in single layer in shallow baking pan with meat side of pieces up. Pour remaining crumbs over top. Drizzle any remaining margarine over all of chicken. Bake at 350°F for 1¼ hours.

SERVES 4

NOTE: A good way to use bread ends.

Oven Fried Herb Chicken

1 chicken, cut up
1 .9-ounce package Good Seasons Cheese Garlic salad dressing mix
2 Tablespoons flour
¼ teaspoon salt
¼ cup soft butter or margarine
1 Tablespoon lemon juice

Wash and dry chicken. Place chicken skin-side up in large flat pan such as cookie sheet or pizza pan. Combine salad dressing mix, flour, and salt, then blend in melted butter and lemon juice. Spread mixture evenly over chicken. Bake in moderate oven, 350°F, for 1¼ hours or until tender.

SERVES 4-6

Mexican Chicken Crepes

1½ cups sour cream
2 garlic cloves, pressed or minced
1½ teaspoons chili powder
1 teaspoon salt
1 teaspoon ground cumin
1 4-ounce can diced California green chiles, drained
2½ cups shredded Monterey Jack cheese, divided
2 cups diced cooked chicken or turkey
1½ cups thinly sliced green onion
10 crepes, made according to your favorite recipe
1 cup shredded Cheddar cheese
2 cups shredded lettuce
1 cup coarsely chopped tomato
1 cup guacamole

Stir together sour cream, garlic, chili powder, salt, cumin, chiles, 1½ cups of Jack cheese, chicken, and green onion. Spoon about ½ cup of the mixture down the center of each crepe; roll up to enclose. Place crepes seam-side down in a single layer in a shallow 3-quart baking dish. Bake covered in a 375°F oven until hot, about 20 minutes. Remove cover and sprinkle evenly with the Cheddar cheese; return to oven and bake uncovered until cheese melts, about 3-5 minutes. To serve, offer lettuce, tomato, 1 cup remaining Jack cheese, and guacamole to sprinkle over individual servings.

SERVES 5-6

NOTE: If made ahead, cover and chill. Then bake at 375°F about 30 minutes.

Sticky Chicken

Flour
Salt and pepper
4 pounds chicken breasts and thighs
½ cup oil
2 envelopes Lipton onion soup
2 28-ounce cans stewed tomatoes
2 cups dry white wine
1½ cups grated Mozzarella cheese

Flour, salt, and pepper the chicken and brown in oil. Combine soup mix, tomatoes, and wine; let stand while browning chicken. Put chicken in two 9 × 13-inch dishes. Pour sauce over and bake 1-1¼ hours at 325°F. Sprinkle with grated Mozzarella cheese and bake 10-15 minutes longer.

SERVES 8

Chicken Livers and Rice

1 cup uncooked long grain white rice
2 cups water
⅛ teaspoon dried thyme leaves
2 sprigs fresh parsley
¼ bay leaf
4 chicken bouillon cubes, divided
1 pound chicken livers
¼ cup flour
¼ cup plus 1 Tablespoon butter or margarine
1 medium onion, sliced into rings
1 garlic clove, peeled and minced
½ cup green pepper seeded and chopped
¼ pound fresh mushrooms, sliced
1 cup boiling water

Combine rice, 2 cups water, thyme, parsley, bay leaf, and 3 bouillon cubes in a heavy saucepan. Bring ingredients to a boil, reducing heat. Cover pan and simmer for 20 minutes or until rice is done. While rice is cooking, coat chicken livers with flour. Melt ¼ cup butter in a skillet over moderate heat (250°F). Add chicken livers and cook about 5 minutes, turning with a slotted spoon, until lightly browned. Remove livers to a plate and set aside. Add the remaining 1 Tablespoon of butter to the skillet. Add onion, garlic, green pepper; mushrooms and cook until tender, stirring occasionally. Dissolve remaining bouillon cube in the 1 cup boiling water. Add dissolved bouillon and reserved chicken livers to vegetables and stir. Cover and place over moderately low heat (225°F); cook about 5 minutes. Serve over the hot rice.

SERVES 6

SEAFOOD

Darlene M. Kosoff

Trout with Pecans

4 trout (8 to 10-inch)
Salt and pepper to taste
Juice of ½ lemon
½ cup butter
½ cup coarsely chopped pecans
¼ cup whole pecan halves
Salt
1-2 Tablespoons butter (optional)
½ lemon, sliced

Place cleaned and scaled fish in a shallow baking dish that is lined with foil and lightly greased. Salt and pepper. Sprinkle with juice from lemon. Bake at 350°F approximately 30 minutes or until fish flakes easily. Meanwhile, melt butter in skillet. Toss chopped pecans in butter until toasted; remove and keep warm. Then toss pecan halves in butter until toasted, remove and save. Reserve butter. Salt nuts. When fish is cooked, take each fish out and carefully remove bones by lifting meat off of top portion, then pulling whole backbone free from lower portion of meat. If desired add 1-2 Tablespoons butter to reserved butter in skillet and place fillets and chopped pecans in skillet to keep warm. To serve, place all fillets on warmed serving dish; spread with chopped pecans and melted butter from skillet. Garnish with lemon slices and toasted pecan halves.

SERVES 4

Pioneers who prided themselves on their smoked native trout went to a great deal of trouble to give their fish a special taste. They would travel to the Elk Lake area where a specific variety of willow grew. Using strong green saplings, they built a conical "wickiup" and thatched it with leaves. From the marshes surrounding the lake, canoe loads of young green willow branches were brought to the improvised smokehouse. The catch of trout was hung from poles inside the top of the wickiup. It took 24 hours to smoke the fish. To maintain the subdued and smoky willow fire in the floor of the smokehouse was the pioneers' most tedious task. The taste of the freshly smoked fish was ample reward for their patience.

Baked Salmon

4-5-pound salmon fillet
½ pound butter
1 garlic clove, crushed
¼ cup ketchup
4 teaspoons soy sauce
2 teaspoons prepared mustard
Dash of Worcestershire sauce
Dash of pepper
1 Tablespoon lemon juice

Place fillet of salmon skin-side down on a foil-lined cookie sheet. Mix remaining ingredients together and heat to simmer, but do not boil. Pour mixture over salmon and bake at 350°F for 35-40 minutes.

SERVES 6-8

Easy Salmon Bake

6-7-pound salmon fillet
2 lemons
Salt and white pepper
Garlic salt
Oregano
¼ cup melted butter
Chopped parsley
2 Tablespoons dry sherry
Paprika (optional)

Place salmon skin-side down on cooking tray. Squeeze juice of 2 lemons ove fish. Sprinkle with salt and pepper. Add hint of garlic salt. Sprinkle liberall with oregano. Pour melted butter over all. Sprinkle with chopped parsley. Slow ly drizzle dry sherry over top. Bake at 350°F for ½ hour or until fish is opaqu and flakes easily. Sprinkle with paprika, if desired, to bring back color to th fish.

SERVES 4-

The Willamette Valley Indian tribes depended a great deal on salmon as mainstay of their diet. The fish were frequently split lengthwise and slow-bake before an open fire, imparting a flavor unequalled by that of modern cookin methods.

Fresh Salmon with Mushrooms and Scallions

2½-3 pounds fresh salmon fillets or steelhead
1 Tablespoon lemon juice
Salt and pepper to taste
½ pound fresh mushrooms, sliced
1 cup sliced green onion with tops
¼ cup butter
1 teaspoon grated lemon peel
½ teaspoon marjoram leaves
Salt and pepper to taste
½ teaspoon garlic powder
Sautéed mushroom buttons
Watercress or parsley sprigs
Sour cream
Caviar (black)

Heat oven to 450°F. Line baking sheet with foil. Place salmon on foil; sprink with lemon juice and salt and pepper. Bake 10 minutes. Remove from ove Cool slightly. Transfer fish to baking dish (dark skin should stick to foil in pa remove any that remains on fillet before placing in baking dish). Saut mushrooms and onion in butter seasoned with lemon peel, marjoram, salt, pe per, and garlic powder, until liquid evaporates. Spread mushroom mixture ove fish. Cover dish with foil, sealing edges. Bake an additional 25-30 minutes c until fish is tender. To serve, garnish with sautéed mushroom buttons an watercress. Pass sour cream and caviar as accompaniments to salmon.

SERVES 4

Whole Stuffed Salmon

3-4-pound whole fresh salmon, steelhead or bass
1 pound bulk sausage
2 medium onions, chopped
1 medium green pepper, seeded and diced
2 cups small bread cubes
2 eggs, slightly beaten
1 teaspoon poultry seasoning
1 teaspoon paprika
1 cup dry white wine
Parsley sprigs
Lemon round slices

Clean and scale fish, leaving head and tail intact. Carefully remove all bones, preserving fish shape as much as possible. Lay fish in well-oiled, foil-lined shallow baking dish. Sauté sausage until partially browned. Add onions and pepper. Cook, stirring occasionally, over medium heat until vegetables are tender and all meat is browned. Drain well. Add sausage mixture to bread crumbs. Stir in eggs and seasonings. Mix thoroughly. Stuff meat mixture into fish. Wrap with strings to hold shape (stuffing will swell somewhat during baking). Pour wine into baking dish. Bake at 350°F for 30-40 minutes or until fish is white and flaky. Add more wine if necessary to keep fish from drying out. Carefully transfer fish to serving platter. Remove strings; garnish with parsley and lemon rounds.

SERVES 6-8

The steelhead begins its life as a rainbow trout in Pacific Northwest rivers and streams. It migrates to the ocean to mature, and returns to fresh water to spawn. During the sea-run, the steelhead flesh turns pink and acquires a flavor much like salmon.

Fillet of Steelhead

1 steelhead fillet
Onion salt to taste
Monosodium glutamate to taste
Mayonnaise to cover
Few pinches Schilling Italian seasoning
Saltine cracker crumbs to cover
½-¾ cube margarine or butter
Lemon pepper seasoning to taste

Sprinkle fillet with onion salt and MSG. Spread fillet generously with mayonnaise, sprinkle with a few pinches of Italian seasoning, and dip in cracker crumbs. Melt the margarine and drizzle over fish. Sprinkle with the lemon pepper seasoning. Bake uncovered at 425°F for 25-35 minutes or until golden brown.

SERVES 3-4

VARIATION: Use salmon instead of steelhead

Sole with Almonds and Green Grapes

6 sole fillets
Flour
Salt and pepper
5 Tablespoons butter or margarine, divided
2 Tablespoons oil
½ cup green grapes, halved
½ cup blanched, slivered almonds
3 Tablespoons white wine or broth
1 Tablespoon lemon juice
Dash Worcestershire sauce

Dust fillets with flour, shaking off excess; then lightly salt and pepper. Melt 2 Tablespoons butter with 2 Tablespoons oil in skillet over medium-hot heat. Sauté sole about 3-4 minutes on each side until lightly browned and cooked through. Carefully lift to a heated platter and keep warm. In same skillet, heat 2 Tablespoons butter and stir in grapes. Cook 2-3 minutes and spoon over sole. In same skillet heat remaining 1 Tablespoon butter, add almonds and sauté until lightly browned. Stir in wine, lemon juice, and Worcestershire; heat and pour over the sole.

SERVES 6

Shrimp-Stuffed Sole

6 serving-size pieces fillet of sole
3 Tablespoon butter or margarine
3 Tablespoons flour
1 cup light cream
½ cup milk
1 cup shredded Gruyere cheese
1 Tablespoon sherry
3 dashes Tabasco (optional)
1½ cups cooked, shelled, deveined shrimp
½ teaspoon salt
½ teaspoon pepper
2 teaspoons parsley flakes

Wash and dry fillets. Melt butter over medium heat; stir in flour, cooking until well blended and bubbly. Remove from heat and gradually stir in cream, then milk. Cook over medium heat until sauce thickens and comes to a boil. Add shredded cheese, stirring until melted. Blend in sherry and Tabasco. Chop shrimp, reserving 6-12 for garnish. In mixing bowl combine chopped shrimp, salt, pepper, and parsley flakes. Blend in 3 Tablespoons of the prepared sauce. Spoon shrimp mixture evenly across center of each fillet. Fold ends of each fillet over stuffing. Place fillets seam side-down in buttered 7½ × 12 × 2-inch baking dish. Pour remaining sauce evenly over top of fillets. Bake at 350°F for 30 minutes or until fish flakes easily and sauce is lightly browned.

SERVES 6

Halibut Steak with Sauce

1-1½ pounds halibut steak (½-inch thick)
Salt and pepper
1 small onion
⅓ cube butter
Juice of ½ lemon
¼-½ cup sour cream
¼-½ cup grated medium sharp Cheddar cheese

Sprinkle halibut steaks with salt and pepper. Place fish in baking dish. Peel a small onion and separate into rings; arrange over halibut. In a saucepan melt butter and add the lemon juice and sour cream. Blend. Pour melted butter sauce over halibut in baking dish. Sprinkle cheese over fish and bake at 350°F for 35 minutes.

SERVES 4-6

Lewis and Clark found a small fish in the Columbia River that they called the anchovy. This prized marine delicacy, the Columbia River Smelt, or eulachon, is caught in immense quantities each spring.

Fish Steaks with Rosemary

4 1-inch thick fish steaks (salmon, swordfish, mackerel)
½ cup melted butter
Salt and pepper to taste
½ teaspoon dried rosemary leaves
Fresh parsley sprigs
Lemon rounds

Wash fish steaks and dry on paper towels. Place in lightly oiled baking dish (may be foil lined for easy cleanup). Pour butter over fish; season with salt and pepper. Sprinkle rosemary leaves over fish. Broil 5 inches from heat, turning once, until fish flakes easily, approximately 10-15 minutes. When fish has been cooked, remove to warmed serving platter. Spoon cooking juices over fish. Garnish with parsley and lemon rounds.

SERVES 4

Crab Soufflé

10 slices bread, crusts trimmed
3 cups crabmeat, tuna or shrimp
1 cup chopped celery
1 cup chopped onion
½ cup mayonnaise
1 cup chopped green pepper
4 eggs
3 cups milk
½ teaspoon salt (optional)
1 10½-ounce can cream of mushroom soup, undiluted
Grated mild or sharp Cheddar cheese
Paprika

Butter a 9 × 13-inch baking dish and line with half of bread slices. Mix together next 5 ingredients and put on top of bread slices in baking dish. Top with remainder of bread slices. Beat together the eggs, milk, and salt. Pour egg mixture over bread and refrigerate overnight. Next day bake at 325°F for 15 minutes; remove from oven and spread undiluted soup over the top. Sprinkle with cheese and paprika. Return to oven and bake 1 hour longer. Allow to set 10-15 minutes before cutting.

SERVES 6-8

Crab and Artichoke Élégante

¼ pound butter
3 Tablespoons minced onion
½ cup flour
1 quart cream, heated to boiling point
½ cup Madeira
Salt and pepper
2 Tablespoons lemon juice
4 cups fresh crabmeat
3 9-ounce packages frozen artichoke hearts, cooked according to directions, or equal amount canned artichoke hearts
6 ounces spaghetti or linguini, cooked and drained
2 cups grated Gruyere or Swiss cheese, divided
Paprika

Preheat oven to 350°F. Melt butter in large heavy pan. When butter sizzles add onion and sauté until golden. Stir in flour, cooking over low heat until flou is pale. Remove from heat. Add cream, stirring vigorously. Return to moderat heat and stir until sauce reaches a boil. Reduce heat and add Madeira. Seaso with salt and pepper; set aside. Pour lemon juice over crabmeat and tos lightly. Quarter artichoke hearts. Combine crab and artichoke hearts. Ad cream sauce. Toss crab mixture with pasta and place in a 6-quart buttere casserole. Stir in half of grated cheese. Sprinkle remaining cheese on top an dust with paprika. Bake 25-30 minutes, or until heated through.

SERVES 10-1

Company Crab Casserole

14-ounce can artichoke hearts, drained
4-ounce can sliced mushrooms, drained
pound fresh or frozen crabmeat, drained
Tablespoons butter
½ Tablespoons flour
½ teaspoon salt
Dash cayenne pepper
1 cup half and half
2 Tablespoons sherry
2 Tablespoons cereal crumbs
1 Tablespoon grated Parmesan cheese
Paprika

ut artichoke hearts in half and place in well-greased shallow 1½-quart sserole. Cover with mushrooms and crabmeat. Melt butter and blend in flour ıd seasonings. Add cream gradually and cook until thick, stirring constantly. ir in sherry. Pour sauce over crabmeat. Combine crumbs and cheese; sprinkle ver sauce. Sprinkle with paprika. Bake in hot 450°F oven for 12-15 minutes ıtil bubbly.

SERVES 4-6

JGGESTION: Good made individually and served with a salad and roll for ncheon.

Company Crab Casserole II

½ pound mushrooms
Tablespoons butter
green onions, chopped
Tablespoons flour
½ cups half and half
½ pound crabmeat
1 teaspoon Worcestershire sauce
¼ cup white wine
1 cup cooked rice
Salt and pepper to taste
1 cup grated Monterey Jack cheese

Cut mushrooms and simmer in butter. Add green onions. Blend in flour; add alf and half and crab. Fold in remaining ingredients except cheese. Turn into asserole and top with cheese. Bake at 350°F until cheese is melted and ubbly.

SERVES 6-8

Crabmeat Delight

1½ cups milk, scalded
1 cup soft bread crumbs
2 cups crabmeat
¼ cup melted butter
2 Tablespoons chopped green pepper
2 Tablespoons chopped pimientoes
1 Tablespoon chopped onion
1 cup grated American cheese
½ teaspoon salt
¼ teaspoon pepper
3 eggs, beaten

Pour milk over bread crumbs. Add remaining ingredients. Pour into buttere casserole. Set in a pan of hot water and bake at 300°F for 1 hour; insert knif blade to test for doneness.

SERVES

Crab A La Martin

1 onion, chopped
1 green pepper, chopped
Oil
1 10½-ounce can tomato soup, undiluted
1 cup mayonnaise
1 pound crabmeat
Bread crumbs
Butter

Brown onion and green pepper in oil. Add tomato soup and mayonnaise. Sti well. Add crabmeat. Mix well and pour into individual shells or casserole Sprinkle with bread crumbs and dot with a few pieces of butter. Bake in moderate 350°F oven approximately 15-20 minutes.

SERVES

Dungeness Crab Fritters

½ pound crabmeat
2 Tablespoons chopped green onion
1 Tablespoon chopped parsley
1 Tablespoon chopped green pepper
2 Tablespoons chopped ripe tomato
2 eggs
1 teaspoon Worcestershire sauce
¼ cup flour
2 teaspoons baking powder
⅛ teaspoon salt
3 Tablespoons butter
Lemon wedges

Thoroughly mix together the first 7 ingredients. Sift the flour, baking powde and salt into the first mixture. Stir until just blended. Fry by Tablespoonfuls i hot butter over moderate-high heat, turning once to brown on both sides Serve immediately accompanied by lemon wedges.

SERVES 4-

Crab Fettuccine

4 Tablespoons butter
2 garlic cloves, minced
4 Tablespoons flour
½ cup sherry or dry white wine
2 cups half and half
½ pound mushrooms, sliced
Butter
⅓ cup Parmesan cheese
Salt and pepper
1 pound crabmeat
Cooked fettuccine

Melt 4 Tablespoons butter in large skillet, add garlic and sauté until soft. Add flour and cook briefly. Gradually add sherry and half and half. Cook until sauce is smooth and thick; set aside. Sauté mushrooms in generous amount of butter. Add mushrooms and any juice to cream sauce. Stir in Parmesan cheese and add salt and pepper to taste. Gently fold in crabmeat. Heat through. Serve over freshly cooked fettuccine, your own or store bought.

SERVES 6

Crepes Celeste

CREPE BATTER
1 cup flour
1 Tablespoon granulated sugar
3 eggs
1 cup milk
2 Tablespoons melted butter

SAUCE:
½ cup sautéed mushrooms
½ cup flour
1 cup milk
¼ cup sherry
½ cup chicken broth
1 egg yolk, beaten
½ cup whipping cream
2 cups crabmeat
¼ cup butter

CREPE BATTER: Combine all ingredients and follow normal procedure for frying. May be made day before.
SAUCE: Melt butter, blend in flour, add milk, sherry, and broth. Stir over medium heat until thickened. Pour a little of this sauce over the egg yolk. Return to rest of sauce with whipping cream. Reserve ½ cup of this sauce and set aside. Add crabmeat and mushrooms to remaining sauce. Fill crepes with this crab mixture. Roll up and place seam-side down in ovenproof dish. Top with ½ cup reserved sauce. Run under broiler to glaze.

SERVES 4-6

Hot Crab Sandwiches

1 6-ounce package cream cheese softened
2 teaspoons lemon juice
1 cup flaked crabmeat
1 Tablespoon chopped onion
½-1 teaspoon chili powder to taste
⅛ teaspoon salt
1 Tablespoon mayonnaise
4 split English muffins

Mix first 7 ingredients. Spread over English muffins; broil until browned.

SERVES

Seafood Quiche

6 ounces crabmeat
¾ pound shrimp (1½ cups)
8 ounces Swiss cheese, chopped
½ cup finely chopped green onion
½ cup finely chopped celery
2 9-inch frozen pie shells or make own crust
1 cup mayonnaise or salad dressin
2 Tablespoons flour
1 cup dry white wine
4 eggs, slightly beaten

Combine crab, shrimp, cheese, onion, and celery. Divide mixture equally b tween pies. Combine mayonnaise, flour, white wine, and eggs; divide and po into pies. Bake at 350°F for 35-40 minutes or until a knife comes out clea May be frozen, unbaked. To serve, bake frozen quiche at 350°F for 50- minutes.

SERVES 10-

Seafood Supreme

Pine Tavern Restaurant

4 cups mixed crab, shrimp, tuna, and any other seafood desired
1 cup soft bread crumbs
2 cups cooked rice
2 Tablespoons chopped pimiento
2 Tablespoons chopped green pepper
2 Tablespoons chopped green onion
1 4-ounce can mushrooms and liquid
1 10½-ounce can mushroom soup
½ cup mayonnaise
½ cup milk
2 Tablespoons capers
2 eggs, beaten

Gently combine all ingredients. Pour into greased casserole and bake at 35 for 30 to 45 minutes.

SERVES

Seafood Lasagne

: ounces lasagne noodles
Tablespoon cooking oil
:old water
: 10½-ounce cans cream of shrimp soup
: 7-ounce cans crabmeat or preferably fresh
: cups cottage cheese
8-ounce package cream cheese, softened
1 large onion, chopped
1 egg
2 teaspoons basil
1 teaspoon salt
½ teaspoon pepper
3-4 medium tomatoes, sliced
2 teaspoons granulated sugar
1½ cups grated Cheddar cheese

:ook noodles and add oil. Drain and cover with cold water; set aside. Heat oup until bubbly, adding flaked crabmeat. Remove from heat; set aside. Blend ottage cheese, cream cheese, onion, egg, basil, salt, and pepper. Line bottom f oiled 9 × 13-inch casserole with layer of noodles and half of the cream heese mixture. Add another layer of noodles and all of the crab-shrimp sauce. 'over with another layer of noodles and rest of cream cheese mixture. Arange tomato slices in single layer on top. Sprinkle with sugar. Cover and efrigerate overnight. Sprinkle with grated cheese and bake at 350°F for 1-1¼ ours. Let stand for 10 minutes before slicing.

SERVES 8

Crab and Shrimp

-1¼ pounds crabmeat
pound fresh or canned small shrimp
green pepper, chopped
cup chopped parsley
2 cups cooked white long grain rice (prepared earlier in the day or day ahead)
1½ cups mayonnaise
2 10-ounce packages frozen peas, thawed, but not cooked
Salt and pepper to taste

ightly mix all ingredients together. Place in greased casserole. Refrigerate and ave covered until ready to cook. Bake covered 1 hour at 350°F.

SERVES 6

Italian-Style Shrimp

1-1½ pounds medium size raw shrimp
⅔ cup butter or margarine
2 Tablespoons minced green onion
2 Tablespoons olive oil
8-10 garlic cloves, minced or pressed
4 teaspoons lemon juice
½ teaspoon salt
½ teaspoon grated lemon peel
¼ cup minced parsley
Dash of liquid hot pepper
Lemon wedges

Shell the shrimp, being careful not to remove the last segment of the tail. De vein and rinse in cold water. In frying pan, melt the butter over medium heat Stir in the onion, oil, garlic, lemon juice, and salt; cook until bubbly. Ad shrimp to pan and cook, stirring occasionally, until they turn pink (5 minutes) Blend in lemon peel, parsley, and hot pepper seasoning; turn into serving dish Garnish with lemon wedges to squeeze over each serving.

SERVES

Shrimp Florentine

½ pound butter
2 Tablespoons flour
1 small onion, diced
1 teaspoon Worcestershire sauce
Pinch of thyme
½ pint whipping cream
1 cup packed grated Cheddar cheese
Jigger of white wine
¼ pound mushrooms, thinly sliced
2 teaspoons butter
1 10½-ounce package frozen spinach, drained
1 pound medium-size fresh shrimp, deveined
Croutons

Melt ½ pound of butter, add flour, onion, and blend. Sprinkle with Worceste shire and pinch of thyme. Slowly add whipping cream and grated chees Blend in wine. Set aside cream sauce. Sauté mushrooms in 2 teaspoons butte Set aside. Place spinach in bottom of casserole dish. Place shrimp on top c spinach. Place sautéed mushrooms on top of shrimp. Pour sauce over all. Plac croutons on top of sauce. Bake covered at 300°F for 20 minutes. May serv with rice.

SERVES 4

Shrimp Casserole Hairpin

- 2½ pounds large raw shrimp
- Boiling water
- 1 Tablespoon fresh lemon juice
- 3 Tablespoons salad oil
- ¾ cup raw rice
- 2 Tablespoons butter
- ¼ cup minced green pepper
- ¼ cup minced green onion
- ¼ teaspoon salt
- ¼ teaspoon pepper
- ⅛ teaspoon cayenne pepper
- ⅛ teaspoon mace
- 1 10½-ounce can condensed tomato soup, undiluted
- 1 cup heavy cream
- ½ cup sherry wine
- ¾ cup slivered almonds, divided

Early in the day, or day before, cook shrimp in boiling water for 5 minutes. Drain. Place in casserole and sprinkle with lemon juice and salad oil. Meanwhile, cook rice. When rice is cooked, place in refrigerator. Drain off liquid from shrimp and refrigerate separately from rice. About 1 hour and 10 minutes before serving, preheat oven to 350°F. In butter sauté green pepper and onion for 5 minutes. Add rice, salt, pepper, cayenne, mace, soup, cream, and sherry. Set aside 8 shrimp to be used later. Add remaining shrimp and ½ cup almonds to cream mixture; toss well. Bake uncovered for 35 minutes, then top with the 8 reserved shrimp and remaining ¼ cup almonds. Bake 20 minutes longer or until mixture is bubbly and shrimp is browned.

SERVES 6-8

Shrimp Casserole

- cups sliced celery (½-inch)
- cup chopped onion
- ½ cup water
- 10½-ounce cans cream of mushroom soup
- 5-ounce can sliced water chestnuts
- ¾ cup chopped green pepper
- 1 6-ounce package cashew nuts, chopped
- ¾ pound cooked shrimp
- 1 4-ounce can mushrooms
- 2 3-ounce cans Chinese chow mein noodles

Cook celery and onion in the water until tender. Drain liquid. Mix all ingredients, except noodles, together. In 9 × 13-inch or 3-quart casserole, place 1 can of noodles. Cover with shrimp sauce. Place other can of noodles over top. Bake 30-45 minutes at 350°F, heating until bubbly throughout.

SERVES 8-10

Herbed-Shrimp Quiche

6 strips crisp bacon, crumbled
1 9-inch unbaked pie shell (preferably in fluted quiche dish)
½ cup diced Mozzarella cheese
¾ cup salad-size cooked, shelled, deveined shrimp
1½ cups light cream or canned milk
½ teaspoon salt
¼ teaspoon pepper
¼ teaspoon rosemary
¼ teaspoon basil
5 eggs
Parsley sprigs (optional)

Preheat oven to 350°F. Sprinkle bacon evenly over bottom of pie shell. Com bine cheese and shrimp. Sprinkle evenly over bacon. Beat remaining ingre dients, except parsley, together (blend 30 seconds in blender if desired) unt eggs are thoroughly blended with milk. Pour egg mixture into pie shell. Bak for 30-40 minutes until eggs are set and knife inserted in center comes ou clean. Serve hot and garnish with parsley, if desired.

SERVES

Shrimp and Chicken Oriental

3½ Tablespoons oil
2 garlic cloves, minced
2 pounds raw shrimp, shelled and deveined
1 pound mushrooms, sliced
1 cup sliced bamboo shoots
1 cup cooked, thinly sliced chicken
4 cups chicken broth, divided
1 teaspoon salt
½ teaspoon monosodium glutamate or Lawry's salt
1½ pounds snow peas or 2 6-ounce packages frozen snow peas, thawed
1 teaspoon granulated sugar
2 Tablespoons cornstarch
Cooked rice or noodles

Heat oil in a skillet. Sauté garlic, shrimp, mushrooms, bamboo shoots, an chicken for 4 minutes, stirring constantly. Transfer to a large saucepan. Add 3 cups broth, salt, and monosodium glutamate. Cover and cook 4 minutes. Ad snow peas and cook 1 minute. Mix together the sugar, cornstarch, and remain ing ½ cup broth to taste. Stir into the sauce until thickened. Cool 1 minut more. Serve with rice or noodles.

SERVES 2

Scampi and Prosciutto

Oregano to taste
5-6 Tablespoons olive oil, divided
12 medium shrimp
12 slices prosciutto or pepper ham
2 garlic cloves, pressed
4 Tablespoons white wine
2 Tablespoons butter
1 Tablespoon lemon juice
1 teaspoon flour (optional)
Chopped parsley

Crush a little oregano (with a mortar and pestle if one is available) into 2 Tablespoons of olive oil. Set aside. Remove shell from shrimp, devein, but leave on tail. Wrap each shrimp with one piece of ham, slightly overlapped. Heat remaining 3-4 Tablespoons olive oil, with garlic added, in a heavy pan. Add the ham-wrapped shrimp and sauté approximately 1 minute. Remove shrimp from pan, brush with reserved olive oil and oregano mixture, and place under broiler for about 2 minutes or until the ham is lightly browned. Drain off oil. In a saucepan, simmer the white wine to reduce a little; then add butter and lemon juice, or make a roux of wine, butter, lemon juice, and 1 teaspoon flour. Spoon over shrimp which has been placed on warm serving platter, sprinkle with parsley, and serve.

SERVES 2-4

The resourceful housewife could beautify her home by making whitewash. She layered spruce limbs and clam shells in a pile as high as she could reach. She ignited the wood and the pile of fresh lime produced after the fire had burned out would provide her with enough whitewash to paint her house inside and out. For extra decoration, she could make a bag and place a ball of bluing inside, dip it into water, and use it to make patterns and designs on the walls.

Spaghetti with Clam Sauce

1 pound spaghetti
3 Tablespoons butter
⅔ cup light cream
2-3 Tablespoons Parmesan cheese
⅛ pound Cheddar cheese, grated
1 6½-ounce can minced clams

Cook spaghetti; drain and return to pan. Reheat slowly and add remaining ingredients, one at a time, mixing well after each addition.

YIELD: 4-6 servings

Empire clams, which can weight four to five pounds each, are found in the estuaries of Coos Bay, Oregon. The large necks of these clams are prepared by scraping off the rough outer skin and splitting the meat into sections. The foot is cleaned and butterflied so it will lie open and flat. These clam pieces are lightly dredged in seasoned flour or cornmeal and quickly panfried until brown and crisp.

Cheese-Clam Fettuccine

6 ounces green spinach noodles (about 4 cups)
¼ pound bacon
½ cup butter
3 garlic cloves, pressed
1 6½-ounce can minced clams, drained, or fresh shelled steamers
1 cup grated Parmesan cheese
Ripe olives (optional)

Cook noodles according to package directions. Meanwhile, cook bacon unti crisp. Drain and crumble; set aside. Melt butter, add garlic and clams. Toss ho drained noodles with clam mixture and grated cheese. Serve on warm platte topped with reserved, crumbled bacon. Garnish with ripe olives, if desired.

SERVES 4-5

Clam Chowder Pie

1 cup rice
2½ cups boiling salted water
1 Tablespoon salad oil
6 slices bacon, cut in pieces
1 cup chopped onion
1 cup chopped celery
1 6½-ounce can minced clams
1 15-ounce can Snow's clam chowder
¼ cup milk
Salt and pepper to taste

Cook rice in boiling water with oil. Reduce heat to very low. Let stand covered for 25 minutes. Lightly brown bacon. Add onion and celery; sauté. Mix together the cooked rice, bacon mixture, clams, clam chowder, milk, and salt and pepper. Bake at 350°F for 45-60 minutes in 2½-quart casserole.

SERVES 6

Pacific Oysters Sauté in Wine Sauce

Wolf Creek Tavern

1 teaspoon coarsely chopped onion
1 teaspoon coarsely chopped green pepper
1 Tablespoon butter, melted
1 Tablespoon sliced fresh mushrooms
1 dozen petite Pacific oysters
1 medium-size fresh tomato, cut into wedges
2 ounces extra-dry vermouth
Lemon juice from 1 wedge

Sauté onion and green pepper in butter until onion is transparent. Add mushrooms and stir. Add oysters and heat through, turning occasionally. Add tomato wedges. Add vermouth and lemon juice. Heat and serve in crockery.

SERVES 2

Happy's Scalloped Oysters

2 cups soda cracker crumbs
1 16-ounce jar tiny oysters, cut into bite-size pieces and drained
Butter
Salt and pepper to taste
1½ cups milk (approximately)

Preheat oven to 325°F. In buttered 2-quart Pyrex dish, layer one-third of bread crumbs, one-third of oysters, dot with butter and salt and pepper. Repeat process, making 2 more layers. Add enough milk to make casserole moist, but without letting milk come to top. Bake in water bath at 325°F for 30 minutes. Serve immediately.

SERVES 8-10

Fried Small Olympia Oysters

Oysters, specifically the tiny Olympias, have long been a delicacy of the Pacific Northwest.

"Drain the oysters in a colander. Then put them in a dish of beaten egg, seasoned with pepper and salt. One egg is sufficient for a quart of oysters. Have ready a bowl of sifted cracker crumbs or finely pounded dried bread crumbs. Take five or six oysters, and with the hand pat them into a cake, and sprinkle the crumbs over them. Fry in butter, taking care that the butter is hot before putting the oysters in the frying pan. When one side is firm, turn with cake turner, and fry the other. They are nice served with cold slaw."

The Web-Foot Cookbook, 1885; Oregon Historical Society

GAME

Terry Maddox

Caution: Any wild game not properly prepared in the field will taste bad, no matter how it is prepared in the kitchen. It is critical that the meat be skinned and cleaned immediately after being shot. If left unattended even for a few hours, the meat will take on a very strong flavor.

In the kitchen, be sure to trim all fat from meat before cooking as the fat will also cause game to have a strong flavor.

Oven Jerky

Meat
Mrs. Wright's Liquid Smoke
Water
Salt

Use any red meat—venison, elk, antelope, wild sheep or even beef. Trim meat removing all fat. Cut into long strips anywhere from 4-8 inches in length. Dilute Mrs. Wright's Liquid Smoke in water using 2 parts liquid smoke to 1 part water. Dip each strip of meat in this solution and lay in flat glass dish. When you have 1 layer of meat in the dish, liberally sprinkle table salt on the meat so you can see the salt. Repeat this process until the dish is about ¾ full. If you have more meat, use another dish, as this solution will become quite juicy and may overflow a dish that is too full. Cover each dish with plastic wrap and set in a cool place for at least 12-24 hours. In a very cool oven, about 140°F or lower if possible, lay the strips (unrinsed) on your oven racks. Place as many racks in your oven as possible to conserve energy. Set a flat pan covered with tinfoil under the bottom rack to catch the drips. Bake for 10-12 hours or until meat is free of moisture, but not brittle. Store in jar or place in freezer for longer storage. This recipe is ideal to use for all those scraps you hate to waste or if your family is not fond of ground game. The better trimmed the meat is, the less chewy. If you like spicier jerky, just add pepper to marinade, but try it without first; you may find this spicy enough. Excellent for snacks for your hunter or school-aged children. Always a hit around our house.

Buffalo Jerk was dried buffalo meat that provided a portable form of nourishment for the travelers of the plains. Buffalo meat was cut into thin strips, salted lightly, then suspended over a bed of hot coals and dried until it was stiff. It could be eaten as it was or softened by cooking it in stews.

Venison/Beef Jerky

5 pounds venison, top round, brisket or flank, free of fat and sliced very thin (¼-⅛-inch thick)
2 Tablespoons salt
2 Tablespoons granulated sugar
3 teaspoons black pepper
1 teaspoon garlic powder
6 teaspoons monosodium glutamate
2 teaspoons liquid smoke

Trim and slice meat and place in dish. Mix the dry ingredients and sprinkle on meat; add the liquid smoke. Cover and refrigerate 24 hours. Place foil on bottom of oven and place meat *directly* on racks. Cook at low temperature, 200°F for 8 hours.

Deer and elk roamed the Oregon country, and the meat of these animals was often the only meat for the pioneer families. It was preserved by drying, salting and canning for the time when the hunter's aim might not be as true.

Baked Venison Steaks

1-1½ pounds meat
Garlic powder to taste
1-1½ cups flour
Salt and pepper to taste
¼-½ cup bacon drippings
¾-1 cup milk

Use any game—elk, venison, antelope, sheep, or even beef. Cut into thin steaks. Pound steaks on both sides and then shake a little garlic powder on each side if you wish to soften the game taste. (Since you are pounding the meat, lesser cuts of game can be used with this recipe.) Lightly coat pounded steaks in flour seasoned with salt and pepper and sauté in bacon fat, browning each side lightly. Reserve leftover flour and bacon fat. Place meat in casserole dish with cover and back in 300°F oven for about ½ hour. With reserved flour and bacon fat make gravy, adding milk to mixture to make creamy. Simmer. Serve meat with gravy on top.

SERVES 4

SUGGESTION: Excellent side dish is mashed potatoes, which can also be topped with gravy.

Venison in Red Wine

2½-3 pounds venison round steak, cut into 1-inch cubes
¼ cup flour
¼ cup butter, melted
½ cup chopped onion
1 Tablespoon dried parsley
1 medium garlic clove, chopped
1 bay leaf
1 teaspoon salt
½ pound fresh mushrooms, sliced
1 cup Burgundy wine
½ cup water
Cooked rice or noodles

Toss meat cubes in flour. Brown lightly in butter. Add onion, parsley, garlic, bay leaf, salt, and mushrooms. Cook until onion is just tender. Slowly add wine and water, stirring constantly. Bring just to boiling, reduce heat and simmer until meat is tender. Add more wine if necessary. Remove bay leaf. Serve over hot cooked rice or hot buttered noodles.

SERVES 6-8

Venison with Sour Cream and Mushrooms

2½ pounds venison tenderloin, cut in ½-inch slices
¾ teaspoon marjoram
Salt and pepper to taste
¼ cup flour
2 Tablespoons shortening
2 medium onions, sliced and separated
½ pound fresh mushrooms, sliced
¼ cup dry sherry
1 beef bouillon cube
½ cup hot water
½ cup sour cream
2 Tablespoons flour

Season meat with marjoram, salt, and pepper. Dredge meat in ¼ cup flour. Heat shortening in a large skillet. Brown meat quickly on both sides. Remove. Reduce heat. Sauté onions and mushrooms until onions are tender. Add sherry, bouillon cube, water, and stir well. Return meat to gravy and continue cooking until meat is medium rare. Combine sour cream and flour. Stir into pan and heat, stirring until gravy thickens (add more sherry if too thick). Do not let gravy boil.

SERVES 4

This recipe works well with beef or pork tenderloin.

Gourmet Venison Stew

3 pounds venison stew meat

MARINADE:
2 medium onions, thinly sliced
1 carrot
2 stalks celery
1 garlic clove
1 teaspoon salt
¼ teaspoon thyme
2 bay leaves
12 black peppercorns
2 cloves
2 cups red wine
½ cup salad oil

STEW:
Faggot of 2 stalks celery, 4 sprigs parsley, ½ bay leaf, 1 sprig thyme
½ cup salad oil
1 cup diced salt pork
12-15 small onions or 1 large onion, chunked
2 carrots, cut on diagonal into 1-inch chunks
2 Tablespoons brown sugar
½ pound fresh mushrooms, sliced
2 Tablespoons flour
1 garlic clove, mashed
⅔ cup red wine
Water
Salt and pepper to taste
Cooked rice

Trim fat from venison and cut into 1 to 2-inch cubes.
MARINADE: Mix and pour marinade over stew meat. Refrigerate at least 24 hours. After 24 hours, remove meat from marinade and dry on paper towels. Strain marinade and *save.*
STEW: Prepare faggot by tying together celery, parsley, bay leaf and thyme. Set aside to add later. In hot oil brown salt pork; add onions. When partially browned, add carrots and sprinkle with brown sugar. Cook until browned. Remove from pan, drain, and set aside. Sauté mushrooms in same pan. When brown, remove, drain, and set aside. Using same pan, brown stew meat. Sprinkle with flour and cook until flour is browned. Add garlic, wine, faggot, reserved marinade, and water to cover meat. Simmer 1 hour until tender. Add the reserved salt pork, onions, carrots, and mushrooms and cook 40 minutes longer. Remove faggot. Season to taste with salt and pepper. Serve over rice.

SERVES 8-1

Venison Shanks with Herbs

4 venison shanks (about 2½ pounds)
2 Tablespoons butter
1½ cups water
1 teaspoon salt
¼ cup flour
2 Tablespoons butter, melted
½ cup water
1 garlic clove, crushed
1 Tablespoon parsley
1 Tablespoon marjoram
1 teaspoon basil
Cooked noodles

In a heavy skillet, brown shanks on all sides in 2 Tablespoons butter. Add 1½ cups water and salt. Cook, covered, over low heat for 1 hour. In a small skillet add flour to 2 Tablespoons butter; cook and stir until flour is brown. Stir in ½ cup water until smooth. Add to meat and stir until smooth. Add herbs. Cover and cook slowly 1 more hour until meat is tender. Add more water during cooking if needed to maintain a good gravy. Place shanks on bed of hot cooked noodles. Spoon gravy over them.

SERVES 4

Pot Roast of Bear

4-5 pound rump roast of bear
4 large potatoes, quartered (with or without skins)
8-10 whole baby carrots
6-8 small boiling onions, peeled

MARINADE
1 cup Burgundy wine
½ cup oil
2 garlic cloves, crushed
¼ cup lemon juice
1 bay leaf
1 teaspoon thyme leaves
1 teaspoon salt
½ teaspoon pepper

Prepare meat by removing fat and bone; tie. Make marinade by combining all ingredients of marinade in a leakproof plastic bag large enough to hold meat. Place meat in bag. Force all air out of bag, twist top and tie securely (this eliminates having to turn meat in marinade). Marinate meat 6-8 hours or overnight in refrigerator. Place meat and marinade in covered roasting pan. Roast at 350°F for 30 minutes per pound. Place vegetables in roaster with meat for last hour of cooking. Make gravy from pan juices, if desired, to serve with meat. Arrange vegetables around meat on large serving platter. Spoon some gravy over meat before carving.

SERVES 4-6

Rabbit Grandmother Style
L'Auberge Restaurant

1 rabbit, cut in pieces
Salt and pepper to taste
Flour
Oil
1 onion, diced
1 stick of celery, diced
1 carrot, diced
2 garlic cloves, chopped
½ cup dry red wine
2-3 cups chicken stock
1 bay leaf
Pinch rosemary
(Roux (butter and flour mix)
Salt and pepper to taste
2 bacon slices
1 dozen cooked pearl onions
½ dozen fresh mushrooms, sliced
Chopped parsley

Sprinkle rabbit with salt and pepper, roll in flour, and sauté in oil until golden. Add onion, celery, carrot, and garlic. Sauté 2 more minutes. Drain off oil and add wine, chicken stock, bay leaf, and rosemary. Simmer slowly and place in deep serving dish. Thicken sauce with roux; add additional salt and pepper to taste. Pour over rabbit in serving dish. Sauté bacon, pearl onions, mushrooms, and place on top of cooked rabbit. Sprinkle with chopped parsley.

SERVES 4

Suggested Menu to Accompany Rabbit

SMALL INDIVIDUAL HORS D'OEUVRE PLATE OF: ½ stuffed egg, along with carrot sliced tomato or cucumber salad.
SOUP: Fresh vegetable soup or light creme soup.
ENTRÉE: Rabbit Grandmother Style, mashed potatoes, buttered brussel sprouts.
DESSERT: Caramel custard.

Old-Fashioned Brunswick Stew

1 large rabbit
2-3 squirrels
Hot water
2 teaspoons salt
½ teaspoon pepper
pound fresh or canned tomatoes, peeled and coarsely diced
cup sliced onion
cup green lima beans
3 medium potatoes, unpeeled, washed and coarsely diced or sliced
1 cup sliced green beans
1 cup fresh or frozen chopped okra
1 cup fresh, frozen or canned corn
Salt and pepper to taste
Garlic powder to taste

In a large kettle cover rabbit and squirrels with hot water. Bring to boil, reduce heat, and simmer until meat is falling off the bones (1-1½ hours). Test by pulling leg: when bone slips out, meat is done. Remove meat from broth and bone. Return meat to pot and add 2 teaspoons salt and ½ teaspoon pepper. Add tomatoes, onion, lima beans, potatoes, and green beans. Simmer until potatoes are done. Add okra and corn. Simmer 5 minutes. Correct seasoning with salt, pepper, and garlic powder. Simmer 5 minutes. Serve hot in bowls with warm buttered bread.

SERVES 6-8

VARIATION: May substitute 1 large cut up stewing chicken for the squirrels and rabbit, but less cooking time is required.

Dressed Roast Pheasant

1 pheasant
12 mushrooms
2 Tablespoons butter
Salt and pepper
4 bacon strips
½ cup brandy

Clean and wash pheasant; place in roasting pan. Chop mushrooms. Sauté in butter and season to taste. Stuff bird with the sautéed mushrooms and butter. Cover breast with bacon. Roast in moderate oven, 350°F, for 40-50 minutes, basting regularly with brandy to keep moist.

SERVES 2-3

Plum-Glazed Wild Duck

2 medium ducks, or 4 small ones
Salt and pepper
Poultry seasoning
1 plus cups water, divided
1 Tablespoon cornstarch

GLAZE:
1 10-ounce jar plum preserves
½ cup frozen orange juice concentrate, thawed
1 Tablespoon vinegar
½ teaspoon Worcestershire sauce
1 Tablespoon brown sugar

Split ducks in half front to back. (If using 4 small ducks, split down back anc butterfly.) Season birds to taste with salt and pepper. Sprinkle with poultry seasoning. Place split-side down on rack in roasting pan. Prick in several places to allow grease to escape. Roast in 350°F oven 20 minutes.

GLAZE: While birds are roasting, combine glaze ingredients in a small pan Heat until preserves melt and sugar dissolves. When birds are done, remove them from oven and place in a baking dish. Spoon glaze over birds. Return tc oven. Baste 2 more times (every 10 minutes) and continue baking until mea tests done, approximately 25-40 more minutes. To serve: Remove birds to serv ing dish and deglaze pan by adding small amount of water to pan and scraping bottom. Then dissolve cornstarch in 1 cup of water and add to the juices in the pan. Heat until boiling and sauce is clear. Serve sauce with birds.

SERVES 4

Anderson Ducks

4-6 wild ducks
Celery pieces with tops (approximately 2 stalks)
Shortening
Salt

Clean, pick, and singe wild ducks. Do not skin. Preheat oven to 375°F. Stu cavity of ducks with lots of celery pieces. Heavily coat skin all over wit shortening. Heavily salt the ducks. Place in 9 × 13-inch baking pan (broiler pa or turkey pan can be used for larger numbers). Bake 50 minutes for 4-6 duck If serving large number of ducks, bake 1 hour. Cut in half with game shears c serve whole. Discard celery stuffing. *Do not use;* it is only to cut wild taste. Th ducks should be moist and juicy.

SERVES

Roast Duck

Vild duck
alt to taste
unpeeled apple per duck
peeled medium onion per duck
1 bacon strip per duck
1 orange slice per duck
1 maraschino cherry per duck

inse ducks well. Sprinkle inside cavity with salt. Place apple and wedge of nion in cavity. Place a strip of bacon over each duck. Roast in a roasting pan, overed with foil. Start at 350°F for 2 hours. Then reduce to 325°F for 2 more ours. Check occasionally to see if ducks are sticking; if necessary add water to an. Remove foil if ducks are not adequately browning during last ½ hour. Garish with an orange slice and maraschino cherry stuck with toothpick on reast of duck.

SERVES 1 duck per person

ashions on the Overland Trail to Oregon were a matter of practicality. Women arted out the journey wearing the popular long dresses of lindsey-woolsey, ashioned with tight long sleeves, sloping shoulders and layers of flannel petti-oats over their bloomers. As the trip progressed, many women tossed modesty side and discarded their skirts in favor of less cumbersome, but properly rotective long flannel bloomers.

Vork clothes were the major garments worn by most men crossing the trail. hirts were cut in two T-shaped pieces and hand sewn with openings left for the ead and arms. Pants, also, were often made from two identical pieces, a back nd a front sewn together. They were held up with a drawstring or belt, and hen one side began to wear, they were just turned around. Buttons were eldom used because of the difficulty in replacing or purchasing them on the ay west.

inding leather boots was nearly impossible. Most women had abandoned their nkle button shoes on the trail in favor of the more comfortable Indian lace-up oots. Moccasins, out of necessity, became the normal footwear for many of the arly settlers. They were readily available from the Indians where were willing trade for goods brought west by the travelers.

Stir-Fried Wild Duck

Breasts of wild duck
1½-2 cups water
2 teaspoons salt
2 teaspoons soda
Kikkoman teriyaki sauce
2-4Tablespoons oil, divided
Fresh vegetables of your choice (suggest celery, onion, carrots, mushrooms)
Cooked rice

Pull the breasts off of the wild duck. Wash and soak in 1½-2 cups water with salt and soda for 20 minutes to ½ hour. Rinse. Dice the duck into pieces about ½-inch square and marinate in Kikkoman teriyaki sauce to cover for 1½-3 hours. Remove from marinade and dry on paper towels; fry quickly in 1-2 Tablespoons oil in hot wok or pan. Remove; clean pan or wok and add 1-2 Tablespoons oil and stir fry fresh vegetables cut into bite-size pieces. When done, add the duck, toss to warm and serve over rice.

SERVES: 1 medium duck breast per person

Wild Duck Breast

1 onion, cut in wedges
3 large celery stalks, sliced diagonally
2 Tablespoons olive oil
2 Tablespoons butter
4 duck breasts, boned, skinned and cut into 1 × ½-inch pieces
3 heaping Tablespoons sesame seeds, divided
½-1 Tablespoon curry, divided
Salt and pepper to taste

In large pan sauté onion and celery in oil and butter until fragrant. Add duck pieces and brown one side, seasoning with ½ sesame seeds and curry, salt, and pepper. Turn duck pieces; brown, and season other side. Cover. Simmer about 7 minutes. Duck is best not too well done.

SERVES

Champagne Peachy Duck

2 medium or 4 small wild ducks
Salt and pepper to taste
1 teaspoon poultry seasoning
1 teaspoon ground ginger
Water
1 10-ounce jar peach preserves
1 cup champagne or dry sparkling wine
8 peach halves (fresh or canned)
8 1-inch pieces candied ginger
Cooked wild rice

Split ducks in half back to front (butterfly small ducks by splitting down back). Season to taste with salt and pepper; sprinkle each bird with poultry seasoning and ginger. Prick skin to permit grease to escape. Broil on a rack until juices run clear when meat is pierced (about ½ hour). Remove from oven. Keep birds warm. Deglaze pan by adding small about of water. Scrape pan drippings into saucepan. Add preserves and stir until they melt. Add the champagne. Cook over medium heat until liquid is reduced by one third. Place birds skin-side up in a baking dish. Spoon sauce over birds and place peach halves around birds. Place 1 piece of ginger in the cavity of each peach. Bake at 350°F for 20 minutes or until desired doneness. Baste birds and fruit after 10 minutes. Serve with wild rice, and of course champagne!

SERVES 4

VARIATION: Remove breasts from bird. Broil with a bacon strip laid over top of each, then follow recipe as for whole duck.

An old pioneer remembers his first years in the Oregon country: "It wasn't so bad. There was venison, fish, wild game: We had plenty of berries. Our principal dish was boiled wheat or hominy and milk and side bacon was used for seasoning. The Indians were friendly. They taught us a lot."

Oregon: End of the Trail, 1951

DESSERTS

Elizabeth F. Gough

Three-Layer Fudge Brownies

FIRST LAYER
2 1-ounce squares unsweetened chocolate
½ cup butter
2 eggs
1 cup granulated sugar
½ cup sifted cake flour
½ teaspoon baking powder
1 teaspoon vanilla
1 cup walnuts, broken

SECOND LAYER
1 cup powdered sugar
⅓ cup butter
½ cup cream

THIRD LAYER:
1 Tablespoon butter
2 1-ounce squares unsweetened chocolate

FIRST LAYER: Melt together chocolate and butter over warm water. Set aside to cool. Beat eggs well, then add sugar slowly. Gradually add the cooled chocolate and butter mixture. Blend in flour, baking powder, vanilla, and walnuts. Pour into a buttered 8 × 8 × 2-inch pan and bake at 350°F for 25 minutes. Cool.

SECOND LAYER: Combine in a saucepan powdered sugar, butter, and cream. Cook to soft ball stage (235°F), stirring occasionally. Spread while hot on cooled brownies.

THIRD LAYER: Melt butter and chocolate together; spread while hot on cooled second layer. Refrigerate 1-2 hours. Cut into squares and serve.

YIELD: 16 2-inch squares

Jeanie's Chocolate-Lovers Brownies

1 cup butter
1 cup granulated sugar
4 eggs
½ teaspoon salt
½ teaspoon baking powder
1 cup flour
1 teaspoon vanilla
1 16-ounce can Hershey's chocolate syrup

FROSTING:
1 cup granulated sugar
¼ cup milk
2 Tablespoons butter
1 6-ounce package Nestle's chocolate chips
1 teaspoon vanilla
½ cup chopped walnuts or pecans

Cream butter and sugar; add eggs and blend well. Add all dry ingredients until well mixed. Add vanilla and chocolate syrup and mix until blended. Pour into greased and floured 9 × 13-inch pan and bake at 350°F for 35-40 minutes.

FROSTING: Bring sugar, milk, and butter to full boil. Remove from heat. Add chocolate chips and vanilla, beating until chips melt. Add chopped nuts and then spread icing over cooled brownies.

YIELD: 22 2-inch bars

Cream Cheese Brownies

1 4-ounce package German sweet chocolate
3 Tablespoons butter
1 3-ounce package cream cheese
2 Tablespoons butter
¼ cup granulated sugar
1 egg
1 Tablespoon flour
½ teaspoon vanilla
2 eggs
¾ cup granulated sugar
½ teaspoon baking powder
¼ teaspoon salt
½ cup unsifted flour
1 teaspoon vanilla
¼ teaspoon almond extract
½ cup chopped nuts
Prepared cream cheese frosting (optional)

Melt German sweet chocolate and 3 Tablespoons butter over very low heat. Stir, then cool. Cream the package of cream cheese with the 2 Tablespoons butter. Gradually add ¼ cup sugar, beating until fluffy. Blend in 1 egg, 1 Tablespoon flour, and ½ teaspoon vanilla. Set aside. Beat the 2 eggs until lemon colored. Slowly add ¾ cup sugar and beat until thick. Add baking powder, salt, and ½ cup flour. Blend in the chocolate mixture, along with 1 teaspoon vanilla, almond extract, and chopped nuts. Spread half the chocolate batter in a greased 8 or 9-inch pan. Cover with cheese mixture. Spoon remaining chocolate batter over top carefully. Zig-zag knife through batter to marble. Bake at 350°F for 35-40 minutes. Cool. Frost if desired with a cream cheese frosting.

YIELD: 16 2-inch squares

Crunch Fudge Sandwich

1 6-ounce package butterscotch chips
½ cup crunchy peanut butter
4 cups Rice Krispies cereal
1 6-ounce package semi-sweet chocolate chips
½ cup sifted powdered sugar
2 Tablespoons butter, softened
1 Tablespoon water

Melt butterscotch chips and peanut butter over *low* heat, stirring constantly until smooth. Add cereal and stir until well coated. Press *half* of the mixture into buttered 8-inch square pan. Chill while preparing fudge mixture. Melt chocolate chips, powdered sugar, butter, and water over hot water; stir until smooth. Spread chocolate over chilled cereal mixture. Spread remaining cereal mixture evenly over top. Press gently and refrigerate until firm. Cut into squares.

YIELD: 24 1½-inch squares

Fudge Meltaways

- ½ cup butter
- ¼ cup granulated sugar
- 1 1-ounce square unsweetened chocolate, melted
- 1 egg
- 2 cups graham cracker crumbs
- 1 cup coconut
- 1 teaspoon vanilla
- ½ cup chopped walnuts or pecans

FROSTING:

- ¼ cup butter
- 1 Tablespoon cream or milk
- 2 cups powdered sugar
- 1 teaspoon vanilla
- 1½ 1-ounce squares unsweetened chocolate, melted

Cream butter and sugar, blending in melted chocolate. Add egg, mixing well. Add graham cracker crumbs, coconut, vanilla, and nuts. Spread in buttered 8 × 8-inch pan. Chill 1 hour. Then frost.

FROSTING: Melt butter, adding cream. Add powdered sugar and blend well. Add vanilla and chocolate. Frost chilled meltaways. Cut into bars.

YIELD: 16 2-inch bars

Peanut Butter Squares

- ½ cup peanut butter
- ½ cup butter
- ½ cup granulated sugar
- ½ cup brown sugar
- egg
- ½ teaspoon vanilla
- cup flour
- ¼ teaspoon baking soda
- ¼ teaspoon salt
- 1 cup uncooked oats or instant
- 1½ cups chocolate chips (9 ounces)
- ⅔ cup powdered sugar, sifted
- ¼ cup peanut butter
- 3-4 Tablespoons milk

Cream ½ cup peanut butter, butter and granulated and brown sugars together. Add egg and vanilla. Add all dry ingredients, blending well. Spread dough into buttered 9 × 13-inch pan and bake at 350°F for 20-25 minutes. Remove from oven and immediately sprinkle chocolate chips on top. Let stand 5 minutes and then spread chips. Combine powdered sugar with ¼ cup peanut butter and milk, adding enough milk to make a thin consistency. Drizzle over the chocolate layer. Cut into bars for serving.

YIELD: 24 2-inch bars

Carob Peanut Bars

3 cups flour
1 cup margarine
1½ cups brown sugar
½ teaspoon salt

TOPPING:
1 6-ounce package butterscotch chips
1 cup carob chips
½ cup light corn syrup
3 Tablespoons margarine
3 Tablespoons water
3 cups raw peanuts

Cream flour, margarine, brown sugar, and salt together. Press into a 10 × 15-inch cookie sheet and bake at 375°F for 10 minutes.
TOPPING: Melt chips, syrup, margarine, and water together and add raw peanuts. Spread over crust and bake at 375°F for 8-10 minutes. Cool and cut.

YIELD: 70 1½-inch bars

Danish Apple Bars

PASTRY DOUGH:
2½ cups flour
1 teaspoon salt
1 cup shortening
Milk
1 egg yolk

FILLING:
1 cup crushed corn cereal (any kind)
10-12 baking apples
1 cup granulated sugar
1 teaspoon cinnamon
1 egg white

TOPPING:
1 cup powdered sugar
1 Tablespoon milk
½ teaspoon vanilla

PASTRY DOUGH: Combine flour and salt; cut in shortening. Add enough milk to egg yolk to make ⅔ cup liquid; mix well. Stir into flour mixture. On floured surface roll out one half of dough and put in bottom of 10 × 15-inch ungreased jelly-roll pan.
FILLING AND TOPPING: Sprinkle crushed cereal on dough. Peel and slice apples and fill crust. Sprinkle with sugar and cinnamon. Roll remaining dough to 10 × 15 inches and place over apples. Score top and seal edges. Beat egg white until frothy; brush on crust. Bake at 350°F for 45-60 minutes. Combine powdered sugar, milk, and vanilla. Drizzle over warm bars.

YIELD: 3 dozen bars

Hungarian Fruit Squares

3 cups flour
1 cup granulated sugar
1 teaspoon baking powder
½ teaspoon salt
1 cup margarine
2 eggs, beaten
2 teaspoons vanilla
¾ cup apricot, peach, or pineapple preserves (choose one)
¾ cup raspberry, strawberry, or blackberry preserves (choose one)

Sift together dry ingredients. With a pastry blender cut in margarine until pieces are size of peas. Add eggs and vanilla, mix well. Set aside and chill one fourth of dough. Press remaining dough onto bottom and sides of ungreased 10½ × 15½-inch jelly-roll pan. Spread half of the dough in the pan with one of the chosen preserves and the remaining half of the dough with the other chosen preserves. Roll chilled reserved dough on lightly floured board; cut into ½-inch strips. Place strips diagonally across preserves to form lattice. Press around edges to seal. Bake at 325°F 30 minutes. Cool. Cut into squares.

YIELD: 30-40 squares

Nanaimo Bars

FIRST LAYER:
½ cup butter
¼ cup granulated sugar
1 egg
5 Tablespoons cocoa
1 teaspoon vanilla
2 cups graham cracker crumbs
cup coconut
½ cup chopped walnuts

SECOND LAYER:
½ cup butter, softened
3 Tablespoons milk
2 Tablespoons instant vanilla pudding
2 cups powdered sugar

THIRD LAYER:
4 1-ounce squares semi-sweet chocolate or 1 6-ounce package chocolate chips

FIRST LAYER: Mix butter, sugar, egg, cocoa, and vanilla over hot water until it resembles custard. Add the crumbs, coconut, and walnuts. Press into a 9 × 9-inch square pan. Cool.
SECOND LAYER: Cream butter, milk, and pudding together, then blend in powdered sugar. Spread over first layer and let stand for 15 minutes.
THIRD LAYER: Melt chocolate and spread over second layer. Cut into squares.

YIELD: 18 1½-inch bars

Macadamia Nut Bars

CRUST:
½ cup butter
1 cup flour
¼ cup granulated sugar
2 Tablespoons flour
½ teaspoon salt
¼ teaspoon baking powder
1 teaspoon vanilla

FILLING:
2 eggs
1½ cups brown sugar
1 cup coarsely chopped Macadamia nuts
½ cup coconut

FROSTING:
2 Tablespoons butter, melted
1¼ cups powdered sugar
2 Tablespoons evaporated or condensed milk

CRUST: Cut butter into flour and sugar with pastry blender, or knives. Press dough into a 9 × 13-inch pan and bake 20 minutes at 350°F. Cool.
FILLING: Mix eggs, brown sugar, nuts, coconut, flour, salt, baking powder, and vanilla together thoroughly and pour over the cooled crust. Bake 20 minutes at 350°F. Cool.
FROSTING: Combine butter, powdered sugar, and milk together. Spread evenly over cooled filling. Cut into squares.

YIELD: 24 2-inch bars

Granola Bars

¾ cup butter or margarine
½ cup brown sugar
½ cup honey
1 teaspoon vanilla
½ teaspoon salt
4½ cups granola-type cereal
⅔ cup chopped nuts, coconut, or sunflower seeds (optional)

In a 3-quart pan melt butter, then add brown sugar, honey, vanilla, and salt stir until blended. Stir in granola and desired nuts, coconut, or sunflower seeds Turn into a well-greased 10 × 15-inch pan. With your hands, press in firmly to form an even layer. Bake uncovered in a 400°F oven until browned and bubbly, about 10-15 minutes. Cool slightly and cut into bars while still warm.

YIELD: 32 bars

Seven-Layer Bars

½ cup butter
1½ cups graham cracker crumbs
1 6-ounce package butterscotch chips
1 6-ounce package chocolate chips
1 7-ounce package shredded coconut
1 cup chopped nuts
1 14-ounce can Eagle Brand milk

Melt butter in a 10½ × 15½-inch pan. Sprinkle graham cracker crumbs over butter and layer butterscotch and chocolate chips over crumbs. Sprinkle coconut and nuts over chips. Pour milk over this mixture and bake at 350°F for 25 minutes. Cut into squares.

YIELD: 32 squares

Pecan Petite Bars

CRUST:
2 cups flour
1 teaspoon baking powder
Dash salt
⅓ cup packed brown sugar
½ cup butter

FILLING:
eggs
½ cup packed brown sugar
⅓ cup flour
1 teaspoon salt
1½ cups dark corn syrup
2 teaspoons vanilla extract
1 cup chopped pecans

ICING:
⅛ cup butter, softened
1 cup powdered sugar
⅛ teaspoon maple extract
Milk

CRUST: Sift together flour, baking powder, and salt. Stir in brown sugar. Cut in butter with pastry blender until well mixed. (It will seem very dry.) Pat evenly into bottom of well-buttered 9 × 13-inch pan and bake at 325°F for 12 minutes.
FILLING: Beat eggs until well mixed but not too light. Add brown sugar, flour, and salt. Blend. Add corn syrup and vanilla. Mix well. Pour over the partly baked crust and sprinkle with pecans. Return to 325°F oven and bake 40-45 minutes. Cut into squares while still warm.
ICING: Blend butter, powdered sugar, maple extract and enough milk to make thin consistency. Drizzle over top of cooled cookies.

YIELD: 24 2-inch bars

VARIATION: Instead of icing, sprinkle with powdered sugar.

Cinnamon-Frosted Raisin Bar

½ cup granulated sugar
1 Tablespoon cornstarch
1 cup water
2 cups raisins
½ cup butter or margarine
1 cup brown sugar
1½ cups sifted flour
½ teaspoon baking soda
½ teaspoon salt
1½ cups quick-cooking oats
1 Tablespoon water

CINNAMON ICING:
1 cup powdered sugar
¼ teaspoon cinnamon
1 Tablespoon milk (approximately)

Mix the sugar and cornstarch together in a saucepan. Add the water and raisins and cook over medium heat until the sauce is thick and clear. Set aside. Cream together butter and brown sugar. Sift together the flour, soda, and salt; add to the butter mixture along with the quick-cooking oats. Mix until crumbly. Firmly press half of this mixture into a 9 × 13-inch (or 7 × 11-inch) pan, depending on desired thickness of bar. Top with the raisin mixture. Stir 1 Tablespoon of water into the remaining half of the crumbs and spoon onto the filling. Spread smooth. Bake at 350°F for 35 minutes. Cut into bars while still warm.
ICING: Mix all icing ingredients together and drizzle over warm bars.

YIELD: 15-20 bars

Graham Cracker Bars

12 whole graham cracker squares, divided (approximately)
1 cup butter or margarine
1 cup granulated sugar
1 egg, slightly beaten
½ cup milk
¾ cup coconut
1 cup chopped walnuts
1 cup graham cracker crumbs

FROSTING:
½ cube butter or margarine, softened
2 cups powdered sugar
1 teaspoon vanilla
Milk or half and half

Place a layer of whole graham crackers on the bottom of a 9 × 13-inch pan Melt butter in saucepan and add the sugar, egg, and milk. Cook, stirring until the mixture comes to a full boil. Add the coconut, walnuts, and graham cracker crumbs. Pour over graham cracker crust. Add another layer of whole graham crackers.
FROSTING: Combine butter, powdered sugar, vanilla, and enough milk to make frosting spreadable. Frost top of bars. Refrigerate until cool. Cut into squares.

YIELD: 20 2-inch squares

Molasses Sugar Cookies

½ cups shortening	4 cups sifted flour
cups granulated sugar	1½ teaspoons cloves
cup molasses	2 teaspoons ginger
eggs	4 teaspoons cinnamon
teaspoons baking soda	1 teaspoon salt
	Granulated sugar

elt shortening and let cool. Add next nine ingredients and stir well. Chill. ɔrm into small balls. Place on ungreased cookie sheet, 2 inches apart. Sprinkle ılls with sugar, but do not flatten. Bake at 375°F for 8-10 minutes. Cool slight-, remove from cookie sheet.

YIELD: 8 dozen cookies

Date Chews

cup chopped dates	½ teaspoon baking soda
cup chopped walnuts	1 teaspoon cream of tartar
cup brown sugar	1 egg, beaten
Tablespoons flour	Granulated sugar

ombine all ingredients except granulated sugar. Press into greased 9 × 9-inch ıking pan. Bake at 350°F for 20 minutes. Let cool just enough to handle, then :oop out by teaspoonfuls, form into balls, and roll in sugar.

YIELD: 30 balls

Chocolate Snappers

½ cups shortening	3½ cups flour
cups granulated sugar	2 teaspoons baking soda
eggs	1 teaspoon cinnamon
cup light corn syrup	½ teaspoon salt
1-ounce squares unsweetened baking chocolate, melted	1½ teaspoons vanilla
	Granulated sugar

ix thoroughly shortening, sugar, and eggs. Add corn syrup and chocolate. lend well. Stir in flour, soda, cinnamon, salt, and vanilla. Chill dough. Roll into inch balls and then in sugar. Bake at 350°F for 12 minutes. Leave on pan to ıll before removing.

YIELD: 6 dozen cookies

Monster Cookies

6 eggs
1 pound brown sugar
1½ teaspoons vanilla
2 cups granulated sugar
4 teaspoons baking soda
½ pound butter
1½ pounds peanut butter (either style)
9 cups oatmeal
½ pound chocolate chips
½ pound M&Ms
¼ cup chopped nuts

Combine all ingredients. Use an ice cream scoop to form balls of dough, the gently flatten dough on cookie sheet. Bake at 350°F for 10-12 minutes.

YIELD: 8 doze

SUGGESTION: This recipe is great to use for bake sales and large gatherings.

Snowflake Cookies

½ cup crunchy peanut butter
¼ cup butter, softened
1 cup powdered sugar
½ cup chopped walnuts
1½ cups Rice Krispies

FROSTING:
1 cup powdered sugar
3 Tablespoons milk (approximately)
½ teaspoon vanilla
Flaked coconut

Cream together peanut butter, butter, and sugar. Add walnuts and Ric Krispies, mix well. Form into balls and put into refrigerator for a short time. FROSTING: Combine powdered sugar, milk, and vanilla. Roll balls in frostir and then in coconut.

YIELD: 2 dozen cooki

Lemon Cookies

1 18½-ounce package lemon cake mix with pudding
2 cups frozen whipped topping, thawed
1 egg
Sifted powdered sugar

Combine cake mix, whipped topping, and egg in large bowl. Stir until mixe Drop by teaspoonfuls into powdered sugar, rolling to coat. Place 1½ inch apart on greased cookie sheet. Bake at 350°F for 10-15 minutes, until lig golden brown. Remove from cookie sheet and cool.

YIELD: 4 dozen cooki

NOTE: An *easy,* chewy cookie.

Sugar Cookies

cup butter
cup powdered sugar
cup granulated sugar
cup oil
eggs
⅓ cups flour, sifted
1 teaspoon baking soda
1 teaspoon salt
1 teaspoon cream of tartar
½ teaspoon lemon extract
½ teaspoon orange extract
Butter
Granulated sugar

ream together butter and sugars. Add oil and mix well. Beat in eggs, one at a me. Sift dry ingredients together and combine with butter mixture. Add exacts and mix well. Chill. Roll into small balls with hands, and place about 2 iches apart on ungreased cookie sheet. Press down with bottom of small glass. ;rease bottom of glass with butter and dip into granulated sugar.) Bake in 25°F oven for 10 minutes.

YIELD: 6 dozen

Egg Nog Sugar Cookies

cup margarine and butter (mixed)
teaspoon salt
teaspoon grated lemon rind
teaspoon nutmeg
cup granulated sugar
eggs
Tablespoons milk
½ cups flour, sifted
½ teaspoon baking soda
1 teaspoon baking powder

BUTTER FROSTING:
¼ pound butter (not margarine)
1 pound powdered sugar, sifted
1 teaspoon vanilla
Milk
Nutmeg
Cherries (optional)

x margarine and butter, salt, lemon rind, nutmeg, sugar, eggs, and milk gether well. Add sifted dry ingredients. Drop by teaspoonfuls on greased okie sheet. Bake at 350°F 8-10 minutes until golden brown.

OSTING: Heat butter to melt, add powdered sugar, vanilla, and enough milk til it is of spreading consistency. When cookies are cool, frost with butter osting and sprinkle with *small* amount of nutmeg. May top with cherry.

YIELD: 4 dozen

Coconut Cookies

2 cups flour
3 teaspoons baking powder
1 teaspoon baking soda
½ teaspoon salt
1 cup shortening or margarine
1 cup granulated sugar
1 cup brown sugar
2 eggs
1 teaspoon vanilla
2 cups one-minute oatmeal
1 cup coconut
1 cup cornflakes

Sift dry ingredients together, then set aside. In a large bowl cream togethe shortening, sugars, and eggs. Combine flour and sugar mixtures. Blend. Ad vanilla, oatmeal, coconut, and cornflakes. Mix well. Drop from spoon ont cookie sheet and bake at 375°F for 10-12 minutes.

YIELD: 5 dozen cooki

Honey was used for sore throats; bark from chittum and cascara trees was us as a laxative; onions were chopped fine and wrapped in a wool cloth, th heated and applied to the chest to relieve a cold or croup; a few drops kerosene were added to sugar for a cold; a "spring tonic" was made fro sulphur and molasses; smoked bacon rind was rubbed on the body to rep mosquitoes; sunflower seeds, onions, and sugar were boiled together to make cough medicine.

Norwegian Lace Cookies

½ cup butter or margarine
1½ cups regular rolled oats
1 egg
⅔ cup granulated sugar
1 teaspoon baking powder
1 Tablespoon flour

Melt butter in small saucepan and pour over oatmeal in bowl. Beat egg un light, then beat in sugar. Add baking powder and flour, blending well. Combi with oatmeal and butter mixture. Drop by teaspoonfuls onto a greased a floured cookie sheet 2-3 inches apart. Bake in a 350°F oven for approximate 8 minutes, or until slightly brown around edges. Cool 1 minute before moving from pan. Note: After several batches, you will probably have regrease and reflour the cookie sheets.

YIELD: 2½ dozen cook

Rice Krispy Cookies

cup butter
cup granulated sugar
egg yolks
½ cups flour
teaspoon salt
¼ teaspoon baking powder
1 teaspoon vanilla
¾ cup quick-cooking oatmeal
¾ cup Rice Krispies

eat the butter, sugar, and egg yolks until creamy. Sift together the flour, salt, nd baking powder, then add to butter mixture along with the vanilla. Blend in atmeal and Rice Krispies. Form cookie dough into 1-inch balls and flatten on ngreased cookie sheet. Bake at 350°F until they start to brown, about 10 inutes.

YIELD: 3 dozen

Peanut Blossoms

cup granulated sugar
cup brown sugar
cup butter or margarine
cup creamy peanut butter
cup milk
eggs
2 teaspoons vanilla
3½ cups sifted flour
2 teaspoons baking soda
1 teaspoon salt
Granulated Sugar
2 10-ounce packages milk chocolate candy kisses

ream sugars, butter, and peanut butter together. Beat in milk, eggs, and anilla. Sift flour, soda, and salt together and stir into egg mixture. Shape into alls, roll in sugar, and place on ungreased baking sheet. Bake at 375°F for 10 inutes. Remove from oven and immediately press a chocolate candy into ach.

YIELD: 7 dozen

quivalents

saltspoonsful of liquid	=	*1 teaspoonful*
wineglassful	=	*4 Tablespoons or ¼ cup*
gills	=	*1 cup*
pound of eggs	=	*9 large or 10 medium*
cups solid butter	=	*1 pound*
utter the size of an egg	=	*¼ cup or 2 ounces*

wentieth Century Cookbook, 1906

Hood River Fresh Apple Cake

2 cups granulated sugar
1 cup shortening
2 eggs
2 cups flour
2 teaspoons baking soda
1 teaspoon cinnamon
½ teaspoon salt
4 cups chopped cooking apples
1 cup chopped nuts

SAUCE:
½ cup packed brown sugar
½ cup granulated sugar
½ cup margarine
½ cup whipping cream
½ teaspoon vanilla

Cream together sugar, shortening, and eggs. Sift the dry ingredients and add t mixture. Add chopped apples and nuts. Bake in a greased 9 × 13-inch pan fc 45 minutes at 350°F.
SAUCE: In a small pan combine sugars, margarine, and whipping cream. Brin mixture to a boil, and then add vanilla. Pour sauce over individual servings c cake. It may be warm or cold, but is particularly good *warm*.

SERVES 1

VARIATION: Instead of pouring sauce over servings of cake, sprinkle powdere sugar on top of cake or cut cake into 1½-inch squares and roll in powdere sugar.

Fresh Apple Bundt Cake

3 cups flour
1 teaspoon salt
1 teaspoon baking soda
1 cup vegetable oil
2 cups granulated sugar
2 eggs
3 cups diced raw cooking apples
1 teaspoon vanilla
1 cup chopped nuts

TOPPING:
½ cup melted butter
¼ cup granulated sugar
1 Tablespoon light corn syrup
1 teaspoon vanilla
Powdered sugar (optional)

Sift together the flour, salt, and soda. Add the rest of the ingredients and m together until well blended. Pour into a greased and floured tube pan. Bake f 1 hour and 15 minutes at 350°F.
TOPPING: Mix the topping ingredients together until blended. Then pour tc ping over hot cake in pan, letting it drizzle down sides. Let cake cool about hour before turning out of pan. If desired, dust the top with powdered sugar.

SERVES 10

'he first apple trees grown in Oregon were started from seeds given to a sea aptain at a dinner in London. He put the seeds in his pocket and forgot them ntil after he had arrived in Oregon. Upon discovering the seeds, he planted 1em and carefully nurtured the young trees until they produced fruit.

Mom's Carrot Cake

cups sugar
eggs
cup cooking oil
cups flour
teaspoons baking soda
teaspoons cinnamon
teaspoon salt
teaspoons vanilla
cups grated carrots
cup chopped nuts
½ cup raisins

FROSTING:
1 8-ounce package cream cheese, softened
½ cup butter or margarine
2 cups powdered sugar
Lemon juice or milk as needed
1 cup chopped nuts

ix together sugar and eggs; add the oil and beat well. Add the dry ingredients the above mixture and beat again. Add the vanilla, carrots, nuts, and raisins mixture and mix well. Pour mixture into three 9-inch greased cake pans and ke 25-30 minutes at 350°F. Let cool and then frost.

ROSTING: Mix together cream cheese, margarine, and powdered sugar. If too iff, add lemon juice or milk until spreading consistency is obtained. Add nuts the mixture and frost cake.

SERVES 8

1847 Henderson Lewelling brought cuttings from pear trees overland with m, planting some of the first pear trees in Oregon. About the same time W.L. olmes was planting fruit trees in the Mt. Pleasant area. By the middle 1850s, regon had many thriving young fruit nurseries that were well stocked with any varieties of pears, apples and peaches.

Cherry Torte

1¼ cups granulated sugar
1 cup flour
1 teaspoon baking soda
1 teaspoon cinnamon
½ teaspoon salt (optional)
½ cup walnuts
1 egg, well beaten
1 Tablespoon butter, melted
2 cups sour cherries, drained (save juice for sauce)
Whipped cream, sweetened

SAUCE:
1 cup cherry juice (drained from cherries)
1 Tablespoon butter, melted
½ cup granulated sugar
1 Tablespoon cornstarch
½ teaspoon salt
Red food color

Combine all dry ingredients and nuts; then add the egg and butter. Fold in th cherries last, being careful not to crush. Bake at 350°F for 30 minutes in an × 8- inch Pyrex dish.
SAUCE: Combine cherry juice, butter, sugar, cornstarch, and salt as for a whi sauce; cook until slightly thick. Add red food coloring so it is a nice red colo Slice cake in squares, put whipped cream over top of cake and pour th thickened sauce over the whipped cream.

SERVES

NOTE: Very festive and soooo good!

Mother's Potato Cake

2 cups granulated sugar
⅔ cup shortening
3 eggs
1 cup mashed potatoes, cooled
½ cup dry cocoa
½ cup milk
2 cups flour
2 teaspoons baking powder
1 teaspoon cinnamon
1 teaspoon nutmeg
½ teaspoon salt
1 cup chopped walnuts

Cream together the sugar, shortening and eggs; add potatoes, cocoa, and mil Blend together the dry ingredients and add to potato mixture. Fold in walnu Grease a 9 × 13-inch pan, and pour in mixture; bake at 350°F for appro imately 25-35 minutes.

SERVES

Spicy Prune Cake

1 teaspoon baking soda
1 teaspoon salt
1 teaspoon nutmeg
1 teaspoon cinnamon
¼ teaspoon allspice
2 cups flour
2 cups granulated sugar
1 cup cooking oil
3 eggs
1 teaspoon vanilla
1 cup buttermilk
1 cup chopped cooked prunes
1 cup chopped walnuts

TOPPING:
½ cup granulated sugar
½ cup butter or margarine
½ cup buttermilk
½ teaspoon baking soda

Sift together the soda, salt, spices, and flour; set aside. Cream together the sugar and oil. Add the eggs, vanilla, and buttermilk; beat until mixture is smooth. Stir in the dry ingredients, prunes, and nuts and beat until smooth. Bake in a greased and floured 9 × 13-inch pan at 350°F for 40-45 minutes.
TOPPING: While cake is baking, combine the ingredients for topping in a sauce pan. Bring ingredients to a rolling boil. When cake is finished baking and while still hot, pierce the top of cake with a fork and spoon topping over cake until all is absorbed. Leave cake in pan.

SERVES 12

Shortcut Bundt Cake

18½-ounce package lemon cake mix
3-ounce package lemon or vanilla pudding
eggs
cup vegetable oil
cup water

GLAZE:
3-5 Tablespoons lemon juice
1½ cups powdered sugar

CREAMY BROWN SUGAR:
1 pint sour cream
⅓ cup packed brown sugar
½ cup fresh or frozen blueberries

rease and flour bundt pan or angel food pan. Mix together cake mix, pudding, ggs, oil, and water in a large bowl. Beat with mixer at medium speed for 2-3 inutes, scraping bottom and sides of bowl with spatula. Pour into prepared an, and bake at 350°F for 35 minutes. Cool on rack for 5-10 minutes before emoving from pan. Frost with glaze and serve with creamy brown sugar.
LAZE: Blend together powdered sugar and lemon juice. Spoon over top and ound sides of cake.
REAMY BROWN SUGAR: Fold sour cream and brown sugar together until oroughly blended. Add blueberries and stir slightly. Serve over a slice of mon cake.

Gooey Chocolate Cake

1 cup buttermilk
1 cup vegetable oil
2 eggs
2 cups flour
2 cups granulated sugar
1 Tablespoon baking soda
1 teaspoon salt
½ cup cocoa
1 cup *strong, hot* coffee

FROSTING:
3-4 1-ounce squares Baker's unsweetened chocolate
3 Tablespoons butter (use real butter for flavor)
1 1-pound box powdered sugar
3-6 Tablespoons strong coffee

Mix together well the buttermilk, oil, and eggs. Set aside. In separate bowl, sift together flour, sugar, soda, and salt. Add cocoa to dry mixture. Combine liquid and dry ingredients and beat well (approximately 2 minutes). Slowly add 1 cup *strong, hot* coffee, beating well. Bake in a greased and floured 9 × 13-inch or 10 × 14-inch Pyrex baking dish at 350°F for 35-40 minutes.
FROSTING: Over low heat melt chocolate and butter or melt in microwave on high for 1½ minutes. (For very dark chocolate frosting, use 4 squares unsweetened chocolate.) Remove from heat and cool slightly. Beat powdered sugar into butter/chocolate mixture. Add 3 Tablespoons of coffee and beat well. Add remaining Tablespoons of coffee in amount necessary to make frosting proper consistency for spreading. When cake has cooled, frost. (Cake may be frosted as a single layer or cut in half and frosted as layer cake.)

SERVES 16

Praline Cake

½ cup butter or margarine
1 pint vanilla ice cream, softened
2 eggs
1½ cups flour
⅔ cup granulated sugar
1 Tablespoon baking powder
½ teaspoon salt
1 cup graham cracker crumbs

TOPPING:
½ cup sour cream or sour half and half
1 cup caramel ice cream topping
½ cup chopped pecans
Ice cream or whipped cream

Melt butter in a 3-quart saucepan; remove from heat. Add ice cream, and the eggs, flour, sugar, baking powder, salt, and cracker crumbs. Mix until smooth. Pour into 9 × 13-inch pan and bake at 350°F for 30-35 minutes.
TOPPING: Combine sour cream and ice cream topping. Pour over warm cake. Top with pecans. Serve with ice cream or whipped cream.

SERVES 1

Chocolate Cookie Sheet Cake

MIXTURE I:
2 cups flour
2 cups granulated sugar
½ teaspoon salt
1 cube margarine, softened
½ cup vegetable oil
4 Tablespoons cocoa
1 cup boiling water

MIXTURE II:
½ cup buttermilk or sour milk (may use milk with 1 Tablespoon vinegar)
½ teaspoon baking soda
2 eggs, beaten
1 teaspoon cinnamon
1 teaspoon vanilla

FROSTING:
1 cube margarine
6 Tablespoons milk
4 Tablespoons cocoa
1 1-pound box powdered sugar
1 teaspoon vanilla
Chopped nuts (optional)

Combine all ingredients for Mixture I and beat well. Then combine and beat Mixture II and add to Mixture I. Blend. Pour into a greased and floured 11 × 17-inch cookie sheet or jelly-roll pan, and bake at 375°F for 18 minutes. During last five minutes of baking time, make frosting and frost cake as soon as removed from oven.

FROSTING: Heat together margarine, milk, and cocoa. Then add sugar and vanilla. Beat well and then frost hot cake. (Frosting will be thin.) Sprinkle with chopped nuts if desired.

SERVES 36

Indian Pound Cake

"Sift a pint of fine yellow Indian (corn) meal and half a pint of wheat flour, and mix them well together. Prepare a nutmeg beaten (grated) and mixed with a tablespoonful of powdered white sugar; and half a pound of fresh butter; adding the spice, with a glass of white wine and a glass of brandy. Having beaten 8 eggs as light as possible, stir them into the butter and sugar a little at a time in turn with the meal. Give the whole a hard stirring; put it into a well-buttered tin pan, and bake it about an hour and a half."

Leslie, Directions for Cookery, 1848

Black Bottom Cupcakes

CREAM CHEESE MIXTURE:
1 8-ounce package cream cheese, softened
1 egg
⅓ cup granulated sugar
⅛ teaspoon salt
6 ounces chocolate chips

CAKE:
1½ cups flour
1 cup granulated sugar
¼ cup cocoa
½ teaspoon salt
1 teaspoon baking soda
1 cup water
⅓ cup cooking oil
1 Tablespoon vinegar
1 teaspoon vanilla
Granulated sugar
Chopped nuts

CREAM CHEESE MIXTURE: Combine cream cheese, egg, sugar, and salt. Beat well, then stir in chocolate chips; set aside.
CAKE: Sift together the dry ingredients. Combine the water, oil, vinegar, and vanilla. Add this to dry ingredients and mix until well combined. Fill paper-lined muffin cups one third full with chocolate cake batter. Top each with a heaping teaspoon of the cream cheese mixture. Sprinkle with sugar and chopped nuts. Bake at 350°F for 30-35 minutes.

SERVES 18

Grandmother's Pound Cake

1 cup shortening or butter
2 cups granulated sugar
2¼ cups sifted all purpose flour
6 eggs
Juice of one lemon
1 teaspoon vanilla
Dash of salt

Use mixer and cream together shortening and sugar. Add flour and eggs alte nately, one at a time to creamed mixture. Add lemon juice, vanilla, and sal Bake 1 hour and 20 minutes in greased and floured angel food cake pan 312°F. Let cool slightly in pan and then turn out on cake rack. Serve plain with the summer fruits.

SERVES 10-

Mile High Cake

18½-ounce package white cake mix
¼-ounce package plain gelatin
cup water
½ pints fresh or frozen berries
½ cup granulated sugar
1 pint whipping cream
2-3 Tablespoons granulated sugar
1 teaspoon vanilla
½ cup sliced fresh berries

ake cake according to the directions for 2 8-inch pans. While cake is baking, oak gelatin in water. Crush 1½ pints berries; add ½ cup sugar and gelatin mixure. Cook together until bubbling (about 10 minutes). Cool cake. With large ronged fork, poke holes in cake, being careful not to go through the bottom f the layers. Pour half of the hot berry liquid into holes. Put cake into efrigerator until liquid sets. Whip cream to form stiff peaks, gradually adding -3 Tablespoons sugar and vanilla. Take one quarter of the whipped cream and dd the remaining half of the cooked berries. Remove cake from pans. Put the ream/berry mixture between the layers. Then use the remaining whipped ream like a frosting and frost the entire cake. Top with ½ cup fresh berries. efrigerate until ready to use.

SERVES 12-16

OTE: Delicious with strawberries. It's like a giant Strawberry Shortcake. It's so asy, and really spectacular.

Egg Nog Refrigerator Cake

cup butter
cups powdered sugar
egg yolks
cup brandy or bourbon
cup slivered almonds, toasted
1 angel food cake (loaf size or *small* round)
Butter
½ pint whipping cream, whipped and sweetened

ream butter and sugar, then beat in egg yolks one at a time. Blend well. Stir brandy and almonds. Cut an angel food cake in about five horizontal slices. n a buttered plate, place a layer of cake and cover top generously with filling ixture, then add another layer of cake, more filling, etc., ending with a layer f cake on top. (Don't put filling on top.) Refrigerate for 24 hours. Just before erving, frost the cake with whipped cream.

SERVES 8-10

Bacardi Rum Cake

1 cup chopped pecans or walnuts
1 18½-ounce package yellow cake mix
1 3¾-ounce package yellow instant vanilla pudding mix
4 eggs
½ cup cold water
½ cup Bacardi dark rum (80 proof)

GLAZE:
¼ pound butter
¼ cup water
1 cup granulated sugar
¼-½ cup Bacardi dark rum (80 proof)

Preheat oven to 325°F. Grease and flour a 10-inch tube or 12-inch bundt pan. Sprinkle the nuts over bottom of pan. Mix next 5 cake ingredients together and pour batter over nuts. Bake 1 hour and cool. Invert on a serving plate.
GLAZE: Melt butter in sauce pan; stir in water and sugar. Boil 5 minutes, stirring constantly. Remove from heat and stir in rum. Prick cake top. Drizzle and smooth prepared glaze evenly over top and sides, allowing cake to absorb glaze. Repeat until glaze is used up.

SERVES 12-1

SUGGESTION: Decorate with whole maraschino cherries and border of sugar frosting or whipped cream. Serve with seedless green grapes dusted with powdered sugar.

Whiskey Pound Cake

1 pound butter
3 cups granulated sugar
8 egg yolks
2 teaspoons vanilla
2 teaspoons almond extract
6 Tablespoons whiskey
3 cups flour
8 egg whites, stiffly beaten
1½ cups pecans, chopped

Cream butter and sugar until fluffy. Add egg yolks one at a time, beating well after each addition. Combine vanilla, almond extract and whiskey; add alternately with flour to creamed mixture. Beat egg whites until stiff and fold into batter. Put one half of the pecans on the bottom of a 10-inch tube pan that has been greased and lined with wax paper. Add all of the batter, and put the remaining nuts on the top of the batter. Bake at 350°F for 1½ hours. This will keep for several days.

SERVES 12-1

Pumpkin Rum Cake

2 16-ounce packages pound cake mix
1 16-ounce can pumpkin
1½ teaspoons pumpkin pie spice

GLAZE:
1 cup granulated sugar
1 cup orange juice
1 2-inch cinnamon stick
¼ cup rum

Prepare pound cake mixes together according to package directions, decreasing water to a total of ⅔ cup and adding the pumpkin and pie spice. Turn into well greased and floured 10-inch fluted tube pan. Bake in 325°F oven 1 hour and 20 minutes or until cake tests done. Cool in pan 10 minutes. Place on serving plate. Using long-tined fork or skewer, punch holes in top of cake at 1-inch intervals.

GLAZE: In saucepan, combine sugar, orange juice and cinnamon stick; bring to boiling. Remove cinnamon and stir in rum. Spoon orange glaze very slowly over cake, a small amount at a time, allowing cake to absorb sauce. Continue until glaze is used. Spoon any glaze that runs onto plate back over cake. Chill until serving time.

SERVES 12-16

Harvey Wallbanger Cake

1 18½-ounce package orange cake mix
1 3¾-ounce package instant vanilla pudding mix
4 eggs
½ cup cooking oil
½ cup orange juice
½ cup Galliano liqueur
2 Tablespoons vodka

GLAZE:
1 cup sifted powdered sugar
1 Tablespoon orange juice
1 Tablespoon Galliano liqueur
1 teaspoon vodka

n a large mixer bowl, combine the cake and the pudding mixes. Add eggs, oil, range juice, Galliano, and vodka. Beat on low speed for 5 minutes, scraping owl frequently. Pour into greased and floured 10-inch fluted tube pan or bundt an. Bake in 350°F oven for 30 minutes. Cool in pan 10 minutes; remove to ack.

LAZE: Combine glaze ingredients and mix well. Then pour glaze over the ake while it is still warm.

SERVES 12-14

An Oregon Cheesecake

1 cup flour, sifted
¼ cup granulated sugar
1 teaspoon grated lemon rind
1 egg yolk
½ cup butter, softened
1 teaspoon vanilla

FILLING:
2½ pounds cream cheese, softened
1¾ cups granulated sugar
3 Tablespoons flour
1½ teaspoons grated orange rind
1½ teaspoons grated lemon rind
¼ teaspoon vanilla
2 egg yolks
5 whole eggs
¼ cup heavy whipping cream, whipped

Mix flour, sugar, and lemon rind; add egg yolk, butter, and vanilla. Blend with fingers. Thinly roll out dough and place approximately half of it on the bottom of a 9-inch spring-form pan without sides. Bake dough circle in oven at 400°F for 5-10 minutes, until dough is slightly colored. Cool dough circle and place sides of spring pan around bottom of pan. Line pan sides with the rest of the dough, sealing bottom with the uncooked side dough.
FILLING: Blend cream cheese, sugar, flour, orange and lemon rind, and vanilla. Add yolks and eggs one at a time, beating throroughly after each addtion. Gently but completely fold in whipped cream. Fill spring-form dough-lined pan and bake at 500°F for 14 minutes. Reduce temperature to 200°F and continue baking for 1 hour or more until filling is completely set and top slightly browned. Remove from oven and cool; refrigerate or freeze.

SERVES 20-25

Quick Cheese Cakes

18 Nabisco vanilla wafers
2 8-ounce packages cream cheese, softened
3 eggs
½ cup granulated sugar

TOPPING:
1 16-ounce package frozen raspberries
⅔ cup granulated sugar
1-1½ Tablespoons cornstarch
1 teaspoon vanilla

Line muffin tins with paper cup liners; place a wafer in the bottom of each. Combine the next four ingredients and fill cups half full with batter. Bake at 375°F for 17-20 minutes. Cool.
TOPPING: Combine all ingredients and cook until thick. Spoon on top of cheese cakes when ready to serve.

SERVES 1

Mom's Cheesecake

3 8-ounce packages cream cheese (room temperature)
5 eggs
1 cup granulated sugar
¼ teaspoon salt
¾ teaspoon almond extract
2 Tablespoons granulated sugar
1½ cups sour cream
½ teaspoon vanilla or lemon extract
Unsweetened chocolate, shaved or grated

Beat cream cheese in electric mixer or with wooden spoon until softened. Add eggs, 1 cup sugar, salt, and almond extract. Beat until smooth and thick. Pour into buttered 9-inch spring-form cake pan. Bake at 325°F 45-50 minutes or until set. Remove from oven and cool in pan on cake rack 20 minutes (top will crack). Mix 2 Tablespoons sugar, sour cream, and vanilla. Pour over cooled cake. Return to oven and bake 10 minutes at 325°F. Cool, then chill in refrigerator. To serve, remove side from pan, put cake on plate, top with shaved or grated chocolate.

SERVES 10-12

Miniature Cheese Cakes

2 8-ounce packages cream cheese, softened
¾ cup granulated sugar
3 eggs, separated
Butter
½ cup graham cracker crumbs
¾ cup sour cream
2½ Tablespoons granulated sugar
1 teaspoon vanilla

Cream together cream cheese and ¾ cup sugar; add slightly beaten egg yolks. Beat egg whites until stiff and fold into cream cheese mixture. Butter 48 miniature muffin tins. Coat with film of crumbs. Fill each cup three quarters full with cream mixture. Bake 15 minutes at 350°F. Remove and cool in tins. Mix sour cream, 2½ Tablespoons sugar, and vanilla. Put a slim teaspoon of this mixture on top of each cake (there is just enough to go around). Bake again 5 minutes at 350°F. May be frozen or refrigerated.

SERVES 24

The pioneers depended on the native wild fruits and berries to add sweetness and pleasure to their often bland diets. The huckleberry, blackberry, Oregon grape, elderberry, and serviceberry provided a refreshing breakfast and many tempting desserts.

White Fruitcake

1 pound butter (not margarine)
2¼ cups granulated sugar
6 egg yolks
2 cups flour
3 ounces lemon extract
1 pound white raisins
¼ pound candied cherries (½ green and ½ red)
¼ pound glazed pineapple
3½ cups chopped pecans (1 pound)
6 egg whites, stiffly beaten
Rum (optional, to taste)

Cream butter and sugar; add egg yolks and blend well. Gradually add flour and lemon. Mix in chopped fruit and nuts. Fold in stiffly beaten egg whites. Bake in wax-paper-lined loaf pan at 225°F for 2-2½ hours. Cool. Tear off paper. Delicious basted with rum. Wrap in cheese cloth and foil and age in refrigerator for one month before serving. Slice thin to serve.

SERVES 15

Christmas Fruitcake

1 14-ounce can Borden's Eagle Brand milk
2 4-ounce boxes ground, shredded coconut
1 1-pound package of assorted fruits (large pieces are best)
1½ cups nuts (whole pieces are best)

Mix the milk with the coconut. Using hands, mix in the assorted fruits and nuts Pour into loaf pan lined with wax paper. Bake in a 300°F oven about 1½ hour or until brown on top. When cool store in refrigerator. Slice servings *very* thin This will keep a long time.

SERVES 15-2

The largest number of settlers who came by the Oregon Trail to the Orego Territory arrived in the 1850s. The population in 1852 was approximatel 13,000. Cholera epidemics along the Trail in 1849, 1850 and 1852 took heav tolls of the would-be settlers, but the promise of gold in the west kept them coming. By the 1860s fewer settlers were coming to Oregon. The completion of the Transcontinental Railroad in the late 1880s provided a speedier and mor comfortable journey.

Old-Fashioned Spiced Apple Pie

FILLING:
4 cups thinly sliced, peeled, and cored apples (a tart, firm variety such as winesap is best)
1 cup granulated sugar
1 teaspoon ground cinnamon
1 teaspoon ground nutmeg
½ teaspoon ground ginger
½ teaspoon ground allspice
¼ teaspoon ground cloves
3 Tablespoons cornstarch or quick-cooking Tapioca
1½ Tablespoons butter

CRUST:
2 cups flour
½ teaspoon salt
⅔ cup shortening (not butter), cool (not necessarily refrigerated)
¼ cup ice water

TOPPING:
¼ cup granulated sugar
1 teaspoon cinnamon

FILLING: Place apples in a large bowl. Sift all ingredients except butter until thoroughly combined. Pour over apples and stir well to coat. Let stand while you make crust (15 minutes). Heat oven to 400°F.

CRUST: Put flour in a medium-size bowl. Sprinkle salt over it. With a fork or pastry blender cut shortening into flour until well blended. Sprinkle ice water over mixture. Stir until just combined. Press mixture down in bowl to form a dry-looking ball. If too dry to stick together, sprinkle with a few drops more ice water. Divide dough into two parts (one third of the dough in one, two thirds of the dough in the other); form into two balls. Using the larger ball, roll dough out on a lightly floured surface to a circle 12 inches in diameter. Spread dough in bottom of 10-inch pie plate. Do not trim edges. Roll out top crust into a rectangle 10 × 12 inches. Cut lengthwise into 1-inch wide strips.

TO ASSEMBLE: Spoon apple mixture into pie shell. Press down well with spoon and make it as level as you can. Dot with 1½ Tablespoons butter. Take 5 strips of crust and lay across top of pie. Use the remaining 5 strips and lay them across the first strips, weaving them into a lattice-work pattern. Moisten the rim of the lower crust and press the ends of the strips to seal them. Roll the excess dough up onto the rim of the pie plate to form a ridge along the edge of the pie. Flute this ridge by pressing your right thumb and index finger on one side of the ridge against your left index finger on the other side of the dough ridge to make a zig-zag design. This ridge of crust also helps to prevent spillovers.

TOPPING: Sprinkle the lattice with the combined topping ingredients. Bake at 400°F for 30-40 minutes or until apples are bubbly and crust is nicely golden.

YIELD: 1 10-inch pie

Blueberry Cream Cheese Pie

½ cup powdered sugar
1 6-ounce package cream cheese, at room temperature
1½-2 cups softened Cool Whip
1 9-inch pie shell, baked, or 1 9-inch graham cracker crust, baked

SAUCE:
1 cup blueberries
⅔ cup water
1 cup granulated sugar
3 Tablespoons cornstarch
⅓ cup water

Blend powdered sugar and cream cheese until smooth. Add Cool Whip and blend all until smooth. Spread in pie shell and cover with slightly cooled blueberry sauce.
SAUCE: Place blueberries and ⅔ cup water in saucepan and simmer for 3 minutes. Mix together sugar and cornstarch, then add ⅓ cup water. Combine this with the blueberries and boil for one minute, stirring constantly. Remove from heat, allow to cool 3-5 minutes. Pour over cream cheese mixture and refrigerate.

YIELD: 8 servings

A delicacy of the early Oregon pioneers was fern pie. It was made from fiddleheads, the tender stalks of young ferns.

Susan's Blueberry Pie

Pastry for 2-crust, 9-inch pie, unbaked
4 cups frozen blueberries
3 Tablespoons flour
1 12-ounce jar pineapple ice cream topping
Butter

Line pie pan with bottom crust. Mix frozen blueberries with flour to coat. Then add pineapple topping and mix. Pour berry mixture into pie shell. Dot filling with butter. Cover with top crust which has slits cut in it. Bake in 400°F oven 35-40 minutes. Serve warm or cold. Can be topped with vanilla ice cream, if desired.

YIELD: 6-8 servings

Rhubarb Custard Pie

Pastry for 2-crust, 10-inch pie, unbaked
4 eggs, beaten
6 Tablespoons flour
⅓ teaspoon salt
¾ teaspoon nutmeg
3 cups granulated sugar
2 Tablespoons granulated sugar
1 Tablespoon flour
6 cups chopped rhubarb (1-inch length pieces)
Butter

Line pie pan with bottom crust. Mix together eggs, 6 Tablespoons flour, salt, nutmeg, and 3 cups sugar. Sprinkle 2 Tablespoons sugar and 1 Tablespoon flour on bottom of prepared crust. Add rhubarb to egg mixture and pour into crust. Dot with butter. Put lattice or regular crust on top and bake at 425°F for 15 minutes; reduce oven to 325°F and bake 45 minutes longer or until set.

YIELD: 10 servings

Strawberry Pie

3 egg whites
½ teaspoon vinegar
¼ teaspoon salt
½ cup granulated sugar
½ teaspoon vanilla
1 9-inch pie shell, baked
2 cups fresh strawberries
⅓ cup granulated sugar
2 Tablespoons cornstarch
½ cup water
Several drops red food coloring
1 cup whipping cream
Sugar (optional)
1 cup fresh strawberries, sliced

Beat egg whites with vinegar and salt until soft peaks form. Gradually add ½ cup sugar and vanilla, beating to stiff peaks. Spread on bottom and sides of baked pie shell. Bake at 325°F for 12 minutes. Let cool. Mash 2 cups of the strawberries. In saucepan blend ⅓ cup sugar and cornstarch. Add water and mashed berries. Cook and stir until mixture thickens and bubbles. Cook for 2 more minutes, then tint with food coloring. Cool slightly. Spread over meringue in pie shell. Chill until set. Whip cream, sweetening with a little sugar, if desired. Spread over pie, decorate with remaining 1 cup berries. Keep refrigerated until ready to serve.

YIELD: 8 servings

Strawberry Cream Cheese Pie

1 1½-ounce envelope whipped topping mix
1 8-ounce package cream cheese
½ cup granulated sugar
1 10-inch graham cracker crust, baked and cooled
1 3-ounce package strawberry flavor gelatin
1 cup boiling water
1-2 pints fresh strawberries, halved and sweetened
Cold water

Prepare whipped topping mix as directed on package. Whip cheese until soft; beat in sugar. Then blend in whipped topping. Pour into baked crust, mounding high at edges. Dissolve gelatin in boiling water. Drain berries, reserving juice, set berries aside. Add enough cold water to reserved juice to make ½ cup. Add liquid to gelatin. Chill until slightly thickened; fold in berries. Pour over top of pie, leaving a narrow rim of cream filling around edge. Chill until gelatin is set, approximately 3 hours.

YIELD: 8-10 servings

Simply Super Pineapple Pie

1 cup flour
1 cup granulated sugar
1 teaspoon salt
½ teaspoon soda
1 egg, slightly beaten
1 20-ounce can crushed pineapple, well drained
3 Tablespoons brown sugar
½ cup shredded coconut
½ cup chopped nuts
Whipped cream or ice cream

In medium-size mixing bowl combine flour, granulated sugar, salt, and soda. Add egg and pineapple; blend. Spread mixture in a well greased 9 or 10-inch pie plate. Combine brown sugar, coconut, and nuts together and sprinkle over pineapple mixture. Bake in a 350°F oven for 45 minutes. Top with whipped cream or ice cream. This is best served slightly warm.

YIELD: 8 servings

Sunny Banana Pie

2 bananas
1 9-inch pie crust, baked
2 cups milk, divided
1 8-ounce package cream cheese, softened
1 5½-ounce package vanilla instant pudding mix
Whipped cream

Slice bananas into baked crust. Add ½ cup milk to cream cheese, mixing well until blended. Add pudding mix and remaining 1½ cups milk. Beat slowly. Pour into crust and refrigerate for at least 1 hour. Serve with whipped cream.

YIELD: 8 servings

Sour Cream Lemon Pie

1 cup granulated sugar
¼ cup cornstarch
3 egg yolks
1 cup milk
¼ cup butter
¼ cup lemon juice
1 Tablespoon grated lemon peel
1 cup sour cream
1 9-inch pie shell, baked
1 cup whipping cream, whipped

Mix sugar and cornstarch together in a saucepan. Add egg yolks, milk, butter, lemon juice, and peel. Cook over medium heat until thick, stirring constantly to avoid scorching. Cool in refrigerator. Stir sour cream into above mixture and pour into baked pie shell. Chill 2 hours. Serve with whipped cream.

YIELD: 8 servings

Lemon Pie

1 8-ounce container Cool Whip
14-ounce can Eagle Brand condensed milk
6-ounce can frozen lemonade, thawed
Juice of 1 lemon
1 9-inch graham cracker crust, baked
Toasted slivered almonds (optional)

Fold together Cool Whip, condensed milk, lemonade, and the lemon juice. Pour into cooled pie crust. Top with optional almonds. Refrigerate pie.

YIELD: 8 servings

Lime Chiffon Pie

1 Tablespoon unflavored gelatin
⅔ cup granulated sugar
¼ teaspoon salt
4 egg yolks
¼ cup water
½ cup fresh lime juice (approximately 3 limes)
3 teaspoons grated lime peel
2-3 drops green food coloring
4 egg whites, at room temperature
½ cup granulated sugar
1 9-inch pie shell, baked

Mix gelatin, ⅔ cup sugar, and salt in top of double boiler. Beat egg yolks, water, and lime juice together; stir into gelatin mixture. Set over boiling water. Thoroughly heat mixture, stirring constantly, and continue cooking 5 minutes to cook egg yolks and dissolve gelatin. Remove from heat and stir in the lime peel and food coloring until blended. Cool. Chill in refrigerator until mixture begins to jell, stirring occasionally. Beat egg whites until frothy. Add the ½ cup sugar gradually, beating well after each addition. Beat until stiff peaks are formed. Fold in the chilled gelatin mixture until thoroughly blended. Turn filling into baked pie shell. Chill until firm.

YIELD: 8 servings

NOTE: This is a very refreshing dessert.

Grasshopper Pie

CRUST:
1¼ cups fine chocolate wafer crumbs
½ cup butter, melted

FILLING:
½ cup milk
20 marshmallows
1 cup whipping cream, whipped
3 Tablespoons creme de cacao
3 Tablespoons creme de menthe
Few drops green food coloring
Whipped cream (optional)
Chocolate curls (optional)

CRUST: Thoroughly blend chocolate wafer crumbs and butter together. Press into a 9-inch pie pan. Chill.
FILLING: Heat milk in double boiler; add marshmallows and stir until melted. Cool thoroughly. Combine whipped cream, creme de cacao, creme de menthe and green food coloring. Fold into cooled marshmallow mixture and pour into chilled pie crust. Chill until firm. May garnish with whipped cream and chocolate curls if desired.

YIELD: 8 servings

Uno Pie

CRUST:
1½ cups ground filberts
3 Tablespoons granulated sugar
½ cup butter, softened

FILLING:
¾ cup granulated sugar
½ cup butter
2 1-ounce squares unsweetened chocolate, melted
1 teaspoon vanilla
2 eggs
Whipped cream, lightly sweetened
Shaved unsweetened chocolate

CRUST: Combine filberts, sugar, and butter together and press into a 9-inch pan. Do not bake.

FILLING: Cream sugar and butter in a small bowl with mixer. Add melted chocolate and vanilla, beating until smooth. Add 1 egg and beat at high speed for 5 minutes. Add second egg and beat an additional 5 minutes. Pour into filbert pie crust. Chill overnight or for several hours. Garnish with whipped cream and shaved chocolate.

YIELD: 8 servings

Eggnog Pie

CRUST:
1¼ cups graham cracker crumbs
¼ cup butter or margarine, softened
¼ cup granulated sugar
¼ teaspoon cinnamon
½ teaspoon nutmeg

FILLING:
1 ¼-ounce envelope unflavored gelatin
¼ cup granulated sugar
¼ teaspoon salt
2 cups prepared eggnog
1 cup whipping cream, whipped
1½ teaspoons vanilla

CRUST: Blend all crust ingredients with a fork. Press into a 9-inch pie plate and bake for 8 minutes at 375°F.

FILLING: Mix gelatin, sugar, and salt. Gradually stir in eggnog. Warm over direct heat until gelatin is dissolved (just below boiling point). Chill until mixture mounds when dropped from a spoon. Fold in whipped cream and vanilla. Heap into pie shell; refrigerate 2-4 hours.

YIELD: 8 servings

Cottage Cheese Pie

1 pint cottage cheese
½ cup granulated sugar
4 eggs
3 Tablespoons butter, softened
¼ cup flour
Pinch of salt
1 teaspoon vanilla
¼ teaspoon nutmeg (optional)
½ cup raisins (optional)
1 8-inch pie shell, unbaked

For a grainy texture: mix first 7 ingredients by hand or in a mixer; add optional nutmeg and raisins and pour into unbaked pie shell. For a smooth texture: combine first 7 ingredients in a food processor or blender and mix until smooth; add optional nutmeg and raisins and pour into unbaked pie shell. Bake for 45 minutes at 350°F.

YIELD: 6 servings

Heavenly Cheese Pie

CRUST:
1½ cups graham cracker crumbs
¼ cup granulated or brown sugar
⅛ teaspoon nutmeg
⅓ cup butter, melted

FILLING:
6 ounces semi-sweet chocolate pieces
1 8-ounce package cream cheese, softened
¾ cup granulated or brown sugar divided
⅛ teaspoon salt
2 eggs, separated
1 cup whipping cream
1 teaspoon vanilla

CRUST: Combine graham cracker crumbs, sugar, nutmeg, and butter; blenc thoroughly. Press mixture into 9-inch pie pan and chill thoroughly.
FILLING: Melt chocolate over hot water (not boiling). Cool about 10 minutes Blend softened cream cheese, ½ cup sugar, and salt. Add egg yolks to crean cheese mixture, one at a time, beating after each addition. Add cooled chocolate Beat egg whites until stiff but not dry. Add ¼ cup sugar gradually to egg whites beating until stiff and glossy. Fold chocolate mixture into meringue. Whip crean until thick and shiny, add vanilla. Fold into chocolate filling. Pour into chilled pie shell. Chill several hours or overnight.

YIELD: 1 9-inch pie

Coffee Toffee Pie

CRUST:
1½ cups chocolate wafer crumbs
¼ cup brown sugar
¼ cup butter or margarine, softened
Few nuts, finely chopped

FIRST LAYER
½ cup butter, softened
¾ cup granulated sugar
1 1-ounce square unsweetened chocolate, melted
2 teaspoons instant coffee
2 eggs

SECOND LAYER:
2 cups cream
2 Tablespoons instant coffee
½ cup powdered sugar
Chocolate curls

CRUST: Mix wafer crumbs, brown sugar, butter, and nuts together. Press mixture into a 9-inch pie pan. Bake at 350°F for 10 minutes. Cool.
FIRST LAYER: In a small bowl beat butter at medium speed until creamy. Gradually add sugar. Beat until light. Mix melted chocolate and instant coffee. When chocolate is cooled, blend into butter mixture. Add 1 egg and beat 5 minutes. Add another egg and beat 5 minutes more. Pour into pie shell and refrigerate overnight.
SECOND LAYER: The next day combine the cream, instant coffee, and powdered sugar. Refrigerate covered for 1 hour. Then whip until stiff. Spread on pie and garnish with chocolate curls. Refrigerate several hours before serving. Remove from refrigerator 5 or 10 minutes before cutting.

YIELD: 8 servings

VARIATION, CRUST:
1 cup flour
¼ cup firmly packed light brown sugar
Dash of salt
1 1-ounce square unsweetened chocolate, grated
¾ cup finely chopped walnuts
⅓ cup shortening
1 teaspoon vanilla
1 Tablespoon water

Place flour, brown sugar, salt, chocolate and nuts in a bowl. Mix in shortening until crumbly. Mix together vanilla and water; drizzle over dry mix, stir with fork until mixed. Press into a 9-inch pie pan and bake 15 minutes at 375°F. Cool.

Heavenly Chocolate Pie

2 egg whites
½ teaspoon vinegar
¼ teaspoon cinnamon
¼ teaspoon salt
¾ cup granulated sugar, divided
1 9-inch pie shell, baked
1 6-ounce package chocolate chips
2 egg yolks
¼ cup water
1 cup whipping cream
½ teaspoon cinnamon

Beat egg whites, vinegar, cinnamon, and salt until stiff, but not dry. Gradually add ½ cup sugar and beat until very stiff. Spread on bottom and sides of baked pie shell. Bake at 325°F for 15-18 minutes until lightly browned. Cool. Melt chips over hot water. Blend in egg yolks and water; stir until smooth. Spread 3 Tablespoons of chocolate mixture on bottom of cooled meringue. Chill remaining chocolate until it begins to thicken. Beat together cream, ¼ cup sugar, and cinnamon until stiff, and spread half of this over chocolate layer in pie shell. Fold remaining chocolate into remaining cream mixture and spread over top of pie. Refrigerate at least 4 hours before serving.

YIELD: 8 servings

Chocolate Velvet Pie

CRUST:
1½ cups chocolate wafer crumbs
⅓ cup margarine, melted

FILLING:
1 8-ounce package cream cheese, softened
½ cup granulated sugar, divided
1 teaspoon vanilla
2 egg yolks
1 6-ounce package chocolate chips, melted
2 egg whites
1 cup whipping cream, whipped
¾ cup chopped pecans

CRUST: Blend wafer crumbs and margarine. Pat into a 9-inch spring form pan and press onto bottom. Bake at 325°F for 10 minutes.
FILLING: To the cream cheese, add ¼ cup sugar and vanilla. Mix well. Beat egg yolks and stir into cream cheese mixture along with melted chocolate chips. Beat egg whites until soft peaks form. Gradually add ¼ cup sugar. Fold into chocolate mixture. Fold whipped cream and pecans into this mixture and pour into crumb crust and freeze.

YIELD: 10-12 servings

Yummy Mocha Pie

CRUST:
6 Tablespoons butter, melted
1½ cups chocolate wafer crumbs

FILLING:
24 marshmallows
½ cup milk
8 1-ounce squares semi-sweet chocolate, or 1½ cups chocolate chips
2 Tablespoons creme de cacao
2 Tablespoons coffee liqueur
1 cup whipping cream, whipped
Grated semi-sweet chocolate

CRUST: Mix butter and wafer crumbs together and press into an 8-inch pie pan. Set aside.

FILLING: Melt marshmallows in milk over low heat. Cool. Melt chocolate over hot water, add liqueurs and pour into marshmallow mixture. Fold in whipped cream and pour into pie shell. Garnish with grated semi-sweet chocolate and freeze.

YIELD: 8-10 servings

Party Pie

egg whites
cup granulated sugar
teaspoon vanilla
teaspoon baking powder
20 round Ritz crackers, broken into small pieces
½ cup chopped walnuts
Whipped cream or Cool Whip
Grated semi-sweet chocolate

Beat egg whites and sugar until stiff. Blend in vanilla and baking powder. Add crackers and walnuts to egg whites and mix. Pour into an ungreased 9-inch pie pan and bake for 30 minutes at 300°F. Cool slightly. Spread with whipped cream and chocolate. Chill.

YIELD: 6 servings

Leila's Pie Crust

cups flour, sifted
½ teaspoons salt
¼ cups shortening
1 egg, beaten
5 Tablespoons water
1 teaspoon vinegar

Sift dry ingredients together. Cut shortening into flour mixture with a pastry blender until consistency of coarse meal. Combine egg, water, and vinegar together and add to dry ingredients. Do not over mix as dough will be heavy. Divide into four equal parts. Wrap in plastic wrap and freeze or use immediately.

YIELD: 4 9-inch crusts

Chocolate Lush

CRUST:
½ cup butter
½ cup chopped or slivered almonds
1 cup flour

FILLING:
1 8-ounce package cream cheese, softened
1 cup powdered sugar
1 cup Cool Whip

TOPPING:
3 cups milk
2 4-ounce packages instant chocolate pudding mix
1 cup Cool Whip
Slivered almonds

CRUST: Mix together butter, almonds, and flour until mealy. Spread into a 9 × 13-inch pan. Bake at 350°F for 15 minutes. Cool.
FILLING: Beat cream cheese and powdered sugar until creamy. Fold in Cool Whip and spread mixture on top of cooled crust.
TOPPING: Mix milk with chocolate pudding mix and let set until thickened. Spread on top of second layer and let set a few minutes. Spread Cool Whip on top. Sprinkle top with slivered almonds.

SERVES 10

VARIATION: Use lemon instant pudding mix instead of the chocolate for Lemon Lush.

Mississippi Mud

1 cup margarine or butter
⅓ cup cocoa
2 cups granulated sugar
1¼ cups flour
4 eggs
1 teaspoon vanilla
1 7-ounce jar marshmallow creme

ICING:
½ pound powdered sugar
½ cube of margarine
4 Tablespoons cocoa
Warm water or milk
½ cup chopped walnuts

Melt margarine and cocoa together; let cool. In bowl blend sugar, flour, and eggs. Add cooled cocoa mixture and vanilla. Bake in a 9 × 13-inch pan 20-25 minutes at 375°F. After taking out of oven, spread marshmallow creme over top. Wait at least 10 minutes and then spread with icing.
ICING: Mix together sugar, margarine, and cocoa. Add warm water or milk until spreadable. After spreading on top of marshmallow creme, sprinkle with nuts.

SERVES 12

Chocolate Lady-Finger Mousse

½ cup granulated sugar
½ cup hot water
4 ounces unsweetened chocolate
4 egg yolks
1 cup butter
1 cup powdered sugar
1 teaspoon vanilla
Dash salt (⅛ teaspoon)
4 egg whites
24 lady finger cakes, split
Whipped cream and chocolate curls

Put sugar, hot water, and unsweetened chocolate in top of double boiler. Stir until chocolate is melted. Beat egg yolks well. Add a small amount of the chocolate to yolks, stirring constantly; then stir yolks into rest of chocolate mixture in double boiler. Cook until thickened. Remove from heat and cool to room temperature. Cream butter and powdered sugar. When chocolate is cool, combine with butter mixture. Add vanilla and salt. Stir well. Beat egg whites very stiff and fold into chocolate mixture. Grease a large loaf pan. Place a layer of 8 lady fingers in the bottom. Spread with half the chocolate mixture. Add another layer of 8 lady fingers and cover with remaining chocolate mixture. Put a final layer of 8 lady fingers, crust side up, on top of chocolate. Chill or freeze until firm (12 hours or overnight). To unmold: slide a sharp knife around edges of pan; invert onto a plate. Flip dessert onto serving plate so clean lady fingers are on top. Slice and serve with whipped cream and chocolate curls for garnish.

SERVES 6-8

Chocolate-Almond Mousse

¼ cup granulated sugar
⅓ cup water
1 6-ounce package semi-sweet chocolate chips
3 Tablespoons dark rum or kirsch
3 egg yolks
½ cup toasted almonds
1½ cups heavy cream

Combine sugar and water in small saucepan and boil for 3 minutes. Using a blender or food processor, break up chocolate chips into small pieces. Add sugar and water mixture, rum, and egg yolks to the chocolate chips and mix well. Add the almonds and mix until they are broken up. Beat the cream until it becomes heavy whipped cream. Carefully fold the chocolate-almond mixture into the whipped cream. Pour mixture into 6 small dessert dishes or 1 pretty serving dish. Chill thoroughly—about 3 hours.

SERVES 6

Amaretto-Creme Meringue

MERINGUE:
4 egg whites, room temperature
½ teaspoon cream of tartar
½ cup plus 3 Tablespoons granulated sugar
⅓ cup granulated sugar

ALMOND BUTTER CREME FILLING:
½ cup whipping cream
4-5 Tablespoons butter, room temperature
¾ cup granulated sugar
1 teaspoon almond extract
4 egg yolks
1½ cups lightly toasted sliced almonds (reserve some for garnish)

AMARETTO CREME FILLING:
1 pint whipping cream
4 Tablespoons powdered sugar
2-3 Tablespoons amaretto liqueur

Fresh camelia, azaleas, or strawberries, etc.

MERINGUE: Preheat oven to 250°F. Trace four 9-inch circles on wax paper and place on foil-covered baking sheets. Beat egg whites with cream of tartar until soft peaks form, then add ½ cup plus 3 Tablespoons sugar very gradually. When the egg whites are stiff, gently fold in the remaining ⅓ cup sugar. Spread this mixture on the four 9-inch circles. Bake 1-1½ hours. Turn off oven and leave in oven at least 3 hours. *Gently* peel off paper.

ALMOND BUTTER CREME FILLING: Whip whipping cream. Then in a separate bowl cream butter and sugar and add almond extract. Add the egg yolks one at a time. Fold this mixture into the whipping cream. Fold in almonds, saving some for garnish on top.

AMARETTO CREME FILLING: Whip whipping cream, then add the powdered sugar. Fold in the liqueur.

ASSEMBLY: Place 1 meringue on serving platter. Spread one quarter of the Almond Butter Creme Filling evenly over the first meringue. Then spread ¼ of the Amaretto Creme over the Almond Butter Creme Filling. Place next meringue layer and repeat process for each of the remaining layers. When finished a spring form may be placed around it, tightly covering with Saran Wrap. Chill at least 18 hours in the freezer. Remove from freezer 20 minutes before serving, then garnish with remaining almonds and flowers or fruit. Cut into wedges for serving your guests.

SERVES 10-1

NOTE: This is worth the rather time-involved preparation.

Cold Amaretto Soufflé

⅓ cup amaretto liqueur
¼-ounce envelopes unflavored gelatin
egg yolks
½ cups granulated sugar
Tablespoon cornstarch
cups milk, scalded
1 Tablespoon vanilla
6 egg whites
Pinch salt
1 Tablespoon granulated sugar
1 pint whipping cream
Toasted, sliced almonds

ombine amaretto and gelatin; set aside to allow gelatin to soften. Beat egg olks with 1½ cups sugar and cornstarch until mixture turns light and forms a bbon. Add scalded milk. Cook over low heat, stirring constantly, until custard ickens. Add gelatin mixture and vanilla; stir to dissolve completely. Cool ightly. Beat egg whites until stiff with a pinch of salt, and 1 Tablespoon sugar. old into custard. Chill, stirring occasionally. Whip cream and fold into custard ixture when not quite set. Fasten foil collar to extend 3 inches above 2-quart ouffle dish. Pour in mixture. Refrigerate 4 hours. Sprinkle with toasted, sliced monds. Remove collar to serve.

SERVES 10-12

Grasshopper Mold

¼-ounce envelopes unflavored gelatin
cup granulated sugar, divided
cup water
egg yolks, well beaten
½ cup creme de menthe
½ cup creme de cacao
6 egg whites
1 pint whipping cream
Chocolate for grating

ix gelatin, ½ cup sugar, and water. Stir in well-beaten egg yolks. Cook slowly ntil thick, but not curdled. Remove from heat and add liqueurs. Keep stirring ntil *cool* and thick. (If it looks curdled, beat with electric beater at this point.) eat egg whites (not too stiff); adding remaining ½ cup sugar. Beat whipping eam. Fold egg whites and whipped cream into liqueur mixture. Pour into fan- glasses for individual servings or one large glass bowl for people to serve emselves. Grate chocolate over the top. Refrigerate.

SERVES 10-12

OTE: It's very important that the first mixture be very cool before folding in e egg whites and cream or it might separate. Also, be sure the egg whites en't beaten until they're dry.

JGGESTION: At Christmas time top with whipping cream and a cherry.

Lemon Dessert

CRUST:
15-20 graham crackers
¼ pound margarine, melted

FILLING:
2 13-ounce cans sweetened, condensed milk
Juice of 4 large lemons

TOPPING:
½ pint whipping cream, whipped
¼ cup granulated sugar
¼ teaspoon almond extract
½ teaspoon vanilla
1 cup chopped pecans

CRUST: Roll graham crackers until fine. Combine cracker crumbs with melted margarine and put into a 9 × 13-inch pan.
FILLING: Combine condensed milk with the lemon juice. Spread this mixture over the crust.
TOPPING: Beat whipping cream, adding sugar, almond extract, and vanilla. Spread over the top of filling. Sprinkle with pecans. Refrigerate 24 hours.

SERVES 1

Blueberries with Lemon Mousse

1 quart fresh blueberries
1 cup granulated sugar, divided
5 egg yolks
Juice of 2 large lemons
5 egg whites
1 cup whipping cream, stiffly whipped
2 teaspoons lemon zest, grated

Wash blueberries; remove stems. Place in glass serving bowl and sprinkle wit ¼ cup of the sugar. Chill. In top of double boiler (do not use aluminum becaus it will affect color and flavor) beat egg yolks with remaining ¾ cup sugar, unt mixture is a light lemon color. Add lemon juice and cook mixture over simme ing water, whisking constantly, until it heavily coats a spoon. (Do not let come to a boil.) Immediately remove from heat and cool mixture. Beat the eg whites until they are stiff, but not dry, and fold them gently into the lemo mixture. Fold in whipped cream and the lemon zest. Stir gently, but well, unt mixture is smooth. Chill. Just before serving, cover the berries with the col mousse.

SERVES

Lemon Angel Dessert

¼-ounce package Knox Gelatine
¼ cup cold water
⅓ cup lemon juice
½ cups granulated sugar, divided
6 eggs, separated
1 loaf-size angel food cake
Whipped cream

)issolve gelatin in water. In double boiler combine lemon juice, ¾ cup sugar, nd egg yolks. Cook mixture until thickened, then add gelatin. Stiffly beat egg vhites, gradually adding remaining ¾ cup sugar. Fold into lemon mixture. Ɜreak angel food cake in pieces and combine with lemon mixture. Put in tube an or oblong 9 × 13-inch pan. Refrigerate. Serve with whipped cream.

SERVES 8

Coupe Deluxe

16-ounce package frozen whole strawberries, defrosted
16-ounce package frozen pineapple chuncks, defrosted
1 16-ounce package frozen peaches, defrosted and sliced
½ cup brandy
1 fifth champagne, iced

ombine fruit and add brandy. Marinate in the refrigerator for at least 1 hour. o serve, fill large goblets half-full of fruit and marinade. Pour champagne over ie fruit at the table.

SERVES 6

ARIATION: Use fresh fruit and add a few blueberries.

Strawberries in Almond Yogurt

pints fresh firm sweet strawberries
cup plain yogurt
2 teaspoons vanilla
1½-2 teaspoons almond extract
¼ cup granulated sugar (or more)

ake several hours in advance. Wash, hull, and drain strawberries (may be lved). Mix together remaining ingredients. Fold in strawberries. Spoon into ampagne glasses and refrigerate. When ready to serve place glasses on a ssert plate with a liner and flower.

SERVES 4

Cherries Jubilee Sunriver

Sunriver Lodge, Oregon

1 28-ounce can dark sweet, pitted cherries, drained (save juice)
Cherry juice (from drained cherries)
1 cup packed brown sugar
1 Tablespoon cornstarch
1 ounce Kirschwasser
1 pint French vanilla ice cream
¼ cup chopped maraschino cherries
¼ cup chopped nuts
1 ounce butter
2 ounces brandy

Drain juice from cherries and save; set cherries aside. Blend cherry juice brown sugar, and cornstarch. Stirring constantly, cook until thickened and clear. Remove from heat, add Kirschwasser. Set aside. Form ice cream into two balls. Roll in chopped maraschino cherries and nuts; set back in freezer until ready to serve.

TABLE SIDE: Preheat chafing dish. Melt butter in hot chafing dish; add cherry juice mixture. Cook until hot and add cherries; add brandy and ignite with match or wand. Stir gently until flame is out. Place ice cream balls, 1 each, in deep serving dish. Spoon hot cherry mixture over and around ice cream balls. Serve immediately.

SERVES 2

Berries A La Romanoff

1 cup heavy cream
1 pint vanilla ice cream
2 quarts strawberries, raspberries, or blueberries
Granulated sugar
1½ ounces cointreau
Fresh berries

Whip the cream until stiff. Soften the ice cream slightly; mix cream and ice cream together. Put in the freezer. Clean the berries, sweeten to taste, and chill. Before serving, remove cream mixture from freezer and leave at room temperature for 15 minutes. Add cointreau to berries; fold into cream mixture. Decorate with a few fresh berries.

SERVES 8-

SUGGESTION: This is great in the winter using frozen blueberries. Easy to make and very elegant. Good served with chocolate mints or wafers.

Chocolate Covered Fruit

24 bite-size chunks fresh or canned pineapple
24 seedless grapes
2 ripe bananas, peeled and cut into 12 slices each
24 marashino cherries with stems
1 12-ounce package semi-sweet chocolate chip pieces
⅔ cup vegetable shortening

Stick wooden toothpicks or cocktail picks into the pineapple, grapes, and bananas. Place fruit, including cherries, on wax-paper-covered cookie sheet (do not allow pieces to touch each other). Freeze at least two hours or until fruit is frozen solid. Make chocolate sauce by placing chocolate pieces and shortening in a 2-cup measure. Place the measuring cup in a pan of hot water *(not boiling)*, stir until melted and smooth. Remove from heat, keeping chocolate mixture in pan of hot water. Dip pieces of frozen fruit into chocolate mixture to coat, do not put fruit back onto pan until chocolate coating has hardened, (it will harden almost immediately). Cover pan with foil and return fruit to freezer as soon as possible after dipping. Freeze. Allow fruit to thaw for 20 minutes to ½ hour before serving.

YIELD: 8 dozen pieces

NOTE: This is a dessert the kids can help you with. You'll welcome the extra hands.

Curried Baked Fruit

16-ounce can pear halves or pieces
16-ounce can sliced cling peaches
16-ounce can pineapple chunks or spears
16-ounce can apricot halves
12 maraschino cherries cut in half
¾ cup light brown sugar
1-3 teaspoons curry powder
⅓ cup butter, melted
⅔ cup slivered almonds

Prepare the day before serving by draining all fruit. Combine sugar, curry powder and melted butter. Arrange fruit and almonds in casserole; pour butter mixture over the fruit and nuts. Bake at 325°F for 1 hour. Refrigerate. Before serving reheat at 350°F.

SERVES 10-12

NOTE: This is a good side dish to serve with poultry, meat, or egg dishes.

Pioneer Plum Pudding

1 cup flour
1 teaspoon salt
1 teaspoon cinnamon
1 teaspoon nutmeg
1 teaspoon allspice
1 cup ground carrots
1 cup ground peeled raw potatoes
1 cup ground suet
1 cup mixed peel (fruit cake mix)
2 cups raisins
1 cup packed brown sugar
1 egg, beaten
1 teaspoon soda dissolved in 3 Tablespoons warm water

HARD SAUCE:
1 cup packed brown sugar
2 Tablespoons flour
2 cups boiling water
¼ teaspoon salt
2 Tablespoons butter
1 teaspoon maple flavoring

Mix well all pudding ingredients. Put in double boiler or mold that is placed on rack in center of canning pot, and steam well for 3 hours. (The pudding should be surrounded by steam for the entire cooking time.) Serve with hard sauce.
HARD SAUCE: Mix together sugar and flour. Add water and salt; boil for 5 minutes. Add butter and flavoring. Serve hot over pudding.

SERVES 12

Apple Pudding

1 cup granulated sugar
¼ cup butter
1-2 eggs
1 cup flour
¼ teaspoon salt
⅔ teaspoon cinnamon
⅔ teaspoon nutmeg
1 teaspoon baking soda
3-4 chopped cooking apples

SAUCE:
½ cup butter
½ cup whipping cream or canned milk
1 cup granulated sugar
Pinch of salt
1½ teaspoons vanilla

Grease and flour a 9-inch baking dish. Cream sugar and butter; then add eggs. Sift dry ingredients and add to cream mixture. Mix in apples slowly. Bake in shallow pan at 350°F for 30 minutes.
SAUCE: Combine and heat all ingredients. Serve hot on pudding.

SERVES 8-

Princess Charlotte Pudding

Henry Thiele's

1 pint milk
½ cup granulated sugar
1 Tablespoon cornstarch
2 eggs
½ ounce granulated gelatin, or ½ small envelope Knox Gelatine
2 ounces water
½ pint whipping cream
Granulated sugar to taste
Vanilla to taste
6-8 medium-size roasted almonds
Tart fruit juice (such as raspberry, strawberry, or loganberry)

In a double boiler combine milk, sugar, cornstarch, and eggs. Stir this cream while cooking until it becomes a very smooth custard cream, and then let it cool to about 60°F. Dissolve the gelatin in water. Heat it a little in order to thoroughly dissolve. Stir gelatin into the custard cream until it begins to set. Beat the whipping cream until it becomes firm; sweeten it according to your taste. Add a little vanilla flavoring. Chop roasted almonds; gently fold into the cooked custard along with the whipped cream. Fill 6 individual molds or one 1-quart mold and let the pudding stand in a cool place for 4-5 hours. Serve with a tart fruit juice.

SERVES 6

Poor Man's Pudding

This recipe has been handed down through the family of Mrs. Albert Geiser, whose parents came to Oregon in 1862.

Bring one quart of milk to boiling point in a skillet, and sprinkle white flour a little at a time slowly, not stirring but gradually "poking" and mixing so it will not get slick and smooth, but ever so slightly lumpy. Keep at high heat but do not boil hard for about 15 minutes.

It should take enough flour to be fairly thick (like cereal) consistency and be served warm with very thick cream, sweetened and flavored generously with cinnamon or nutmeg or both."

Josephine County Historical Society

Apple Oatmeal Crunch

4 cups sliced cooking apples
¾ cup granulated sugar
2 Tablespoons flour
½ cup packed brown sugar
½ cup flour
½ cup butter or margarine
⅔ cup rolled oats
1 Tablespoon cinnamon
Whipped cream or ice cream

Put apples, sugar, and 2 Tablespoons flour in a 9-inch buttered baking dish. Mix brown sugar and ½ cup flour; then cut in the butter. Add the oats and cinnamon. Put this over the apples and bake for 1 hour at 300°F. Serve warm with whipped cream or ice cream. This is also good cold.

SERVES 6-8

Apple-Mincemeat Dumplings Flambé

6 large firm apples
1 pound prepared mincemeat
Dough for 2-crust pie
1 Tablespoon cinnamon
½ cup granulated sugar
1 egg
Vanilla ice cream

FLAMBÉ:
¼ cup rum
¼ cup brandy

Working from stem end of apple, use a grapefruit spoon to scoop our core of apple, leaving bottom (blossom end) intact. Fill each hollow to top with mincemeat. Divide pie crust dough into 6 portions. Roll out each portion into a circle large enough to cover apples. Place each filled apple in center of circle and pull dough up to completely cover apple sealing crust edges with water. Combine cinnamon and sugar. Beat egg until lemon colored. Brush each apple all over with egg. Roll apples in (or thoroughly sprinkle with) cinnamon mixture. Place in lightly buttered baking dish so that apples do not tough. Bake at 375°F for 35-40 minutes or until apples are just tender and crusts are golden (reduce heat if browning too fast). Test for doneness with small skewer. Remove to serving dishes. Place 1 apple and 1 scoop vanilla ice cream in each dish.
FLAMBÉ: Heat rum and brandy together in small pan. Just before serving, light and pour over apples.

SERVES 6

NOTE: To serve cold, top each dumpling with large scoop of whipped cream or Cool Whip. To freeze, prepare dumplings. Freeze before baking. Defrost; brush with egg and coat in sugar, bake and serve as directed.

Mincemeat Crescents

FILLING:
1 9-ounce package dry None Such mincemeat or mincemeat filling for 1 8-inch pie (approximately 2 cups)
1 16-ounce can applesauce
1 cup finely chopped cooking apples
½ pound raisins

CRUST:
1 teaspoon salt
3 cups flour
1 cup solid shortening
½ cup ice water
1 egg, beaten
3 Tablespoons milk

FILLING: Prepare mincemeat according to package directions. While still warm, add remaining ingredients. Cook 5 minutes over medium heat until apples are tender. (If prepared mincemeat is used, heat to boiling, then add remaining ingredients and continue recipe.) Cool.

CRUST: Sprinkle salt over flour. Cut shortening into flour with pastry fork until well blended. Add ice water and mix until all flour is worked in. Knead slightly in bowl. Add a few drops more water if necessary to work in all flour. Divide dough into 3 balls. Using one ball at a time, roll out to ¼-inch thick on a lightly floured surface and cut into 3-inch rounds using biscuit cutter or wide mouth glass. Repeat until all dough is rolled and cut. Heat oven to 400°F. Lay rounds on lightly floured surface. Spoon 1 teaspoon mincemeat filling on each round. Fold in half and seal edges with tines of a fork. Place crescents on a cookie sheet. Brush tops with beaten egg combined with milk. Bake 15 minutes or until tops are golden. Serve warm or cold.

YIELD: 5 dozen

NOTE: To freeze, seal in air tight container, leaving small airspace. Keeps well for months.

Pecan Tasties

1 3-ounce package cream cheese
1 cube butter
1 cup flour
Dash of salt

FILLING:
¾ cup packed brown sugar
1 large egg, well beaten
1 teaspoon vanilla
Dash of salt
1 Tablespoon light corn syrup
1 teaspoon butter, melted
¾ cup or more chopped pecans

Let cheese and butter soften at room temperature. Combine with flour and salt; mix well. Press into 24 small tart tins.

FILLING: Mix filling ingredients together. Fill shells and bake at 350°F for 15 minutes.

YIELD: 24 small servings

Graham Cracker Greek Dessert

1 pound butter
1 pound powdered sugar
4 egg yolks
1½ teaspoons vanilla
4 Tablespoons cocoa
1 16-ounce box of graham crackers
3 cups cold strong black coffee
½ pound ground salted almonds

Cream butter and sugar; beat at least 15 minutes. Add egg yolks and vanilla and beat well. Separate into 2 parts. To half, add cocoa and mix well. Set aside. Dip eight graham crackers, each quickly, with the fingers, into the cold coffee, and lay on tray for serving, putting crackers 3 one way and 5 the other way. Spread thinly with white mixture. Add another layer of dipped crackers and spread thinly with the chocolate mixture. Do this, alternating white and chocolate mixture, until you have a stack 6-7 crackers high. Ice top and sides with the chocolate mixture and sprinkle with the ground almonds. Put in refrigerator and remove 2 hours before serving so it will mellow. Return unused portion to refrigerator.

SERVES 20-3

Chocolate Eclairs

SHELLS:
1 cube butter or margarine
1 cup water
1 cup flour
Pinch of salt
4 eggs

FILLING:
1 5½-ounce package vanilla pudding
2 cups milk
½ pint whipping cream
Chocolate frosting

SHELLS: Add butter to boiling water; stir until melted. Add flour and salt; sti vigorously until mixture is smooth. Cool slightly; add eggs one at a time; bea vigorously after each egg is added. Place mounds on teflon cookie sheet; us spoon to elongate for eclairs or leave round for cream puffs. (Makes 12 larg shells or 16 medium shells.) Bake at 400°F for 40 minutes.
FILLING: Cook vanilla pudding with milk over medium heat until it boil Remove from heat and cool. Whip whipping cream and fold into cooled pu ding.
TO ASSEMBLE: Cut shells in half and spoon in filling. Frost shells with favorit chocolate frosting and refrigerate.

SERVES 12-1

French Mint Dessert

4 1-ounce squares unsweetened chocolate
1 cup butter
2 cups powdered sugar
1 teaspon peppermint extract
4 eggs
2 teaspoons vanilla
½ cup vanilla wafer crumbs
Whipped cream, sweetened
Cherry or walnuts

Melt and cool chocolate. Beat butter and powdered sugar until fluffy. Add cooled chocolate and peppermint to butter mixture. Add eggs one at a time, beating well after each addition. Add vanilla. Put a thin layer of wafer crumbs in each bottom of 12 paper-lined cupcake pans. Fill liners three quarters full with mint mixture. Top with sweetened whipped cream and garnish with a cherry on top or nuts. Freeze.

SERVES 12

VARIATION: May add 1 cup chopped nuts to mixture. May fill liners ½ full to make 24 small but rich desserts.

Fool's Paradise

1½ cups homemade rich chocolate fudge sauce
8 pints (or 4 quarts) various flavors (compatible) high-quality ice cream
1 cube butter, melted
1 8½-ounce package Nabisco Famous Chocolate Wafers ground into fine crumbs
1 12-ounce package peanut brittle, crumbled very fine

Make fudge sauce (any good recipe). Slightly soften all of the flavors of ice cream. Combine melted butter and cookie crumbs, pressing into bottom of 10-inch spring form pan. Bake at 400°F for 8 minutes. Cool. Using 4 of the pints of ice cream, spread each one over one quarter of the crumb crust. Freeze until firm. Pour ¾ cup fudge sauce over ice cream in cookie crust. Freeze. Using the other 4 pints of ice cream, spread each one over one quarter of the ice cream and fudge sauce layers. Freeze until firm. Pour the remaining ¾ cup fudge sauce over the frozen dessert. Freeze. Top with peanut brittle crumb topping and freeze several hours.

SERVES 20

NOTE: This dessert will gain you raves and pounds!!!

French Vanilla Ice Cream

6 eggs, slightly beaten
2 pints whipping cream
1 pint half and half
1 13-ounce can evaporated milk
1 can water
2 cups granulated sugar
2 Tablespoons vanilla
Dash salt

Combine ingredients and freeze according to directions on ice cream freezer.

YIELD: 3-4 quarts

Ice Cream Dessert

1 12-ounce box vanilla wafers, crushed (approximately 4 cups)
½ cup chopped pecans
¾ cup melted butter
½ gallon vanilla ice cream (softened)

CHOCOLATE SAUCE:
1 cup granulated sugar
1 cup milk
3 Tablespoons cocoa
3 Tablespoons flour

Combine crushed wafers, pecans, and butter. Spread half of mixture in 9 × 13-inch pan. Spread ice cream on top of crumb mixture. Top with remaining crumbs. Freeze. Combine all sauce ingredients and cook until thick. Serve dessert with chocolate sauce.

SERVES 9-12

Toffee Crunch

1 quart vanilla or coffee ice cream (or ½ of each)
½ pound See's English Toffee, crumbled to pea size
1 8½-ounce package Nabisco Famous Chocolate Wafers, crushed
Shaved chocolate

Mix softened ice cream and candy. Line a 9 × 13-inch pan with waxed paper allowing an extra 3-4 inches of paper on each end. Put two thirds of cookie crumbs on bottom of pan. Spread ice cream mixture on top. Put remaining one third crumbs on top of ice cream. Fold wax paper ends over and *press down* gently. Freeze 8 hours. Garnish with shaved chocolate. Cut into squares and serve.

SERVES 9-1

Caramels

1 cup granulated sugar
½ cup brown sugar
½ cup light corn syrup
1½ cups cream
4 Tablespoons butter (real butter)
1 teaspoon vanilla

Combine all ingredients except vanilla in a saucepan. Cook and stir over medium heat until mixture boils. Continue cooking, stirring occasionally, to firm ball stage (248°F), 30-45 minutes. Remove from heat and stir in vanilla. Pour into buttered 9 × 5 × 3-inch loaf pan. Cool. Cut and wrap in wax paper.

YIELD: 3 dozen

English Toffee

1 cup butter
1⅓ cups granulated sugar
1 Tablespoon light corn syrup
3 Tablespoons water
1½ cups toasted blanched almond bits

COATING:
4 4½-ounce milk chocolate candy bars
1 cup almond bits

In a large heavy pan add butter, sugar, corn syrup, and water. Cook, stirring occasionally, to the hard crack stage (300°F). Remove from heat and stir in 1½ cups almond bits. Spread mixture in a well-greased 9 × 13-inch pan. Cool.
COATING: Melt the chocolate bars. Turn cooled candy out onto waxed paper and spread with one half of the chocolate. Sprinkle with ½ cup almond bits. Let this set. Then turn the candy over and spread the other side with remaining chocolate and rest of almond bits. Chill to firm. Break into pieces.

YIELD: 24 pieces

Church Windows

½ cup margarine
1 12-ounce package chocolate chips
1 10½-ounce package colored miniature marshmalows
1 cup chopped walnuts
1 cup flaked coconut (optional)

In top of double boiler, melt together margarine and chocolate chips. Place marshmallows and nuts in large bowl. Pour chocolate mixture over marshmallows and nuts, blending carefully. Sprinkle ⅓ cup coconut on a piece of wax paper, and pour one third of marshmallow mixture on paper. Roll the paper into an oblong, or tube shape. Repeat for 2 more rolls. Refrigerate for at least 1 hour. Before slicing, pull away and remove wax paper from rolls. Slice each roll into about 12 pieces. Keep refrigerated!

YIELD: 3 dozen

"Never beat fudge as soon as it is taken from the fire. Pour first into cold bowl and then beat. You will find that it is much creamier."

Klamath County Museum

Bon Bons

1 cup peanut butter
1 cup powdered sugar
1 cup chopped nuts
1 cup chopped dates
1 6-ounce package chocolate chips

Mix peanut butter, powdered sugar, nuts, and dates together in bowl. Form mixture into round balls the size of shelled walnuts and chill. Melt chocolate chips in top of double boiler and dip individual balls in melted chocolate. Place on cookie sheets lined with wax paper. Chill.

YIELD: 3½ dozen

Truffles

8 ounces dark sweet chocolate (Baker's German)
5 Tablespoons water
8 Tablespoons sweet butter
3 Tablespoons light rum
Grated dark sweet chocolate
Candy papers

Cut chocolate into small pieces and put in an ovenproof pan with water. Melt in oven to prevent burning. Cut butter into small pieces and add a little at a time to melted chocolate. Blend well. Stir in rum and cool in refrigerator for easier handling. Shape into ¾-inch diameter balls and roll in grated chocolate. Place each ball in a candy paper.

YIELD: 25-30

Candied Pretzels

2 pounds white almond bark
2 cups Rice Krispies
2 cups small pretzels
1½ cups mixed salted nuts
2 cups Captain Crunch peanut butter cereal

Melt almond bark in double boiler over hot water. Combine the remaining ingredients in a large bowl and add melted almond bark. Stir to coat. Spread candy out on a cookie sheet covered with wax paper. When cool break into bite-size pieces.

YIELD: Approximately 3 dozen pieces

Peanut Butter Clusters

½ cup peanut butter
1 6-ounce package butterscotch chips
1 cup peanuts (either Spanish with skins or plain)

Over low heat melt together the peanut butter and the butterscotch chips. Remove from heat and stir in peanuts. Drop by spoonfuls onto cookie sheet covered with wax paper. Refrigerate. When hard, remove from cookie sheet and place in another container. Store in the refrigerator, as they will get soft after being at room temperature for an hour or two.

YIELD: 2 dozen

Walnut Candy

2 cups granulated sugar
½ cup water
⅛ teaspoon salt
2 Tablespoons corn syrup
⅔ teaspoon mint extract
4 rounded Tablespoons marshmallow creme
6 cups large walnuts

Cook sugar, water, salt, and corn syrup to soft ball stage (235°F). Add mint and marshmallow creme. When melted add nuts and remove from heat. Working quickly, fold in nuts until all are coated. Pour out on large piece of wax paper and spread with spoon. When cool enough to handle, start separating the nuts. Allow to cool completely before serving.

YIELD: 3-4 dozen pieces

Sugar-Glazed Walnuts

cup granulated sugar
½ cup water
½ teaspoon salt
1 teaspoon cinnamon
1½ teaspoons vanilla
2½ cups walnut halves

Combine and cook sugar, water, salt, and cinnamon to soft ball stage (236°F) *without* stirring. Remove from heat, add vanilla and walnuts. Stir gently until the nuts are well coated and the mixture becomes creamy. Turn out on wax paper. Separate the walnut halves as they cool.

YIELD: 2 dozen pieces

MICROWAVE

Betty R. Stockman

Rondelé Mushrooms

12 large fresh mushrooms (about 2 inches in diameter)
¼-½ cup finely chopped onion
2 ounces Rondelé cheese (garlic herb)
¼ cup fine dry bread crumbs
2½ ounces canned chicken salad (Underwood makes a good one)
¼-½ cup chopped parsley
1 egg, beaten
Parsley (garnish)

Wash and stem mushrooms. Dry them with a paper towel. Chop stems fine and combine with onion. Cover and microwave at High for 4 minutes, stirring once after 2 minutes. Add the Rondelé cheese, bread crumbs, chicken salad, parsley, and egg to the hot stems and onion. Stuff each mushroom cap with about 1 Tablespoon of mixture. Place stuffed caps in microwave dish in a circle. Microwave at High 3-4 minutes, turning after 2 minutes. Serve hot. Garnish with parsley.

YIELD: 12 mushrooms

Hot Crab Dip

1 8-ounce package cream cheese
1 Tablespoon milk
1 6½-ounce can crab
Dash pepper
2 Tablespoons chopped onion
1½ teaspoons horseradish
¼ teaspoon salt
Slivered almonds to taste

Blend all ingredients and microwave 3-4 minutes, stirring once.

YIELD: 1½ cups

Mexican Bean Dip

1 16-ounce can refried beans
1 cup grated Cheddar cheese
½ cup chopped green onion
¼-½ teaspoon salt
½ teaspoon cumin
½ teaspoon coriander
2 Tablespoons green taco sauce
Corn chips

Combine all ingredients except chips in a glass dish. Heat in microwave for 5 minutes, stirring 3 times. Serve with corn chips.

YIELD: 2 cups

Omelet

1 teaspoon butter
3 eggs
1 Tablespoon water
½ teaspoon salt

OPTIONAL FILLINGS:
½ cup grated Cheddar cheese
½ cup chili
½ avocado, diced
½ tomato, chopped

In 9-inch glass pie pan, melt butter (15 seconds). Combine eggs, water and salt; beat until well mixed. Pour over butter. Cover tightly with plastic wrap. Cook 1 minute; stir to move eggs toward center. Cover again with plastic wrap and cook 1 minute. Let stand 1 minute before loosening with rubber scraper. Sprinkle with grated cheese, chili, etc. Fold over and heat another 15 seconds.

SERVES 4-6

Sunrise Bacon and Egg

1 thick slice of bacon
1 egg

Wrap bacon around inside edges of Pyrex custard cup. Cook in microwave approximately 1-2 minutes on High, until bacon is well cooked, but not crisp. (Will vary with thickness of bacon.) Remove from oven and pour off grease. Crack egg into center of bacon. (Bacon will shrink to bottom during cooking.) Pierce yolk of egg lightly with fork. Place custard cup in microwave and cook 1 minute on High. Remove from cup with spoon and serve on plate. Recipe may be increased. Cooking times will also increase accordingly. Keep an eye on it!

SERVES 1

Denver Brunch

6 slices bacon
6 eggs
⅓ cup milk
½ cup mayonnaise
¼ cup chopped pimiento
¼ teaspoon salt
¼ cup chopped green pepper
Tomato slices

Microwave bacon 5-6 minutes. Crumble and set aside. Combine eggs, milk, and mayonnaise in bowl; beat well with rotary beater. Stir in bacon and remaining ingredients, except tomato. Pour into a lightly greased 8-inch square baking dish. Cover with plastic wrap. Microwave for 6-7 minutes or until center is almost set. Rest covered for 5 minutes. Garnish with tomato slices and serve.

SERVES

Impossible Quiche Lorraine

5 strips bacon
1 9-inch pie shell, baked
1 cup grated Swiss cheese
¼ cup grated Parmesan cheese
Mushrooms (optional)
Broccoli (optional)
½ teaspoon salt
½ teaspoon freeze-dried chives
4 eggs
1⅓ cups evaporated milk
½ Tablespoon chopped onion
⅛ teaspoon nutmeg
⅛ teaspoon cayenne pepper

Cook and crumble bacon. Cover bottom of pie shell with cheeses and bacon. Combine rest of ingredients; beat thoroughly. Cook mixture in microwave 2-3 minutes. Stir and pour into pie shell. Cook 6 minutes or longer. Rotate twice during cooking. Let rest 10 minutes.

SERVES 4-6

Swiss Broccoli Custard

2 10-ounce packages frozen chopped broccoli
1 cup half and half
4 medium eggs, beaten
1½ cups shredded Swiss cheese
¼ cup biscuit mix
½ teaspoon onion salt
Pepper and paprika to taste
2 Tablespoons butter or margarine
Bacon curls (optional garnish)

Thaw broccoli in microwave 6 minutes. Press in strainer to remove all liquid. Mix broccoli with half and half and eggs. Dredge cheese with biscuit mix and seasonings. Stir in broccoli mixture. Melt butter 45 seconds, spread over bottom and sides of baking dish. Pour in broccoli mixture and cook 10 minutes. Stir from outside edge into center at half time. Let stand covered 10 minutes. To serve cut in wedges and garnish with bacon curls if desired.

SERVES 8

VARIATION: Use spinach or green beans for broccoli.

Stuffed Cabbage Rolls

1 medium-size green cabbage
2 eggs
1 teaspoon seasoned salt
1 teaspoon Worcestershire sauce
1 small onion, finely chopped
1 pound ground beef
½ cup uncooked quick-cooking (1 minute) rice
1 10½-ounce can tomato soup
2 Tablespoons brown sugar
½ teaspoon cinnamon
1 Tablespoon lemon juice

Wrap head of cabbage in wax paper and microwave 6-7 minutes or until leaves have softened. Remove 12 cabbage leaves; cut off thick part of leaf (about 2 inches). In bowl combine eggs, salt, Worcestershire sauce, onion, ground beef, and rice; beat together with fork. Spoon ¼ cup of meat mixture on each leaf. Fold in sides and roll ends over meat. Place rolls, seam-side down, in 2-quart baking dish. Combine soup, sugar, cinnamon, and lemon juice. Pour over cabbage rolls. Cook covered with wax paper 13-16 minutes or until cabbage is tender. Spoon sauce over cabbage during cooking to keep moist.

YIELD: 12 rolls, 4-6 servings

VARIATION: To prepare separated cabbage leaves place head of cabbage in 4-quart deep casserole with 2 Tablespoons water. Cover and cook 8 minutes. Then continue as above.

Glazed Carrots

1 pound carrots, sliced
¼ teaspoon salt
⅛ teaspoon nutmeg
3 Tablespoons orange juice
1 Tablespoon butter

Combine all ingredients in a 1-quart glass casserole. Cook covered 6-7 minutes, stirring halfway through cooking time. Rest covered 5 minutes.

SERVES 4-6

Tangy Cheese Cauliflower

1 medium-size head cauliflower
½ cup mayonnaise
¼ teaspoon onion salt
1-2 teaspoons prepared mustard
¾ cup shredded sharp Cheddar cheese
Paprika or parsley

Remove woody base from cauliflower, leaving cauliflower whole. Cook cauliflower 6-7 minutes per pound in a wax paper covering. Carry Over cook 5 minutes. In a 2-cup glass measure, mix mayonnaise, salt, and mustard; heat 30 seconds. Spread over cauliflower. Sprinkle cauliflower with cheese. Microwave approximately 30 seconds to melt cheese. Garnish with paprika or parsley.

SERVES 6

Fresh Corn in the Husk

4 ears of corn in husks
Cold water

Remove any dry outside leaves from corn husks. Soak corn in cold water for 5 minutes. Place ears of corn in a dish and cook on High in microwave for 12 minutes. (For additional ears, allow 3 minutes cooking time on High for each ear of corn.) Peel husks down from top of ear. The silk will peal away with the husk.

YIELD: 4 ears

Savory Cheese Potatoes

6 medium potatoes
¼ cup butter or margarine
½ teaspoon onion salt
½ pint sour cream
2 Tablespoons chives
½ teaspoon salt
1 10½-ounce can cream of chicken soup, undiluted
2 cups shredded Cheddar cheese
Dry bread crumbs or crushed croutons

Boil potatoes, with skins on, in microwave 22-24 minutes. Cool. Peel and shred. In a 9 × 12-inch casserole dish, microwave butter 1 minute on Medium High. Blend in onion salt, sour cream, chives, salt, soup, and Cheddar cheese, reserving a little cheese to sprinkle on top. Add potatoes, mix well and cover with plastic wrap. Cook 8 minutes on Medium High. Sprinkle with bread crumbs and remaining cheese and cook on Medium High 3-4 minutes until hot.

SERVES 10-12

Wilted Lettuce Salad

5 slices bacon
1 head leaf lettuce, torn into bite-size pieces
2 green onions, sliced
2 Tablespoons cider vinegar
1 Tablespoon granulated sugar
2 Tablespoons water
½ teaspoon salt
¼ teaspoon dry mustard
¼ teaspoon pepper

Cook bacon in a glass dish, covered with paper towel, 3-4 minutes or until crisp. Reserve 2 Tablespoons drippings for dressing. Set bacon aside. Combine lettuce and onions in salad bowl; refrigerate until ready to serve. Pour vinegar into 1-cup measure. Add reserved bacon drippings, sugar, water, salt, mustard, and pepper. Cook uncovered 1 minute or until mixture boils; stir to dissolve sugar. Pour over salad greens, tossing to coat. Garnish with crumbled bacon.

SERVES 6

VARIATION: Use fresh spinach for lettuce.

Cheesy Vegetables

¼ cup bread crumbs, seasoned with garlic salt and thyme
¼ cup grated Parmesan or Romano cheese
1 teaspoon paprika
1 head cauliflower, zucchini, mushrooms, or other fresh vegetables, cut into uniform-size pieces
⅓ cup butter or margarine, melted

Mix bread crumbs, cheese and paprika in plastic or paper bag. Dip vegetable pieces in butter or margarine. Drop vegetables in bag of dry mixture and shake to coat. Arrange in dish and cover with paper towel. Microwave 5-6 minutes or until tender.

YIELD: 2-4 cups

Seasoned Rice

2 cups water
1 cup long grain rice
¼ cup dehydrated onion or ½ fresh onion, chopped
2 teaspoons or 2 cubes chicken or or beef bouillon
1 Tablespoon fresh parsley or 1 teaspoon dried parsley
½ bay leaf

Mix all ingredients in a 2-quart glass casserole dish. Cover and cook on High in microwave 12-14 minutes. Let stand 10 minutes, or until all water is absorbed.

SERVES 4-6

NOTE: To reheat leftovers, add about 2 Tablespoons water for each cup of cooked rice. Cook on High until thoroughly heated.

Teriyaki Meat Loaf

1½-2 pounds ground beef
½ cup chopped onion
¼ cup milk
1 egg
2 slices bread, cubed

SAUCE:
¼ cup soy sauce
¼ cup granulated sugar
½ garlic clove, minced
2 teaspoons mayonnaise
½ teaspoon monosodium glutamate

Mix meat and onion together. Combine milk and egg; add cubed bread. Stir into meat mixture. Mix sauce ingredients together. Add half the sauce to the meat mixture. Place in loaf pan. Bake 8 minutes on High. Drain grease. Pour remaining sauce over meat loaf. Bake 15-20 minutes on Roast cycle, or until meat is no longer pink. Let stand in microwave 5 minutes.

SERVES 6

Sweet and Sour Meatballs

1 pound ground beef
1 egg
1 Tablespoon cornstarch
2 Tablespoons chopped onion
1 teaspoon salt
Dash pepper
1 15¼-ounce can pineapple chunks
1 tomato, quartered
Cooked rice

SAUCE:
½ cup granulated sugar
3 Tablespoons cornstarch
Drained juice from pineapple chunks (about 1 cup)
1 Tablespoon soy sauce
3 Tablespoons vinegar

Combine all ingredients except pineapple, tomato, and rice. Form a tablespoon of meat mixture around each pineapple chunk. Place in shallow baking dish. Set aside. Combine all sauce ingredients in 2-cup measure. Stir. Cook uncovered 4-5 minutes or until mixture begins to boil, stirring once. Set aside. Cook meatballs uncovered 5-7 minutes. Drain off grease. Pour prepared sauce over meatballs. Top with remaining pineapple chunks and tomato. Serve over rice.

SERVES 4-6

Enchilada Casserole

1 pound ground beef
1 small onion, chopped
1 $10\frac{1}{2}$-ounce can cream of mushroom soup
1 $10\frac{1}{2}$-ounce can cream of of chicken soup
1 15-ounce can enchilada sauce or 1 15-ounce can tomato sauce
1 dozen corn tortillias, cut in eighths, or taco chips
$\frac{1}{2}$ cup pitted ripe olives, sliced
1 4-ounce can chopped green chiles (optional)
1 pound Cheddar cheese, grated

Crumble ground beef in collander. Set in bowl and cook in microwave for 6 minutes, stirring and "breaking up" beef once or twice during cooking period. Remove from microwave and put drained meat into large bowl. Stir in onion, soups, and enchilada sauce; cook 5 minutes. Add tortillas, olives, and chiles. Stir to combine ingredients. Place in 9 × 13-inch glass dish and cook 5 minutes. Top with cheese and return to microwave to melt, about 1-2 minutes.

SERVES 8-10

Buffalo was a major part of the diet of the overland travelers to Oregon in the early 1800s. Most parts were spit roasted or pan fried, but the hump meat was almost always boiled. The heavy ribs were held for the evening meal when there was more time to cook them.

Summer Sausage

3 pounds ground beef
3 teaspoons meat curing salt (Morton's Tender Quick)
1 Tablespoon liquid smoke
1 teaspoon oregano
1 teaspoon ground pepper
$1\frac{1}{2}$ teaspoons garlic salt
Nylon netting or cheese cloth

Combine first 6 ingredients and refrigerate for 24 hours. Form into 3 12-inch sausages. Roll each in a piece of nylon netting. Secure ends of netting with string or rubber band. Bake all 3 rolls at once on meat rack for 20 minutes on Low. Rearrange and turn over. Bake an additional 25 minutes on Low. To cook just one roll, baking time reduces to 18-20 minutes on Low, turning at half time.

YIELD: 3 rolls

SUGGESTION: Excellent served with homemade mustard.

Crispy Teriyaki Chicken

½ cup soy sauce
¼ cup vegetable oil
1½ teaspoons dry mustard
½ teaspoon ground ginger
⅛ teaspoon pepper
1 teaspoon garlic powder
2 Tablespoons granulated sugar
6-8 chicken breasts

Mix all ingredients except chicken. Place chicken in single layer in a shallow glass dish. Pour sauce over chicken. Let stand for 30 minutes. Drain off sauce and cook chicken in microwave for 10 minutes on each side. Brush on sauce as chicken is cooking. For crispness brush on additional sauce and broil for 3 minutes per side in conventional oven.

SERVES 6-8

Herb Chicken Breasts

¼ cup butter
¼ teaspoon garlic powder
¼ teaspoon pepper
⅛ teaspoon oregano
1 teaspoon salt
2 whole or halved chicken breasts (2 pounds)
¼ cup dry white wine
Cooked rice or noodles

Place butter in 2-quart baking dish and melt 30-40 seconds. Add seasonings to butter; mix well. Skin chicken breasts and roll in butter. Place skin side down, with thick side edges to outside of dish. Cover with pierced plastic wrap. Cook 10 minutes on High. Carefully remove wrap; turn chicken over and pour on wine. Cook on High 6-8 minutes (fork tender). Let stand 5 minutes. Serve over rice or noodles.

SERVES 4

Chicken Delight

1 3-pound chicken
4 Tablespoons butter
Paprika (optional)
1¼ cup uncooked rice
1 10½-ounce can cream of mushroom soup
1 soup can water
1 small onion, sliced
½ cup sliced mushrooms
¼ cup chopped green pepper
½ package dried onion soup

Cut up chicken and sauté in butter. Roll in paprika if desired. Mix all other ingredients together and put in rectangular baking dish. Put chicken on top and microwave for 30 minutes. Let rest 10 minutes before serving.

SERVES 6-8

Mandarin Game Hen

1 Cornish game hen (1-1½ pounds)
1 Tablespoon salad oil
2 Tablespoons Kitchen Bouquet
⅓ cup orange juice concentrate
Soy sauce to taste
Garlic powder to taste
2 Tablespoons orange marmalade
1 11-ounce can mandarin oranges, drained

RICE MIXTURE:
1 cup quick rice
2 teaspoons grated orange rind
½ cup raisins
1 cup boiling water
2 chicken bouillon cubes

Split game hen with kitchen shears. Brush with salad oil, then with Kitchen Bouquet. Combine rice mixture ingredients and place in bottom of glass baking dish. Place hen breast side down on top of rice mixture. Cover and cook 10 minutes, turning dish if necessary. Remove and place hen breast up. Baste with marinade of orange juice, soy sauce, and garlic powder. Then baste with marmalade. Cover and bake 10 minutes more. Remove; garnish with oranges. Let stand for 10 minutes.

SERVES 2

Turkey Bunwiches

4 hamburger buns, toasted
1 cup cooked chopped turkey
1 Tablespoon instant minced onion
1 teaspoon parsley flakes
1 egg, hard cooked and chopped
½ cup mayonnaise
½ cup shredded sharp Cheddar cheese
Salt and pepper

Place bottom half of buns on paper-towel-lined plate. Combine remaining ingredients and spread filling on bottom half of buns. Then place remaining half of bun on top to make "bunwiches." Heat in microwave on Medium for 4-5½ minutes or until heated through.

SERVES 4

VARIATION: Use any leftover cooked poultry or meat instead of turkey.

Hot Turkey Salad

2 cups diced cooked turkey
1 cup thinly sliced celery
½ cup slivered almonds
½ teaspoon salt
2 teaspoons grated onion
1 cup mayonnaise
1-2 Tablespoons lemon juice
½ cup shredded Cheddar cheese
1 cup crushed potato chips

Combine turkey, celery, almonds, salt, onion, mayonnaise, and lemon juice. Spoon into a 1½-quart casserole. Bake in microwave oven 4 minutes or until mixture is heated. Sprinkle cheese and then crushed potato chips over the top of the turkey mixture and microwave 1-2 minutes longer.

SERVES 4

VARIATION: Chicken, shrimp, or tuna may be substituted for the turkey.

Nathanial Wyeth, a Boston merchant, led the first caravan of settlers across the Oregon Trail. The group of New England farmers and their wagons left from St. Joseph, Missouri in the spring of 1832. They followed the Missouri and Kansas rivers, eventually abandoning their wagons. With pack horses they continued up to the Platte and the Sweetwater rivers, crossing the South Pass of the Rockies at the Snake river. They arrived at Walla Walla, Washington on September 18, 1832, and thus became the first settlers to travel the Oregon Trail.

Oven-Baked Fish

1 egg, slightly beaten
1 Tablespoon lemon juice
½ teaspoon salt
Dash pepper
1 pound fish fillets
½ cup cornflake crumbs

Beat together egg, lemon juice, salt, and pepper in shallow bowl. Dip fish into egg mixture, coat with crumbs. Arrange in 8 × 12-inch baking dish. Cover with paper towel. Cook about 4 minutes or until fish flakes apart easily.

SERVES 4

Snappy Red Snapper

1½-2 pounds fresh red snapper fillets, skinned and boned
1 small tomato, chopped
½ cup chopped onion
½ cup chopped green pepper
4 Tablespoons butter or margarine
4 ounces mushrooms, sliced
3 Tablespoons chili sauce
2 Tablespoons lemon juice
2 teaspoons capers
2 teaspoons dried parsley
¼ teaspoon garlic powder
½ teaspoon dried thyme, crushed
¼ teaspoon salt
4-6 dashes bottled hot pepper sauce
¼ cup dry white wine
¼ pound cocktail shrimp

Cut fish into 4-inch chunks. Set aside. In 7 × 12-inch glass baking dish, combine all ingredients *except* fish, wine, and shrimp. Cover with wax paper. Cook on High for 6 minutes, until butter melts and vegetables are tender. Stir in wine. Place fish on top; spoon some of sauce over. Cook covered on High for 8-10 minutes or until fish flakes when tested with a fork and is almost done. Sprinkle shrimp on top; cover, cook for 2 more minutes on High. Serve with a slotted spoon, and put vegetables on top of fish on each plate.

SERVES 4-6

Salmon Roast

2-3 pound salmon roast
2 Tablespoons butter
2 Tablespoons lemon juice
Salt and pepper
Onion
Celery
Paprika

Place salmon on cooking rack. In glass cup melt butter; add lemon juice. Salt and pepper inside of salmon; pour butter mixture inside and over outside of salmon. Slice onion and celery and fill inside of roast. Secure with toothpicks. Sprinkle with paprika for color. Cook 5 minutes per pound. Turn salmon over at half time.

SERVES 4-6

Shrimp Scampi

2 Tablespoons butter
1½ teaspoons lemon juice
1½ teaspoons parsley flakes
⅛ teaspoons garlic powder
⅛ teaspoon salt
½ pound shrimp (fresh or defrosted frozen)

Combine all ingredients except shrimp and cook on High for 1 minute. Add the shrimp (drained well if frozen) and microwave 1½ minutes more or until shrimp is pink. Stir halfway through cooking time.

SERVES 4

Sherried Shrimp Rockefeller

2 10-ounce packages frozen chopped spinach
16 medium-size raw shrimp, peeled and deveined (about ¾-1 pound)
1 10½-ounce can condensed cream of shrimp soup
1 cup Cheddar cheese
3 Tablespoons sherry
2 slices fresh bread, torn into small pieces
3 Tablespoons butter
Paprika

In 2-quart baking dish place frozen spinach blocks and cook 3 minutes. Break up blocks and cook 3 more minutes until just thawed. Drain well; squeeze out as much juice as possible. Spread over bottom of 9 × 13-inch casserole. Distribute shrimp evenly over spinach. In 1-quart measuring cup stir together the soup, cheese, and sherry. Cook 4 minutes, stirring after 2 minutes, until cheese is melted. Pour over casserole. In small bowl combine bread and butter. Cook 1 minute, stirring after ½ minute, until butter is distributed among bread pieces. Distribute bread pieces over top of casserole. Sprinkle with paprika. Cook uncovered 12-14 minutes, giving dish quarter turn after 6 minutes. Let stand covered 5 minutes before serving.

SERVES 4

Fishermen of Scandinavia found the cold North Pacific, with its rugged coastline and bountiful fish harvest, much like their homeland. Other immigrants from farming countries settled in the fertile Willamette Valley to establish dairy and agricultural farms. The town of Astoria, with its sailing, fishing and shipbuilding industries, attracted many Finns. The lumber industry drew numbers of hearty Swedes, as did the excellent wheat growing land of Morrow county and the Nehalem valley.

Baked Apples

4 large crisp baking apples
1 heaping Tablespoon white raisins
¼-⅓ cup sherry
¼ cup chopped pecans
1 teaspoon cinnamon-sugar mixture
¼ cup raspberry jam
Whipped cream

Core and remove all peel from apples except for a broad ring around the base. Place raisins and sherry in a glass measuring cup and cook 1 minute. Drain raisins. Divide raisins and pecans equally among apple cavities. Sprinkle with cinnamon-sugar and cover with raspberry preserves. Place apples in 2-quart round glass casserole, cover loosely with wax paper and cook 4 minutes. Rotate dish half turn and cook an additional 4 minutes, or until apples are just tender. Serve warm, topped with whipped cream.

SERVES 4

Applesauce

4 medium cooking apples, peeled and quartered
½ cup water
¼-½ cup granulated sugar
½ teaspoon cinnamon

In 2½-quart casserole, combine apples and water. Cover and cook 7-9 minutes, or until fruit is soft but not mushy. Add sugar to taste and press through colander or sieve, if desired. Season with cinnamon.

SERVES 4-6

Peanut Brittle

1 cup raw Spanish peanuts
1 cup granulated sugar
½ cup light corn syrup
½ teaspoon salt
1 teaspoon vanilla
1 teaspoon margarine
1 teaspoon baking soda

In 1½-quart casserole, stir together peanuts, sugar, syrup, and salt. Microwave 7-8 minutes, stirring after 4 minutes. Add vanilla and margarine; blend well. Cook 1-2 minutes more. (Peanuts will brown lightly and the syrup will be very hot.) Add soda and gently stir until light and foamy. Pour onto lightly greased cookie sheet. Cool ½-1 hour. Store in airtight container.

YIELD: 10 × 15-inch pan

Granola Energy Bars

½ cup sesame seeds
½ cup shelled sunflower seeds
¼ cup wheat germ
¾ honey
¾ cup chunky peanut butter
3 cups oat flakes
½ cup walnuts, filberts, or almonds
⅓ cup diced dried apricots
⅓ cup diced dried prunes
⅓ cup raisins

Spread the sesame seeds in a 7 × 11-inch baking dish and cook uncovered in the microwave for 5 minutes or until seeds are golden brown. Stir seeds several times while cooking. Set aside. Follow same procedure for sunflower seeds and wheat germ. Place honey in a 2-quart bowl and microwave 2½ minutes. Add peanut butter and cook 1 minute longer. Combine sunflower seeds, wheat germ, honey mixture, oat flakes, nuts, apricots, prunes, and raisins; mix well. Spread half of the sesame seeds back into the baking dish. Press the oat mixture into the pan. Sprinkle top with remaining sesame seeds and press firmly. Chill 1 hour. Cut into bars and wrap each in plastic wrap. Wrapped bars will keep indefinitely.

YIELD: 2½ dozen bars

Peanut Butter Snacks

1 cup granulated sugar
1 cup light corn syrup
1 cup creamy or crunchy peanut butter
6-8 cups cornflakes

Stir together sugar, syrup, and peanut butter. Cook in microwave for 6 minutes. Stir to blend while cooking. Add cornflakes and stir well. Drop by teaspoonfuls on wax-paper-covered cookie sheet. Refrigerate to set.

YIELD: 4 dozen

Fudge-Like Brownie

1 cube frozen butter
2 1-ounce squares unsweetened chocolate
1 cup granulated sugar
2 eggs
½ cup flour
1 teaspoon vanilla
⅓ cup chopped nuts

Melt butter and chocolate in an 8-inch square pan for 2½ minutes. After 1 minute, break chocolate up and continue stirring every 30 seconds. Add sugar, eggs, flour, vanilla, and nuts, stirring after each ingredient. Cook 4 minutes on Roast (70%), 5 minutes on High. Elevate dish and rotate as necessary. Top should be slightly sticky when done. Cut when cool.

YIELD: 16 squares

Creamy Lemon Sauce

1 3-ounce package cream cheese
3 Tablespoons milk
½ teaspoon grated lemon peel
2 teaspoons lemon juice
¼ teaspoon ground ginger
¼ teaspoon salt

In 2-cup measure, soften cream cheese about 20 seconds; stir until smooth. Add remaining ingredients. Cook until simmering (about 1-2 minutes). Serve to accompany fish.

YIELD: 1 cup

Cucumber Sauce

¼ cup sour cream
¼ cup mayonnaise
½ cup chopped, seeded cucumber
½ teaspoon salt
½ teaspoon dill weed
1 Tablespoon lemon juice

Mix all ingredients in bowl. Microwave 1½ minutes; stir. Serve warm with baked or broiled fish, or cold with raw vegetables.

YIELD: 1 cup

Early Oregonians were frequently subjected to peculiar hazards from living in such "wild" country. The rivers would swell from the melting snows of the high mountains and often remain flooded for weeks. One such flood occurred on the Columbia River in 1894. The river began to rise in mid-May and did not crest until June 7th. It then took just as long to return to a normal flow. In the town of St. Helens, Oregon, Dr. Edwin Ross, the pharmacist, watched the flood approach his store. Realizing the need to continue services and to protect his valuable inventory, he rented a vacant scow, poled it to his store, loaded his goods aboard, and then tied it to an oak tree in the center of town. People would come to his floating drugstore by boat for the duration of the flood and as the waters began to recede, he poled his "store" back to his pharmacy building and returned his merchandise to the shelves.

Coconut Pecan Topping

¾ cup packed brown sugar
2 Tablespoons milk
6 Tablespoons butter
½ cup chopped pecans
1 cup coconut

Combine brown sugar, milk, and butter in 1-quart measure. Cook 2-2½ minutes on High, stirring after 1 minute. Blend in pecans and coconut. Spread while warm on cooled cake.

YIELD: 1½ cups

Instant Berry Jam

1½ cups whole berries (strawberries, raspberries, blueberries, blackberries, or boysenberries; thawed if frozen)
¾ cup granulated sugar
2 teaspoons lemon juice
¼ teaspoon butter or margarine

Wash berries, remove stems or hulls, and crush evenly in a bowl. You should have 1 cup crushed berries. In a 3-quart casserole stir together berries, sugar, lemon juice, and butter. Cook uncovered in microwave for 8 minutes, stirring every 2 minutes, until it reaches desired thickness. Serve warm or cool. Store in covered jar in refrigerator.

YIELD: 1 cup

Recipe Timing Adjustment Chart For Microwave Ovens

600-700 Watt Ovens	500-600 Watt Ovens Add 15%	400-500 Watt Ovens Add 35%
15 sec.	17 sec.	20 sec.
30 sec.	35 sec.	41 sec.
1 min.	1 min. 9 sec.	1 min. 21 sec.
2 min.	2 min. 22 sec.	2 min. 42 sec.
3 min.	3 min. 27 sec.	4 min. 3 sec.
4 min.	4 min. 36 sec.	5 min. 24 sec.
5 min.	5 min. 45 sec.	6 min. 45 sec.
10 min.	11 min. 30 sec.	13 min. 30 sec.
15 min.	17 min. 15 sec.	20 min. 15 sec.
20 min.	23 min.	27 min.
25 min.	28 min. 45 sec.	33 mins. 45 sec.
30 min.	34 min. 30 sec.	40 mins. 30 sec.

Temperature Equivalents

High	—	100%
Sauté	—	90%
Reheat	—	80%
Roast	—	70%
Bake	—	60%
Simmer	—	50%
Braise	—	40%
Defrost	—	30%
Low	—	20%
Warm	—	10%

All recipes should be prepared on High, Full Power, or 100% unless otherwis indicated.

References to the terms "rest," "setting time," or "standing time," appear i some microwave recipe instructions. These terms are used in regard to period of carryover cooking which takes place when food is removed from th oven and allowed to stand. This is necessary for the heat to equalize and fo cooking to finish. Resting times vary depending on the size, moisture conten volume and density of the food. Approximate standing times are:

1-3 minutes for small items (bacon, cupcakes, peas, corn, etc.)
5 minutes for most vegetables, cakes, sauces, etc.
10 minutes for main dishes, casseroles, and more dense foods such as chicke and meat loaf.
15 minutes for large roasts, turkeys, and hams.

Helpful Hints for Microwave Cooking

To cook ground beef in microwave, crumble 1 pound meat in collander and set in bowl to catch drippings. Microwave on high for 6 minutes, stirring and breaking up every 2 minutes.

When cooked chicken is needed for casseroles, first microwave chicken breasts for 10 minutes on high. Then skin, debone and chop; proceed with recipe.

To help prevent sogginess of hot sandwiches, place a paper towel under the bread while heating.

To dry parsley, celery leaves and other herbs, pat semi-dry between paper towel, place in microwave, and heat 1-3 minutes (mixing every 30 seconds). Remove from oven, cool, and rub between towel to crumble.

Soften hard-as-rock brown sugar by setting box in microwave with a cup of hot water. Cook 2 minutes for ½ box, 4 minutes for a full box.

To crisp soggy potato chips or pretzels, heat for 15-30 seconds; let stand for 2 minutes.

When cooking any vegetable with a skin, such as a potato, prick it in several places to prevent it from exploding. When cooking frozen vegetables in plastic pouches, prick the pouches.

Your microwave produces the best cooking results when foods are arranged in a circular or donut-shaped pattern.

Microwaves first cook food on the outer edges of the dish, therefore more dense food should be arranged toward the outside.

Stirring moves cool portions of the food to edges of dish for faster and more uniform cooking.

When shopping for microwave cookware, look for deep dishes, either round or with rounded or oval corners.

When a recipe calls for food to be elevated and you do not have a rack in your microwave, an upside-down glass pan or dish works well.

Generally foods cooked in the microwave oven require one fourth the conventional cooking time. However, most porous foods (cakes, quick breads, etc.) will bake in less than one fourth the time.

Decrease the liquid in your conventional recipe by approximately one fourth when converting to microwave cooking.

POTPOURRI

Bonnie B. Phipps

Peanut Butter Pizza

1 package yeast
1 cup very warm water
2 teaspoons honey
1 Tablespoon vegetable oil
1 teaspoon salt
2 cups whole wheat flour or
1 cup whole wheat flour and
1 cup regular flour
Oil

Corn meal
1 cup peanut butter
¼ cup honey
¼ cup raisins
¼ cup sesame seeds
¼ cup shelled sunflower seeds
¼ cup shredded coconut
¼ chopped nuts
½ cup shredded Mozzarella cheese

Sprinkle yeast over water in medium-size bowl and stir to dissolve. Let stand 10 minutes until bubbly. Stir in honey, 1 Tablespoon oil, and salt. Add flour and beat until smooth. Turn out onto lightly floured surface, adding more flour if necessary. Knead for 10 minutes or until smooth and elastic. Roll out to make a 15-inch circle. Oil a 14-inch pizza pan and sprinkle with corn meal. Fit dough onto pan. Press with fingers around edge to keep flat. Let rest 15 minutes. Bake in preheated 450°F oven for 15 minutes. Remove from the oven. Lower oven temperature to 350°F. Combine peanut butter and honey in small bowl; spread over pizza. Sprinkle with raisins, seeds, coconut, and nuts. Sprinkle cheese over top. Return to oven and bake at 350°F for 10 minutes, or until crust is brown and crisp.

SERVES 4-5

Easy Popcorn Balls

6 Tablespoons margarine
3 cups miniature marshmallows
3 Tablespoons flavored gelatin (any flavor)

3 quarts unsalted popped corn
Margarine (to butter hands)

Melt 6 Tablespoons margarine in large pan; add marshmallows. Stir until melted. Blend in the gelatin. Place the popped corn in a large bowl or Dutch oven (give yourself room to stir!), pour the gelatin mixture over the popped corn, and stir. Butter your hands and form corn into balls. Be sure to work quickly as it gets sticky when it cools down!

YIELD: 8-10

Cracker Jacks

2 cups granulated sugar
½ cup dark molasses
½ cup water
1 teaspoon baking soda
5 quarts popped corn
Peanuts (as desired)

Combine sugar, molasses, and water in saucepan and bring to soft ball stage (235°F). Take off heat and add soda. Mix popped corn with peanuts and pour sugar mixture over all. Stir to coat evenly.

YIELD: 5 quarts

Frozen Orange Treats

1 3-ounce package orange flavored gelatin
½ cup granulated sugar
2 cups boiling water
2 cups orange juice

Dissolve gelatin and sugar in boiling water. Add orange juice. Pour into ice cube trays or pop molds and freeze. Can also be made in paper-lined muffin tins.

SERVES 12-14

Finger Jello

3 3-ounce packages flavored gelatin (any flavor)
4 cups boiling water
4 ¼-ounce envelopes Knox Gelatine

Put all ingredients in bowl and stir until dissolved. Pour into 9 × 13-inch pan and refrigerate. Cut into squares or use cookie cutters.

YIELD: 40-50 medium treats

NOTE: A fun treat or preschool snack.

Roasted Pumpkin Seeds

2 cups pumpkin seeds (pull off strands but do not wash)
1½ Tablespoons oil
1½ teaspoons salt

Mix all ingredients and put on cookie sheet. Bake in a 250°F oven for 45-6 minutes. Stir occasionally.

YIELD: Approximately 2 cup

Granola I

6 cups rolled oats
1 cup firmly packed brown sugar
1 cup wheat germ
½ cup bran flakes (optional)
1 cup shredded coconut (optional)
1½ cups salted nuts, chopped or not (optional)
1 cup shelled sunflower seeds (optional)
1½ cups raisins (optional)
1 cup unshelled sesame seeds (optional)
½ cup vegetable oil
½-¾ cup honey
2 teaspoons vanilla

Combine all dry ingredients to be used, mixing thoroughly. Add liquids to dry ingredients, mixing thoroughly. Grease 2 large 10 × 15-inch rimmed baking sheets. Divide granola and spread evenly on baking sheets. Bake uncovered in 325°F oven for 15-20 minutes, stirring 2-3 times. Remove from oven. Stir occasionally while cooling. When completely cool store in airtight containers.

YIELD: Depends on number of ingredients used.

Granola II

6 cups old-fashioned oatmeal
1 cup cut almonds
1 cup unrefined sesame seeds
1 cup shelled sunflower seeds
1 cup shredded coconut
1 cup soy flour
1 cup powdered milk (*non*-instant)
1 cup wheat germ
1 cup cashews
¾ cup honey
½ cup vegetable oil

Combine the dry ingredients. In a separate bowl mix the honey and oil. Combine dry and moist ingredients. Divide and spread on 2 cookie sheets. Bake at 300°F for 1 hour or until browned.

YIELD: 4-5 quarts

The Manzanita, a red barked evergreen bush, produced a small, dry, and tasteless fruit that was crushed into a fine meal by the Indians of Oregon. This meal was then used to make a rich and delicious cider.

Dough Art

2 cups flour
1 cup salt
1 cup water
Model paints

Blend together the flour and salt. Add water a little at a time. Knead dough 7-10 minutes until firm. Pat dough to desired thickness. Mold or cut out design. (May use cookie cutters for Christmas tree ornaments. Be sure to poke a hole for string!) Bake at 325°F for 35-60 minutes, depending on thickness. If air bubbles occur, stick with a needle while baking. Use model paints for decorating.

Playdough

1 cup flour
½ cup salt
1 Tablespoon salad oil
1 Tablespoon alum
1 cup boiling water
Food coloring

Combine flour, salt, oil, and alum. Add the boiling water and stir until a ball forms. Add food coloring of choice, and work into dough. Store in plastic bags in refrigerator. Can be doubled!

YIELD: 1 cup ball

Finger Paint

1½ cups laundry starch
Cold water
1 quart boiling water
1½ cups talc
1½ cups soap flakes
1 Tablespoon powdered tempera paint

Mix laundry starch with a little cold water until creamy. Add the boiling water. Cool until glossy looking and add talc. Cool slightly. Then add soap flakes, stirring until distributed. Mix in tempera paint—any color. Children can "paint" directly on a formica table. Prints can be made by pressing a clean piece of paper onto the painted surface. Be sure to press *all* of paper onto painted surface for a complete print. Paint can be stored in an airtight jar. Add warm water if it is too thick.

Finger Painting

Shaving cream

Tempera paint

Spray "Dad's" shaving cream on a piece of white paper. Add or sprinkle dry tempera (poster paint) into the cream and let the child go to town!

Crayon Meltings

Tray

Aluminum foil

Crayons

Warm tray with foil on top. Using crayons, have child color a picture on the foil; it will melt on the foil. When the child is finished take a plain piece of paper and lay it over the tray and press. It makes a print of the picture.

Old Fashioned Root Beer

"Use strong bottles with patent stoppers or tie corks in securely. Use a stone crock or granite vessell in which to let drinks stand while 'working.' Fresh roots from the woods are always preferable to dried herbs. Select a cool place in which to store drinks; the longer they stand in a warm place after bottling, the more effervescent they will become! When filling bottles, fill to within an inch of the top.

1 cake compressed yeast
2 ounces Sassafras root
2 ounces Juniper Berries
1 ounce Dandelion root
4 pounds sugar
1 ounce Hops or Ginger Root
4 gallons water
2 ounces Wintergreen

Wash roots well in cold water. Add juniper berries (crushed) and hops. Pour 8 quarts boiling water over root mixture and boil slowly 20 minutes. Strain through flannel bag. Add sugar and remaining 8 quarts water. Allow to stand until lukewarm. Dissolve yeast in a little cool water. Add to root liquid. Stir well. Let settle then strain again and bottle. Cork tightly. Keep in a warm room 5 to 6 hours, then store in a ***cool*** *place. Put on ice as required for use."*

The Fleischman Company, Excellent Recipes for Baking Raised Bread, 1912

A Good Toilet Soap

"For toilet soap, dissolve one can of lye in quart of cold water. Fry out five pounds of mutton tallow until perfectly pure. Have the grease as cool as it can be without congealing, then pour it, a few drops at a time and beating constantly, into the dissolved lye. Stir into the mixture four ounces of glycerin and half an ounce of oil of bergamot or of oil of lavender, as preferred. Or, if one does not care for either of these odors, use oil of geranium instead, as this gives a pleasant perfume. When all the ingredients are blended, beat in two tablespoonfuls each of powdered borax and ammonia, whip hard, line a pan with paper, and pour the soap into it."

Josephine County Historical Society

Make-Your-Own-Casserole

1 cup main ingredient
1 cup second ingredient
1-2 cups starchy ingredient
1½ cups binder (*eg.*, can of soup)
¼ cup of a "goodie"
Seasoning
Topping

1. Decide on a main ingredient such as tuna, chicken, turkey, ham, seafood or a vegetable. Place 1 cup of main ingredient in a large bowl.
2. Measure and add 1 cup of a second ingredient such as sliced celery or mushrooms, chopped hard-cooked eggs, a package of frozen peas, or another cup of the main ingredient.
3. Add 1-2 cups of a starchy ingredient such as crushed potato chips, croutons cooked noodles or rice.
4. Add 1½ cups of a binder such as cream sauce; mayonnaise; sour cream; or cream of mushroom, celery or chicken soup.
5. Add ¼ cup of a "goodie" such as sliced pimiento, sliced olives, water chestnuts, chopped almonds or cashews, or 2 Tablespoons of capers.
6. Add seasoning such as 1-2 Tablespoons lemon juice, sherry, soy sauce or Worcestershire sauce; a minced clove of garlic; ¼ cup chopped onion or green pepper; 2 teaspoons of curry powder; or ½ cup or more grated cheese.
7. Mix together thoroughly. If the mixture seems dry add ¼-½ cup of cream milk or chicken stock. Place in buttered casserole dish.
8. Spread over the top toasted buttered crumbs, chopped nuts, grated cheese or use Chinese noodles or crushed potato chips if these were not used as the starchy ingredient.
9. Bake at 350°F for 30-45 minutes. Use the longer cooking time if you have used uncooked celery, green pepper or onion as an ingredient.

Substitutions

Instead of:	Use:
1 teaspoon baking powder	¼ teaspoon baking soda plus ½ teaspoon cream of tartar
1 cup buttermilk	1 cup milk plus 1 Tablespoon lemon juice or vinegar (let stand 5 minutes, beat well)
3 ounces semi-sweet chocolate	2 squares unsweetened chocolate plus 2 Tablespoons granulated sugar, or ⅓ cup unsweetened cocoa plus 2 Tablespoons granulated sugar and 2 Tablespoons butter or margarine
1 square (1 ounce) unsweetened chocolate	3 Tablespoons unsweetened cocoa plus 1 Tablespoon butter or margarine
1 cup corn syrup	¾ cup granulated sugar plus ½ cup water
1 Tablespoon cornstarch	2 Tablespoons flour or 1 Tablespoon arrowroot
1 cup cake flour	1 cup all purpose flour minus 2 Tablespoons
1 medium-size garlic clove	⅛ teaspoon garlic powder
1 Tablespoon prepared mustard	1 teaspoon dry mustard plus 1 Tablespoon vinegar
1 cup self-rising flour	1 cup all purpose flour plus 1½ teaspoons baking powder and ¼ teaspoon salt
1 Tablespoon tomato paste	1 Tablespoon tomato ketchup
1 cup tomato juice	½ cup tomato sauce plus ½ cup water
1 6-ounce can tomato paste	2 8-ounce cans tomato sauce (reduce other liquids)
1 can (10¾-ounce) condensed tomato soup	1 8-ounce can tomato sauce and ¼ cup water

Equivalents

Beans, green	1 pound	3 cups cut (uncooked)
Beans, dried	½ pound	1 cup
Bread	2 slices	1 cup crumbs
Butter	½ cup (8 Tablespoons)	1 stick
Butter, packed solid	2 cups	1 pound
Carrots	7-9 carrots (2 cups cooked)	1 pound
Chocolate	1 square	1 ounce
Chocolate	1 square	3-4 Tablespoon, grated
Cocoa	4 cups	1 pound
Coffee, ground	(5 cups (80 Tablespoons)	40-50 servings, 1 pound
Cheese	4-4½ cups	1 pound
Cheese, grated	1 cup	¼ pound
Cheese, cream	3-ounce package	6 Tablespoons
Cream, heavy	½ pint	2 cups whipped
Cucumbers	2 6-inch cucumbers	1 pound
Dates, pitted	2 cups	1 pound
Eggs	1	¼ cup
Egg white	1	1½ Tablespoons
Egg yolk	1	1 Tablespoon
Egg whites	4 to 6	½ cup
Egg yolks	6 to 7	½ cup
Flour, all purpose, sifted	4 cups	1 pound
Flour, cake	4½-5 cups	1 pound
Graham cracker crumbs	11 crackers	1 cup, rolled fine
Lemon	1 juiced	2-3 Tablespoons
Macaroni	1 cup	2 cups cooked
Meat, cooked and diced	2 cups	1 pound
Meat, crab	2 cups	1 pound
Marshmallows	16	¼ pound (1 large equals 10 miniature)
Milk, condensed	1¼ cups	14-ounce can
Milk, evaporated	⅔ cup	6-ounce can
Milk, evaporated	1⅔ cup	14½-ounce can
Noodles	1 cup raw	1½ cups cooked
Nuts, shelled	2 cups coarsely chopped	½ pound
Orange	1 juiced	½ cup or 6-8 Tablespoons
Peas, in pod	1 pound	1-1½ cups shelled or 1 cup cooked

Potatoes, white	1 pound	2-5 medium, 2-3 cups cooked, mashed
Prunes	1 pound	4 cups cooked
Punch	4 quarts	About 40 punch cups
Raisins, seedless	1 pound	3 cups
Rice, raw	2¼ cups	1 pound
Rice	1 cup uncooked	About 3 cups cooked
Saccharin	¼ grain	1 teaspoon sugar
Spinach	1 pound	2-2½ quarts raw or 1½ cups cooked
Sucaryl	1 tablet	1 teaspoon sugar
Sugar, granulated	2 cups	1 pound
Sugar, brown (firmly packed)	2¼ cups	1 pound (1 box)
Sugar, confectioners	3-3½ cups	1 pound (1 box)
Tea, loose	1 pound	5 cups (about 155 teacup servings)

The Yield from Citrus Fruits

ORANGES:
3 medium oranges yield 1 cup of juice
1 medium orange yields 4 teaspoons grated rind
1 medium orange, unpeeled, yields ⅔-¾ cup of purée
1 medium orange yields ⅔ cup slivered rind
1 medium orange yields 10-12 sections

GRAPEFRUIT:
1 medium grapefruit yields ⅔ cup juice
1 medium grapefruit yields 3-4 Tablespoons grated rind
1 medium grapefruit yields 1⅓ cups slivered rind
1 grapefruit yields 10-12 sections

LEMONS:
6 medium lemons yield 1 cup of juice
1 medium lemon yields 1 Tablespoon grated rind
1 medium lemon yields ⅓ cup slivered rind

LIMES:
1 medium lime yields 2 Tablespoons of juice
1 medium lime yields 2 teaspoons grated rind
1 medium lime yields about 3 Tablespoons slivered rind

Citrus fruits yield more juice if they stand in boiling water a few minutes before squeezing, or if rolled on work surface before squeezing. If you are going to use the rind in some way, always grate or peel before placing the fruit in boiling water.

Table of Measurements and Equivalents in U.S. and Metric

U.S.	EQUIVALENTS	METRIC*
		volume-milliliters
Dash	Less than ⅛ teaspoon	
1 teaspoon	60 drops	5 ml.
1 Tablespoon	3 teaspoons	15 ml.
2 Tablespoons	1 fluid ounce	30 ml.
4 Tablespoons	¼ cup	60 ml.
5⅓ Tablespoons	⅓ cup	80 ml.
6 Tablespoons	⅜ cup	90 ml.
8 Tablespoons	½ cup	120 ml.
10⅔ Tablespoons	⅔ cup	160 ml.
12 Tablespoons	¾ cup	180 ml.
16 Tablespoons	1 cup or 8 ounces	240 ml.
1 cup	½ pint or 8 fluid ounces	240 ml.
2 cups	1 pint	480 ml.
1 pint	16 ounces	480 ml. or .473 liter
1 quart	2 pints	960 ml. or .95 liter
2.1 pints	1.05 quarts or .26 gallons	1 liter
2 quarts	½ gallon	
4 quarts	1 gallon	3.8 liters
		weight-grams
1 ounce	16 drams	28 grams
1 pound	16 ounces	454 grams
1 pound	2 cups liquid	
1 kilogram	2.20 pounds	

Temperature Conversion from Fahrenheit to Celsius*

FAHRENHEIT	200	225	250	275	300	325	350	375
CELSIUS	93	106	121	135	149	163	176	191
FAHRENHEIT	400	425	450	475	500	550		
CELSIUS	205	218	231	246	260	288		

**These are round figures. The important thing to remember in cooking is to use relative amounts in measuring.*

Pan and Baking Dish Sizes

4-cup baking dish:
- 9-inch pie plate
- 8-inch layer cake pan
- 7⅜ × 3⅝-inch loaf pan

6-cup baking dish:
- 8 or 9-inch layer cake pan
- 10-inch pie plate
- 8½ × 3⅝-inch loaf pan

8-cup baking dish:
- 8 × 8-inch square pan
- 11 × 7-inch baking pan
- 9 × 5-inch loaf pan

10-cup baking dish:
- 9 × 9-inch square pan
- 11¾ × 7½-inch baking pan
- 15 × 10-inch jelly-roll pan

12-cup baking dish and over:	
13½ × 8½-inch glass baking pan	12 cups
13 × 9-inch metal baking pan	15 cups
14 × 10½-inch roasting pan	19 cups

VOLUME OF SPECIAL BAKING PANS

Tube pans:	
7½ × 3-inch bundt pan	6 cups
9 × 3½-inch bundt pan	9 cups
9 × 3½-inch angel cake pan	12 cups
10 × 3¾-inch bundt pan	12 cups
10 × 4-inch angel cake pan	18 cups
Mold:	
7 × 5½ × 4-inch mold	6 cups
Springform pans:	
8 × 3-inch pan	12 cups
9 × 3-inch pan	16 cups
Ring molds:	
8½ × 2¼-inch mold	4½ cups
9¼ × 2¾-inch mold	8 cups
Brioche pan:	
9½ × 3¼-inch pan	8 cups

INDEX

Terry Maddox

BIBLOGRAPHY

Dictionary of Oregon History; Howard Corning (ed.), Binsford and Mort, Portland, Oregon, 1956.

Directions For Cookery; Leslie (ed.), New York, New York, 1848.

Excellent Recipes for Baking Raised Bread; The Fleischman Co., Cincinnati, Ohio, 1912.

Forest Trees of the Pacific Coast; W.A. Eliot, G.P. Putnam and Sons, New York, New York, 1938.

Frontier Living; Edwin Tunis, World Publishing Co., Cleveland, Ohio, 1961.

Oregon: End of the Trail; Writer's Program for Oregon, Binsford and Mort, Portland, Oregon, 1951.

Oregon in the USA; F. Haines and B. Tucker, Cascade Pacific Books, Portland, Oregon, 1955.

Our Wagon Train is Lost; Peterson, American Gothic Publications, Eugene, Oregon, 1975.

Season of Harvest: Recollections of Lane County; Youth and Senior Exchange Project, Lane County Youth and Children's Services, Eugene, Oregon, 1975.

Some More Good Things to Eat; Helen Armstrong, Chicago, Illinois, 1907.

The Early History of Eugene; Frederica Coons, Double D Printing Co., Eugene, Oregon, 1957.

Twentieth Century Cookbook; Ladies Aid Society of the First Christian Church, The Dalles, Oregon, 1906.

Eugene Register-Guard; Eugene, Oregon.

A TASTE OF OREGON

Junior League of Eugene • 2839 Willamette Street • Eugene, Oregon 97405

Name ______________________________

Address ______________________________

City ____________________ State __________ Zip __________

Please send ______ copies of "A TASTE OF OREGON" at $11.95 per copy plus $1.50 per copy to cover postage and handling. Make check payable to "A TASTE OF OREGON."

☐ Visa

☐ Master Charge

Inter Bank No. ☐☐☐☐

Card No. ☐☐☐☐☐☐☐☐☐☐☐☐☐☐☐☐

Signature ____________________ Exp. Date __________

On orders of one hundred or more copies, postage and handling will be paid by the Junior League of Eugene.

- -

A TASTE OF OREGON

Junior League of Eugene • 2839 Willamette Street • Eugene, Oregon 97405

Name ______________________________

Address ______________________________

City ____________________ State __________ Zip __________

Please send ______ copies of "A TASTE OF OREGON" at $11.95 per copy plus $1.50 per copy to cover postage and handling. Make check payable to "A TASTE OF OREGON."

☐ Visa

☐ Master Charge

Inter Bank No. ☐☐☐☐

Card No. ☐☐☐☐☐☐☐☐☐☐☐☐☐☐☐☐

Signature ____________________ Exp. Date __________

On orders of one hundred or more copies, postage and handling will be paid by the Junior League of Eugene.

- -

A TASTE OF OREGON

Junior League of Eugene • 2839 Willamette Street • Eugene, Oregon 97405

Name ______________________________

Address ______________________________

City ____________________ State __________ Zip __________

Please send ______ copies of "A TASTE OF OREGON" at $11.95 per copy plus $1.50 per copy to cover postage and handling. Make check payable to "A TASTE OF OREGON."

☐ Visa

☐ Master Charge

Inter Bank No. ☐☐☐☐

Card No. ☐☐☐☐☐☐☐☐☐☐☐☐☐☐☐☐

Signature ____________________ Exp. Date __________

On orders of one hundred or more copies, postage and handling will be paid by the Junior League of Eugene.